the Rolling Stones

James Phelge

a cappella

Library of Congress Cataloging-in-Publication Data

Phelge, James.
    Nankering with the Rolling Stones : the untold story of the early days / James Phelge.
        p. cm.
    Includes index.
    ISBN 1-55652-373-4
    1. Rolling Stones. 2. Rock musicians—England—Biography. I. Title.

ML421.R64P5 2000
782.42166'092'2—dc21
[B]   99-054413

Published by A Cappella Books
An imprint of Chicago Review Press, Incorporated
814 N. Franklin Street
Chicago, Illinois 60610
ISBN 1-55652-373-4
Printed in the United States of America
5 4 3 2 1

Reading Instructions

Thank you for purchasing a copy of *Nankering with the Rolling Stones*.

All the things you are about to read in the pages of this book are absolutely true and as they happened.

This book is intended to be a serious work of art and you should treat it as such by reading it properly. Should you find yourself inadvertently laughing at any of the contents, please follow the instructions below.

Put the book down immediately and take a large dose of some depressant-type drug. Do not attempt to read another page for at least 24 hours.

You may find some printing errors in this edition. Well . . . they are not actually printing errors but a test to make sure you have paid attention. If you spot one of these you are reading the book correctly.

As most of you know nothing about music I have only mentioned Pat Boone once—I find it best to educate people slowly.

Do not try and copy any of the stunts in this book—only professionals can get away with this kind of shit. *You* may end up being arrested.

Do not tell anyone how this book ends. You will make yourself look stupid. The reason for this is that every book has a different ending.

Keith does not really swear—I am just trying to make him look like a hero.

If you enjoy reading this book then read it again. If you enjoy reading it a second time you are in need of some serious psychiatric care available from Buncha Asshole Serious Illnesses Center.

If your name is John Grisham or Robert Ludlum: this is what writing is all about, not that tacky crap about lawyers and spies that you two turn out. So eat shit.

James Phelge

The gateway to hell. The legendary place where it all began. (photo courtesy of the author)

Gimme Shelter—Edith Grove, the scene of the early crimes, today. The much-repaired house is now a shelter for abused women. (photo courtesy of the author)

The Stones mixing drinks with David Jacobs of *Juke Box Jury* and pop star Adam Faith (with blond hair). Jacobs was probably born in the dinner suit. (photo courtesy of Rex USA Ltd.)

The Chelsea pie stall where we ate late at night is still there today. It still sells the same food and is the only place in London I can afford to eat. (photo courtesy of the author)

You can't always get what you want—but the Stones can nowadays. This is the drugstore in Chelsea close to Edith Grove where I queued with Mick. Not to be confused with another store that came later and was actually named The Chelsea Drugstore. (photo courtesy of the author)

A blow job for Keith. Proof that the Stones did actually wash their hair despite the "unwashed" image. Even I looked OK in the mirror. (photo courtesy of Rex USA Ltd.)

VOODOO LOUNGE

Wembley. July 11, 1995

IT HAD NEVER been like this at the beginning. Back then you could turn up at the stage door and say, "I'm with the Rolling Stones." They just took your word for it and let you in. Then the Stones played at the Empire Pool, nowadays called the Arena. Today they are playing inside the huge football stadium next door. In the old days you would be here so many times with the band that you were on first-name terms with the security staff. They would open the gate in readiness when they saw you coming and let you walk straight through. I did not know anyone here now.

This time I am furnished with a VIP badge but struggling to get anywhere. Even with this pass they are still reluctant to let you proceed without the utmost difficulty. Nobody has heard of the people you were told to ask for, let alone where to find them. Eventually in the Voodoo Lounge hospitality bar for celebrities I find a friendly journalist who queries the pass I am wearing. He explains this particular pass is for a more exclusive area than where I currently find myself and directs me to the place I should have been an hour or more previously.

I make my way out to a gray warehouse-type building across the way from the main stadium. Inside, a makeshift construction of black curtaining forms another hospitality suite, which is full of people waiting. Now and again the curtains part and someone passes through to what looks like a vast unloading area. I ask a guy going through the opening if he knows the contact I need. "Yeah," he replies, "I'm the tour manager. I'll mention you're here."

The lady I had spoken with on the phone but never met appears a few minutes later and I follow her across the unloading area. Charlie is just standing there watching some items being moved and at first I nearly walk past him. When I speak, he looks bewildered for a moment until the penny drops. It's a brief chat lasting only a few seconds and then we're continuing on to another makeshift lounge. People here look like tour personnel, or maybe they are press. Across this lounge and out the other side is yet another area containing several portable buildings similar to motor homes. I note one marked "Make-Up" and another marked "Guitars" as I pass.

Walking round between the mobiles, we come to one with an open door through which I can see his back as he is standing there, playing music on a keyboard. We wait until he finishes and then the lady, Sherry, calls out, "Keith, Phelge is here."

MICK WAS STANDING sideways looking around from behind the square-shaped Reslo microphone, his mouth open and his tongue pressed against his lower teeth as he considered what to say next. He was using the few seconds to take a breather as the smoke-filled air mingled with the sweat of the audience and drifted toward him. Keith was propped up against the parapet on the right, tuning his guitar and occasionally turning to his old Harmony amplifier, balanced on some crates, to adjust the volume.

The 15-inch-high stage always looked cramped with six of them up there, especially as the new bass player's speaker cabinet seemed enormous compared with the rest of the equipment the band possessed. The drummer in the middle was adjusting his snare; he also had to contend with the pianist on his left, whose stool was jammed tight up against his kit.

"Yeah, one two, one two, yeah." Mick's mind seemed made up now and he began checking that the Reslo was still functioning. You never knew with Reslos; they could be pigs if they wanted.

"Yeah, we're looking for another person to share a flat in Chelsea," he said in a couldn't-care-less tone. "Anyone interested let us know; the share of the rent's four pounds a week."

He paused, looking for some sign of interest, but none came. Then he announced, "The next one's a Chuck Berry number called 'Sweet Little Sixteen.'"

Brian, who had his back to the crowd, gulped down a final mouthful of beer and turned round, his face deadpan but his guitar ready. Keith looked up as well to see if there were any takers and then looked back at Mick and fixed his cigarette to the end of his guitar.

It was a new Harmony he played now and not the old blonde deep-bodied guitar somebody had made for him. Mick gave a final stare and stood away from the microphone, mouthing something across to Keith who started counting time to the drummer. Keith's fingers picked out the intro, and they were on the way into "Sweet Little Sixteen."

It was January 1963 and right then I had not yet decided upon being James Phelge, although I had dropped my "Mumbles" nickname and the beatnik image that came complete with donkey jacket, beard, and curly pipe. I now wore a short black corduroy coat, the fashion gimmick for me being to have the buttons done all the way up to the neck for an Edwardian effect. I had been toying with the idea of removing the collar—it seemed to have no function—but did not want to spoil the coat. I had also grown long sideburns on my elongated college-boy hairstyle. The name stayed on though—my friend Fengey still called me Mumbles, as did the other guys. Mumbles had been derived from a habit I had formed of pausing and clicking my fingers as I considered how to answer the simplest questions. Someone had likened it to the way Marlon Brando acted and told me I always mumbled like him when I spoke. I felt I needed a change.

It was another Saturday night at the Ealing Club in West London and I was at the far end of the small dance floor, drinking with Fengey. We had been coming down each week for some months since before the Rolling Stones had taken over the whole gig. Alexis Korner and Cyril Davies had moved on elsewhere and the new young crowd was growing gradually. There were some nice-looking girls here too.

There were a few guys we hung out with at the bar who seemed to be led by Eric the Mod, who would occasionally get up and sing, although right now he was over by the bar talking with Doug and another guy nicknamed Pretty Mick. Meanwhile Rowan was being his usual extrovert self up near the stage, dancing with some girls. He always seemed to need so much space and I could never really make up my mind whether he was dancing or leaping about, but guessed he was dancing.

During the interval Fengey and I had made our usual trip up the stairs and across the road to the small off license and bought a quarter bottle of Scotch each. We would smuggle it back into the club and use it to supplement the beer we bought from the bar during the rest of the evening. We were now taking occasional sips of the whisky and Fengey was talking about guitars again.

"I think it cost about 75 quid; it looks all right. I wonder how it plays. I'll ask him later. I wouldn't mind having a go on it, but I don't suppose he'll let me," he said, laughing as he imagined what Keith would say.

"That girl Rose is over there, man. I'd rather have a go on her than Keith's guitar," I said. "Let's go over and talk to Eric so we can look at her at the same time."

I led Fengey over to the bar. Eric was talking to the others about the Flamingo Club up town, saying that Blues Incorporated was now playing there on certain nights. Not wishing to stop his flow of conversation, I continued to talk with Fengey while looking at Rose.

"I think I might ask Jagger about this flat in Chelsea and see about moving up there. What do you think?" I asked Fengey, seeking reassurance.

"What do you want to move up there with them for? You've got a nice place now." He sounded puzzled.

"I don't know. A flat in Chelsea sounds all right, probably a bit more action up there as well; don't forget I work that way anyhow," I replied, trying to make a case.

"Yeah, but I wouldn't move house to go to work," said Fengey.

The real truth was that I thought Chelsea sounded glamorous, with its reputation for artists and society types. Whenever you read the papers, it always seemed as if Chelsea was the part of London where it all happened. I also imagined the flat would be something special and pictured it in some expensive block. I knew these guys a bit anyway and they seemed all right so that helped. I did not know anyone else who lived there and this seemed like a good opportunity to discover Chelsea, so why not? I decided to see Mick later.

The band had done a few more numbers by now and Brian was sliding his bottleneck up and down the strings of his guitar the way he always did when playing lead on Bo Diddley songs. Mick was cavorting about the front of the stage and shaking a pair of maracas. It always escalated into a frenzy toward the end of the evening and the dancers would stamp their feet on the floor to accent the final two beats of the Diddley riff. The noise added a crescendo to the mounting excitement. Rowan was still down there waving his college scarf about in the air, and now was the time to go and join in before it all finished.

The Stones, like most other bands, always played a couple of extra numbers and ran over the supposed closing time. I danced out the last few songs with the long-haired girl who wore a bolero-type hat and high boots. Eventually the bartender signaled that it really was finally time. "C'mon now!" he called out before the band could start again.

"Yeah, thanks for coming, everybody," announced Mick. "We'll be down the Red Lion in Sutton on Wednesday if you'd like to come along. That's the Red Lion in Sutton and we'll be back here next week. Thanks again for coming and goodnight."

The band began to relax, looking pleased with themselves. We were hanging around finishing our drinks, watching the club gradually clear out as everyone trooped reluctantly up the stairs. We called "Goodbye" here and there to those we knew. Fengey dumped his empty Scotch bottle, then turned to me to speak.

"That's another Saturday night done for. You coming for fish and chips then, Mumbles?" The meal served out of newspaper had become part of our Saturday night routine on the journey home.

"Yeah, sure I am, but you'll have to hang on for a minute. I've just gotta go up and find out about this flat."

I wandered slowly up the stage with hands thrust deep inside my coat pockets and stood there. The band was winding up cables and dismantling the equipment. Keith looked across to where I stood and took no notice. Mick turned round with a harmonica in his hand, then nodded when he saw me.

"Yeah, tell me a bit about this flat you mentioned earlier," I said to him. He looked surprised and asked in return, "Are you interested?"

"Yeah, maybe, what's it like?" I said.

He turned to the others and said, "He's interested in the flat," then paused for a second waiting to see if anyone disapproved. Keith looked at me blankly with his mousey face, then shrugged and turned away.

"We're looking for a fourth person to share with us and the rent's four pounds a week each," said Mick.

"Sound's OK. Who lives there?" I asked him.

"It's me, Keith, and Brian," Mick said. "You want to come over and see it?"

"No, I guess it's OK. Whereabouts is it?" I said to him.

"It's 102 Edith Grove, Chelsea, near the Kings Road. Do you know it?" he asked as he stepped down from the stage.

I pictured a 10-story block with the bottom half painted white. "No, but don't worry—I'll find it," I said. "When's a good time to come?"

"Anytime. How about Tuesday, that all right?"

"Yeah, that's fine, in the afternoon?"

"Yeah, great. Just give two knocks on the door."

I SAT IN the car as Eddie steered us through the London traffic. He had never heard of the Rolling Stones, and they would not have conformed to his image of would-be pop stars. He was a men's hairdresser, and one of his clients was Adam Faith, who at the time was making hit records alongside Cliff Richard. I had not seen Eddie for a while, but he was the only person I knew who had a car and would give me a lift with the few belongings I wanted to transport to the flat in Chelsea. I had been with him on several backstage visits to Adam Faith's dressing rooms around the theaters including the London Palladium. Eddie's image of a pop star was clean-cut with a mohair suit and hair that never messed up. On one visit to the Palladium we had met the suave-looking Everly Brothers, both dressed immaculately in suits and long, dark, expensive-looking coats. I wondered what he was going to think when he saw the Stones, but in the end I need not have worried.

I was back working in the printing industry after leaving it for a job as a general gardening laborer where I had met Fengey. He played guitar and was interested in the blues and consequently introduced me to the Ealing club about a year before. I was more interested in playing drums and had taken lessons from a well-known drummer on the London jazz circuit, but never owned a proper kit. The nearest I had was some biscuit tins with polythene bags stretched over the top, which I used when Fengey came to my place for a session. He would play guitar and I would beat the biscuit tins, but mostly we drank beer instead.

Before Ealing I had never heard this type of blues music and spent my early teenage years just listening to the rock and roll and teenbeat music on the radio. I had about 15 pop records and five or six albums, which made up my entire record collection. Then I started listening to modern jazz and developed an interest in the drums. The clothes I wore in the course of the laboring job were similar to the kind that beatniks or hippies were wearing at the time, so Fengey and I adapted our work clothing and dressed that way too. We did it to be different from other people our age who were still wearing the suits and relatively smart clothes then associated with pop idols. The next step from that would have been conformity with society, following the usual route of steady job and a girlfriend with whom you would then settle down. This was a natural progression expected of you, which a lot of my friends followed. Fengey and I grew beards, smoked pipes filled with cheap tobacco, and went around looking unwashed. We enjoyed the effect this Bohemian artistic appearance had on some people.

For the best part I had endured a very unhappy childhood, which consisted of begging for food and being beaten, both mentally and physically. By the time I escaped that situation at 15 years of age I was very downtrodden and introverted and had difficulty communicating with people in general. It all happened overnight, and I went from being repressed and bullied to virtually total freedom and found it difficult to come to terms with.

At first I had a very resentful attitude toward adults who I saw as aggressors of my liberty. It took me a long time to adjust to the fact I was able to express myself. Then I was able to branch out with my sense of humor. I would purposely tell people supposed jokes that were not really jokes at all—just simple stories that sounded like they could be jokes, but with bizarre endings. One of the stories was about a guy named Oppenheimer who stopped to look in a toy shop window at the model of a crane. Around the crane were some tin soldiers. Oppenheimer turned to his friend and said, "Look at all the ants." Then I would laugh at the punch line as the listener struggled to grasp the gag. I could see them thinking about it for hours afterward. People wondered what you were talking about. Then I found you could also affect them without the use of words. One example of this was when I took the lid off an empty treacle tin and then removed the bottom with a can opener so all that remained was the empty shell. I tied a length of cotton around it and hung it from the ceiling in my bedroom. I just did it because nobody else did. Nobody knew what it meant except me. I used to lie in bed watching it and saw it as the world with a hole through the middle through which everyone fell because they copied a routine of life without asking why. Everyone did the same things every day as if they had to. It was as if they wanted to do nothing else but follow the route taken before.

Eddie saw it and said, "Why have you got a fucking treacle tin hanging on the ceiling?" He looked bewildered and thought I was mad. That was the whole point but he couldn't see it. Just like the clothes, something unusual affected people by throwing them off balance. You did something they would not have done and you were considered nuts. Then on the way to the Ealing club in our beatnik clothes people thought we were unclean or maybe even stupid, and so as to put them off us further we made out we had fleas. Fengey would say, "Hey, I went to the clinic today, and they gave me this new powder to sprinkle on myself," and we would carry on from there. We always had plenty of space on the crowded underground.

I thought the other guys on the garden laboring job were totally stupid and lived boring lives. They were relatively young but looked haunted by responsibility and worry. I used to tell them, "Hey, come to the Ealing club and see this band called the Rolling Stones." Then I would pick up a shovel and hold it like a guitar and go through a routine of mouthing the guitar parts and singing "Sweet Little Sixteen" right there in the middle of the street we were working on. "If they look and sound anything like you, Mumbles, they should be locked up," was all they said. I used to reply, "Yeah, maybe, but you guys already are and can't see it."

Then I decided the beatnik thing was not really me at all and that I did not need to dress up to be eccentric. I thought people were mistaking me for a figure of entertainment and that was not really my objective. The better way was to dress as myself and then see how people reacted.

I always viewed the older generation as regimented because most men had been in the army. It was as if they had all been trained to conform to a pattern and style without asking questions. You needed your hair cut once a month and wore your best clothes on Sundays. If you worked hard and toed the line, you could earn the money to buy a television.

I wanted to show people that nothing happened if you did something considered odd or outrageous or stupid. Many people's attitude at the time was, "You can't do that!" So you immediately did it as if to say, "Hey, look, I've just done it and nothing's changed. The house hasn't fallen down and it's still Thursday." In order to do that it was necessary to be way over the top, like using a sledgehammer to crack a walnut. It never occurred to me there were some other guys pulling faces at each other and doing something similar.

We gradually made our way toward the flat passing through Earls Court where there were crowds of people milling around, creating a buzzing atmosphere. After that we drove along Redcliffe Gardens with its many elegant houses and exclusive-looking squares. The farther down we traveled, however, the more the properties began to deteriorate until we found ourselves in Edith Grove. My grand vision of Chelsea had disappeared. There were no fashionable apartment blocks—just rows of drab and dilapidated houses begging for repair, and it was more the edge of Fulham than Chelsea. Eddie pulled the car up outside number 102 and we climbed out.

"You're not going to live in this fucking dump, are you?" he looked at me and sounded shocked.

"If it's 102, it looks like I am. It's probably better inside," I answered hopefully but unconvinced.

He looked up at the house as I unloaded some plastic carrier bags and a case from the boot of his car.

"Are you sure you haven't changed your mind? I'll give you a lift back if you want," Eddie said, looking at the rest of the street.

Having come this far I was not going to be deterred so easily, and after we had said our good-byes, I watched him drive away. I imagined him wishing he had a faster car to get out of the area. Then he was out of sight and it was too late to change my mind.

The house had two pillars that supported a porch over the doorway. To the left were some iron railings with a gate leading down to the basement. I noticed the cream paint on the lower half of the building was beginning to flake away. After climbing the few steps I lifted the knocker on the door then banged it twice and waited for someone to answer. A few seconds later I heard some footsteps, and Mick opened the door.

"Oh, hello, come in, it's straight up the stairs on the first floor. Go straight up."

It did not look any better on the inside. The hallway was gloomy and everything seemed brown and dismal as I climbed the lino-covered stairs to the first landing. The kitchen was straight ahead, and as I turned left, I had my first glimpse of the communal toilet before continuing up a few more steps to the next landing. The bedroom was on the right opposite more stairs to the bathroom and the flat above. The lounge was straight ahead so I followed Mick in.

The place would have been perfect as a replica of a World War II battlefront, but as a room it was a complete shambles. Over in the far right-hand corner was an unmade bed looking as if it had just been dumped there. A table covered with dirty plates, cups, knives, and other crap stood in the bay window. To my immediate right stood a dark-colored radiogram, the kind where you pulled a flap down on the top half to gain access to the deck and the radio. The flap was down now, sagging under the weight of a pile of records. There were more records on top of the gram and yet more on the floor. The carpet had probably been colored once but now it was just grime, an almost perfect match for the wallpaper, which was hanging off in places.

"This is Keith and that's Brian," said Mick by way of introduction.

I knew that anyway, but at least it broke the ice. Brian was standing by the table and said, "Hello." Keith, who did not seem all that interested, lay sprawled out on the remains of a sofa covered with dirty washing playing his guitar. He nodded. "Hi."

It was not the same as meeting in the club. Potential flatmates need to suss each other out, so after a few moments of silence Brian asked where I was from and what I did and we chatted for a few minutes.

Then he asked, "What's your favorite song?" He probably meant one the Stones played, but I didn't realize.

"'Moonlight in Vermont,'" I answered.

"'Moonlight in Vermont'?" Mick looked taken aback, and I heard Keith chuckle in the background.

"Yeah, 'Moonlight in Vermont,'" I answered. "Do you do that one?"

Mick looked at Brian, who looked at Keith, who looked back up at Mick. He seemed to be asking himself was I for real or putting him on. Then he turned it round and came back grinning. "Yeah, but we only use it for rehearsing."

"Oh, that's good. I'll have to come down. Can you play some now?" I said to Keith, who was laughing.

He stood up and put down his guitar. "No, I'll do it later. What records have you got in the bag?" he asked.

"Go ahead and take a look," I said nodding toward the bag that contained one LP and some singles.

He delved inside the plastic bag and pulled out the album.

"A fucking Perry Como LP," he said, laughing some more. The others were laughing too.

"Hey! It's got 'Route 66' on it," said Keith, reading the track list.

"Let's have a look," said Mick, taking the record as Keith pulled out the singles.

"Is it the same one we are trying to do?" asked Brian.

"He's only got a Cliff Richard record as well and Three Stars," continued Keith, as if to say, "So this is who buys this shit."

"Is this Chuck Berry's 'Route 66'?" asked Mick.

"I don't know. I didn't know he did it," I replied.

"Put it on and have a listen," said Brian, holding the cover. "See if it is."

Mick went over to the gram and moved some records aside and put the album on. Perry Como and the orchestra came out of the speakers.

"It *is* the same 'Route 66,'" said Brian. Then to Mick, "Why don't you get the words down?"

"For chrissakes, take it off," said Keith.

"Yeah, hang on," said Mick. "I'll get some paper and write down the words first."

"Take the fucking thing off," said Keith impatiently.

Mick put the track on again and perched on the edge of the sofa writing down the words. I noted he was still wearing his overcoat.

"Do you like it?" I asked.

"It's fucking horrible. Take it off," said Keith, lounging back on the sofa.

So there we were—I'd just arrived and was sitting around with the Rolling Stones listening to Perry Como. It seemed we were all going to get along just fine. Mick played it three more times until he had finished writing all the words down. When Mick had finished, Keith leapt over to the record player. He hastily removed the Como album then said, "Thank Christ, let's have some Chuck Berry."

It was only once I had been in the kitchen that I realized the lounge was the luxury part of the flat. The only thing left that was capable of being operated was the kettle that was now trying to boil water on the ancient stove. The sink was not actually visible because piled to the top was every imaginable utensil you could think of. Saucepans, frying pans, plates, knives, and forks—everything was in there, half-filled with water. I had no idea of what lay at the bottom, but judging by the grease-covered tiles around the sink it was going to be sticky. There were about 20 milk bottles standing around like soldiers, their contents happily growing a nice green mould. I was wondering if it glowed in the dark and would light up all the empty tins, dozens of which had been left lying anywhere with their tops open and contents gone.

Brian had rinsed some cups under the single tap, which only provided cold water, and was waiting for the kettle to boil. As we stood there he began sorting through the food from my other bag and held up one of the cans I had brought.

"Sausalene? Sausalene? What's Sausalene?" He was using what I would come to know as his puzzled "nankering" voice. Keith and Mick were standing there looking on amused.

"It's a health food made out of soya beans," I told him.

"Soya beans? Sausalene? Soya beans?" Brian was still nankering in the puzzled voice.

"Yeah, they're made to taste like sausages." I informed him further.

"Made to taste like sausages? Soya beans?" he queried.

"Yeah!" I guessed he knew nothing of health food.

"Soya beans? Sausages? Sausalene? Sounds like shit to me. What else you got?" He picked up a small brown packet. "What's this?"

"That's rice," I said. Mick and Keith still stood there, clearly amused.

"Rice?" said Brian as if it was something new.

"Yeah, you boil it and then mix it with the Sausalene for a meal," I explained simply.

"Boil it and mix it with the shit? Haven't you got any real food?" he asked in mock disbelief.

"It's better than no food. You should try it sometime," I said, not imagining he would.

After smelling some milk to make sure it had not gone completely off, Brian made the coffee then passed the cups around. Amazingly there was nothing floating round on the top.

"I reckon we should go up the Ernie," said Keith.

"What's the Ernie?" I asked.

"That's the café at the top of the road—we call it the Ernie 'cos all the workmen go there and sit reading the paper and calling each other Ernie. You'll see when we go up there."

The rear bedroom of the flat was to the left as you came out of the lounge. As you entered the room Mick's bed was immediately in front of you. Behind the door to the right were two more beds—the first was to be mine, the other belonged to Keith. Brian had commandeered the remaining bed in the front room and slept there on his own. Mick had some sort of cabinet next to his bed and there was a large wardrobe with a mirrored door in the corner opposite Keith's bed. Needless to say the remainder of the room was a perfect match to the rest of the flat, with drab brown walls and grimed carpet. The windows were so dirty that at first glance I thought someone had boarded them up.

After four or five days I settled in and we seemed more at ease with each other, and even the food I had bought had disappeared, despite Brian's mockery. I had seen the other tenants in the building when they came out to use the toilet. There was a couple living upstairs and some girls who lived below. We never socialized with any of them, but we did talk to the girls below now and then. We thought the couple upstairs seemed a bit "la-di-dah"—they seemed to look down on us and avoided talking to anyone. Mick said they were "a bit off," so he called them "the Offers."

WE WERE IN the lower part of Edith Grove, so when you left the building and turned left, the street led up to some traffic lights where the Kings Road ran across. This particular area was called World's End, aptly named I thought after a nearby public house. Once you had walked up the Grove and turned right at the lights there was a row of shops. On the opposite side of the road was another parade of shops, the first one being a dairy owned by our landlord. A few doors along from there stood the Ernie, which was a typical workman's café. The food was cheap and they gave you a fair portion.

Keith was right. Most of the men read papers, wore overalls, and rolled their own cigarettes. They could also be heard talking, mainly about their jobs, and Brian and Keith would imitate their voices and mannerisms. They would sit there mimicking the conversation in bored tones about dumb facts. Even ordering a meal involved a routine, which the boys copied.

"'Allo, Ernie, ya gonna 'ave one slice or two then? Aw, all right then, if you're 'avin' two slices, fink I'll 'ave two as well. 'Ad a good day then 'ave ya Ern'? Fings must be lookin' up, I see ya got some new overalls then."

The whole meal from start to finish would be accomplished with this type of nonsense, which fitted in perfectly.

We would come here often and received a few strange looks because of our longer-than-average hair, but on the whole nobody took too much notice.

Mick was studying at the London School of Economics (LSE) during the day and often would not return until late evening. I worked in

Fulham making plates for a lithographic printer and usually arrived back about six. This Thursday Mick was back early as they were rehearsing at the Wetherby Arms, another nearby pub. It was just Mick, Keith, and Brian sitting at a table in the back room as they ran through a few numbers at low volume. In fact you would not really have been aware that a band, or part of one, was rehearsing.

They looked like three bedraggled guys who had made up an excuse to come into the pub because they had nowhere else to go. You could somehow sense the pub's landlord did not object to them having guitars as long as they never made a noise. Mick sat cross-legged at the table with a Reslo in his hand and mouthed a few words now and then as Keith and Brian fiddled with their guitars. The whole session was very subdued. It was not designed as a practice to improve the band's sound but more just a way of learning the sequences of new songs. It did not look much of a rehearsal to me, more just something to do while trying to make your drink last as long as possible. Anyone who may have been expecting some form of free entertainment would have been disappointed. If they had started playing some of their usual blues tunes at full tilt, the boys would probably have been thrown out. The regulars who used the pub sat in the front bar, oblivious or uninterested in the youngsters with guitars who did not play anything.

I was in the kitchen on the following Saturday morning polishing my fashionable "Chelsea boots" when Brian and Keith came in.

"What're you cleaning your shoes for?" demanded Keith.

"Because they're fucking dirty," I replied. "They need some polish."

"How fucking Ernie," sneered Keith.

"Why's that?" I asked him.

"Only fucking Ernies clean their shoes. What's the point?" Keith chided. "They only get dirty again."

I looked at Keith's shoes. No, they had not been cleaned recently. Probably never, judging by the scuff marks all over them.

"Oi always cleans me shoes first thing in the mornin' Bert," said the nankering Brian. "Gotta 'ave me shoes cleaned."

"Nankering" was a Stones art form one of them had created, although I never knew which and never thought of asking. You could just use a nankering voice that sounded as if it could have a West Country or similar accent. Or you could do a "full nanker," which meant pulling your lower eyelids down with the first finger of each hand. Then you would place the second finger of each hand on each nostril and push your nose up toward your eyes. The idea was to take on an alien personality to deride what the boys thought were absurd opinions or actions. It would also be used to make absurd suggestions to each other. Right then I was the subject of nankering derision.

"Why's that then, Sid?" Keith said, nankering back with his hands on his face.

"Cos' the foreman says Oi gotta 'ave clean shoes and overalls, Bert," said Brian.

"Oh, gotta do what the foreman says, can't come to work unless your overalls are clean, Sid," replied Keith.

"That's right, Bert. Don't want t' lose me job, do I?" nankered Brian.

I could tell that if you were not careful, these guys would walk all over you if you let them. While they went on with their bantering I considered how to gain the offensive and surprise them. Finally I decided upon a course.

"Have you ever had a job?" I asked Keith.

"Yeah, I worked in the Post Office for a morning. I didn't like it so I never went back in the afternoon."

Brian laughed and put the kettle on for some coffee.

"Before that I was at Sidcup Art College," Keith answered and waited for the next question.

"What were you doing there?" I asked. Then I turned my head to the left, chose a spot, and gobbed on the wall. I looked back at Keith and asked, "Anything interesting?"

There followed a few seconds' silence as both their mouths and their eyes opened in shock.

"Aw, Keith, did you see that? Look what he's done. Fucking horrible. He's gobbed on the wall," Brian called out.

"Ah, for fuck's sake, man!" said Keith.

"I can't believe it," said Brian.

Both of them stared at me for a few seconds, then saw the funny side and burst into laughter.

I took a pencil from my pocket and drew a ring around the gob on the wall. "This is called a Yellow Humphrey," I explained, writing the name alongside it as Mick walked in.

"Look what Phelge has done. We were standing here talking and he just gobbed on the wall," explained Brian, grimacing.

Mick looked and winced. "Oh, no," he groaned, shaking his head in disbelief. He searched for a cup in the sink.

"That's called a Yellow Humphrey," I explained to him. Seeing him looking slightly reviled I continued. "And this is a Scarlet Jerkins." I gobbed on the wall again for Mick to see firsthand.

He cringed and looked away, then groaned, "Oh no, that's so fucking off. Maybe we should have him as personal manager," he suggested to the others with a smile.

On Saturdays Stu would arrive at the flat in his van along with Bill and his equipment. After picking everyone up he would then drive everyone over to Ealing for the gig. Stu contrasted sharply with the other members of the band, although this never bothered him. He wore baggy sweaters most of the time, some with patterns such as a line of horses following each other around the garment. It seemed he had a collection of them, and other times he would arrive dressed in one with an equally hideous selection of multicolored zigzag hoops. The pockets on his trousers always seemed to be under constant threat from the contents—wallets and notebooks, keys and pens all looking as if they were going to fall out at any second. Every pocket seemed full and you felt that if you needed an item such as a pair of scissors he would pull it out for you there and then. Brian or Keith would sometimes poke fun at his clothes but Stu ignored their remarks. He always seemed to feel that his clothes served their purpose and that was all that mattered. If he had knocked at your door he could have passed as any type of general tradesman. That was until he was on stage playing blues piano with the Stones.

This particular night was like any other, except for Keith's fit. The gig had finished and we were the only ones remaining, packing up the gear. The lights in the club were out except behind the bar, which was now closed and being cleaned. On either side of the small dance floor was an upholstered bench seat, and I was sitting on the left-hand side when suddenly Keith collapsed on the floor. His body began shaking with spasmodic jerks and a gurgling noise started coming from his throat.

"Keith, Keith, what's the matter?" Brian cried. "Quick! Help!"

"What is it, Keith, are you all right?" Mick asked bending over him.

Charlie bent down. "What's wrong with him?"

Keith was shaking from head to foot with foam coming from his mouth.

"He looks really ill," said Brian. "Lift him up onto the seat."

The three of them struggled with his still-contorting body, lifted then half-dropped him on the seat while he continued to struggle for air. Bill looked ashen and horrified.

"Keith, try and tell us what's wrong," said Mick, holding Keith's shoulders and trying to keep him still.

"Do you need some help?" the barman called as he came out from behind the bar.

"It's Keith. He's having some sort of fit and we don't know what to do," Brian said, sounding panicked.

"Do you think we should call an ambulance?" I asked. "He looks like shit."

Whether Keith could hear what was going on I did not know, but the spasms seemed worse now and the barman hurried over and looked down at him. "Jesus Christ, he looks terrible," he said. "Does this happen often?"

"Now and again," said Brian. "He has these kinds of fits. This one's bad."

The barman leaned over to look at Keith's face.

"Give him some air, let him breathe," Brian ordered. "Mick, hold his head."

Charlie looked round helplessly at the barman. "What do you think we should do?"

"He needs an ambulance. It's no good looking at him," I said to the barman.

He looked across at me, then back at Keith and made a decision. "I'll get him some brandy," he said on his way back to the bar.

"Brandy?" said Brian watching the barman holding a glass up to the optics. "What good's that?"

"Yeah, brandy, it will do him good," said the barman. "Help steady his nerves. Hold him up and we'll get him to sip it," called the barman as he hurried back.

They held Keith up and put the glass to his mouth. "Try to sip it slowly," said the barman. Keith sipped until the glass was empty. The shaking seemed to subside for a few seconds.

"He's stopped shaking," said Brian. "You were right about the brandy. Are you all right, Keith?"

Keith half sat up and looked around as if he was coming to and then suddenly relapsed again, shaking on the seat.

"Do you think we should try another one?" asked Brian.

The barman rushed off and came back carrying the refilled glass and held it out. Keith suddenly sat bolt upright and grabbed the glass from the barman. Then in one swift movement he put the glass to his lips and downed the drink in one gulp.

"What's been going on?" he asked as if nothing had happened. "C'mon, let's go." Then he stood up and handed the glass back to the barman before marching briskly out of the club.

Outside we all absolutely collapsed with hysterics at Keith's spur-of-the-moment imitation fit. That was with the exception of Stu who was shaking his head sadly. "C'mon you hooligans, get in the van," he ordered. Then turning to me he said, "You're almost as bad as them."

We laughed virtually all the way back to Edith Grove. This was the first time Keith had pulled this particular stunt. In fact I had only realized halfway through that it was a gag thought up by Keith to get a free drink.

By the time we arrived back at the flat it was long past midnight. We made some coffee and hung around talking and smoking before finally going to bed. There was not much to do the next day and we all stayed in bed until the early afternoon. This was not an unusual occurrence for the Stones, who often had nothing else to do.

One evening when I returned from work, I found all three of them still in bed. Brian had managed the trip from his room and was lying in my bed talking to Keith and Mick, who had taken a day off from college. They were discussing having two girl singers rehearse with the band to provide backing vocals. I knew that Mick had been trying to date Cleo, one of the girls, and my impression was that the proposed arrangement was more for his benefit than the band's. Whatever the reason, the idea proved short-lived and was soon forgotten.

Some evenings during the week we visited clubs in London and on another Keith and I cleaned up the kitchen—not a pleasant task. We set about that by pouring hot water over everything to melt as much of the grease as possible before one of us had to put his hand into the sink to touch anything. Gradually, with a lot of scraping, we made our way down to the sink's surface and cleaned that a bit too. With the bottles and cans cleared and dumped it did not look too bad. It only took about a week for Brian to fix it back again.

My favorite R&B number at the time was "Goin' to New York" by Jimmy Reed, which featured on an album among the vast record collection at Edith Grove, which I gradually sorted my way through. Everything by Chuck Berry and Bo Diddley must have been there with an occasional Elvis and Howlin' Wolf. The singles were a different matter with the selection made up of country, blues, and rock, all by American artists. It seemed impossible to play them all. Many of them I had never heard of before and from these I found a few favorites, which I played regularly. Some of them were favorites of the other guys too and ended up being covered by the Stones. One of the artists was someone I had never heard of before named Arthur Alexander. I thought the name sounded odd, but his recording of "You Better Move On" had an appealing, off-beat rhythm. Among the other records weighing the gram down were "Poison Ivy" and "Louie, Louie." The stack of records contained nothing in the way of guitar instrumentals that had been popular during the early '60s.

Brian and I were in the lounge, which doubled as his bedroom, huddling around the electric fire the following Saturday morning. Keith had gone out and Mick was still in bed. Brian was relating some of his background and telling me about his strict upbringing. He had studied a great deal, gaining several good educational qualifications. He also came from a good musical background, but as there was no music scene to speak of in Cheltenham he had decided to come to London. Since arriving he had only had a couple of short-term jobs, which he never really talked about in detail. He occasionally received letters addressed to L. B. H. Jones and I asked him what the initials stood for. *L* was for Lewis and *B* was Brian, he had replied. I asked him about the *H*.

"I'm not telling you that—it's so awful; it's embarrassing. I'll never tell anybody so don't ask me again."

I felt it was time to drop the issue—for the time being—and changed the subject. "Didn't I see a letter from you some time back in one of the music papers?"

"Yeah, before Christmas. I've still got a copy of it somewhere. Do you want to see it?" he asked with a hint of eagerness.

"No, I read it. I remember it had the band's name at the bottom," I answered. Although I didn't recall the letter's content, I didn't particularly want to read it again.

"I've also written to the BBC trying to get an audition for the band," he said in a hopeful tone. "Though I haven't heard anything back from them as yet."

"What, for *Saturday Club*?" I asked but got no answer. Suddenly Keith burst in looking pleased with himself and carrying a parcel under his arm.

"Ah, it's come," said Brian, suddenly excited.

"Yeah, I got it, man. Just turned up this morning." Keith was wearing a scarf around his neck, shivering from the cold outside. Maybe it was inside. He passed the package to Brian and stood warming his hands in front of the pathetic-looking fire, trying to absorb some heat. Brian undid the package, pulled out the record and studied the cover.

"Aaah, see what he's using this time. Look at this guitar, Keith. He's got a square Gretsch."

It was the latest Bo Diddley album, ordered from the States, and as usual Bo was on the cover with his trademark, an unusual-looking guitar. He always came up with something different on each album cover. We stood there grinning, admiring Bo's humor.

R&B records were seldom imported into the U.K., and the only reliable source for them was direct from the States. Over the coming months various Chuck Berry and Bo Diddley albums on the Chess label would arrive and were the source of many new songs for the band's repertoire. Each arrival generated the same routine with the ritual studying of the cover. Everyone seemed to be trying to savor the precious moments of anticipation before playing the first track, when all would finally be revealed. To be loved or rejected.

The Bo Diddley album was at full blast when Mick joined us. Mornings were never a buoyant time for him—he always seemed to struggle for the first few hours of the day, but on this occasion he had somehow found the will to make it around the door into the front room. He sat on the edge of Brian's bed, and I thought he was not going to make it through the first track, but he seemed to gain life as the record played.

Brian and Keith evaluated each track as it came as either being "knockout" or "too slow" and then "Let's listen to it again, see if we can use it."

Eventually when the usable tracks had been picked out they would be rehearsed acoustically in the front room over the next few days. Quite often the first real test was at the first available gig. The rehearsals at the Wetherby Arms were virtually nonexistent—although we lived locally, Bill, Charlie, and Stu were in the suburbs. There was never a full rehearsal at the pub with all the band members and all the equipment.

Repairs and replacements to the equipment took precedence over paying the rent almost every week. The amplifiers seemed to go wrong on a regular basis and the Reslo mikes packed up seemingly at will, costing £12 a time to replace. The harmonicas also had a fairly short life span and although they only cost about four shillings and sixpence each, there had to be a different one for each key.

Everything had to be ready and perfect for the only regular weekly gig—Saturdays at Ealing. The Red Lion gig in Sutton was every other Wednesday, while the Marquee Club only booked the Stones for occasional Thursdays.

The Marquee was probably the best showcase for the band, for two reasons: it was a major venue, and it was in Oxford Street, the heart of London's West End. It was a large club compared to Ealing and always seemed fairly empty by comparison despite the presence of some of the band's regular followers. Although this following grew each week, it still remained just a large handful of cult mod people.

The Marquee was essentially a jazz club. It seemed the management at the Marquee did not take too kindly to the type of people the band was attracting. It had been difficult enough at first with the Stones' music and image. Now there were the strangely dressed people, whose clean image and sharp dressing formed an odd contrast to the band they were following and to the polo-necked jazz people. The jazzers would stand there all night with a half pint of beer and click their fingers to the music. These new freaks danced. Well sort of; it was mainly stamping their feet and waving their arms. "Most uncool way to behave, man," you could hear the jazzers whisper.

The only non-jazzer who appeared to be readily accepted by the management was "Big" Pete Deucher, a would-be country artist. Rumor said Big Pete was quite wealthy and had also been given the key to the city of Nashville, country music's mecca. Basically he came across to us as just another big strummer on the guitar from the left-over days of Skiffle, with songs like "Footprints in the Snow" and "Midnight Special." He did not like the Stones either—yobbos with electric guitars and long hair. There was even a rumor that Big Pete had tried to have the Stones banned from ever setting foot through the door.

Despite the mixed reception, the members of the band were grateful for the gig, not because of the small amount of money earned but simply just because it was a gig. It was somewhere to play and gain exposure for the band and its music. On Thursdays at the Marquee they were the support group to the Cyril Davies All Star R&B Group. Cyril's band blended blues and rock and roll rhythm featuring Carlo Little and Ricky Brown on drums and bass. Both ex-members of the Screaming Lord Sutch band, they could put down a solid beat all night. Nicky Hopkins played some amazing piano and a guy named Bernie Watson would sometimes totally ignore the audience, turning his back upon them as his guitar played like magic. Whenever he did this it came across that he was trying to hide the secret of his ability. The highlight of Cyril's set was a tune they later recorded called "Country Line Special." Cyril blew his harmonica and the crowd to a frenzy every time with that one.

One or two people used to "guest" with the All Stars, notably Long John Baldry, a good vocalist also doing the blues circuit at this time whose three-piece suit contrasted sharply with other artists and made him look like a blues version of Frank Sinatra.

Perhaps inevitably, the Stones proved to be more popular than Cyril's All Star band, or at least they received a stronger reaction. I thought it was several factors: Mick was younger than Cyril and a bit more trendy and the Stones also came across as antiestablishment. Also they were more a guitar band with just a harmonica here and there and some occasional piano. The two different lead sounds of Brian and Keith formed a more versatile arrangement. As good as Cyril was, having harmonica as virtual lead on every number could get tedious. The other factor was that the Stones' followers came to see the Stones, not Cyril. Although they started as second billing to the All Stars, after three weeks they attained equal status and this seemed to breed discontent all round. The Stones wanted some extra money as their section of the crowd was growing and the club was beginning to appear fairly full, but their request was refused. Maybe it was Cyril's way of maintaining his advantage, but whatever the cause the Stones left the Marquee after four weeks at the end of January. Consequently a much-needed gig ended up being surrendered on a matter of principle.

Losing the Marquee came at a time when the Stones really needed more exposure. Only a few days before they had heard the Beatles performing on BBC's *Saturday Club*. Why we were up so early on a Saturday I wasn't sure. When I came back from buying cigarettes, Brian was standing next to the radiogram having just tuned in to the Beatles' pending broadcast. It was the first time we had ever tuned in to *Saturday Club*.

Snippets of news had been in the music press about the band from Liverpool who were making a steady impact and Brian wanted to hear them. After 10 minutes or so the Beatles came on and Brian's face dropped. In a panic-stricken voice he called for Keith to come and listen. I was standing about three feet away from the radio while Brian and Keith crowded themselves right over it. As the Beatles played "Love Me Do," Keith bent right over, transfixed as if he could see the band.

"Oh, no," said Brian. "Listen to that. They're doing it!"

"Hang on, let's hear the guitar," said Keith listening intently. "Fuck it."

"They've got harmonies too," said Brian "It's just what we didn't want."

I listened and thought the Beatles sounded OK, but so what? Just another group. "What's the problem?" I asked.

"Can't you hear?" Said Keith "They're using a harmonica—they've beaten us to it."

"They're into the same blues thing as us," said Brian. "We'll have to listen to see what else they do later."

I liked the song and I could hear the harmonica, but I did not think the music sounded anything like the Stones. Brian's point was that the Beatles were using the bluesy sound and that if they took off successfully, everyone else would copy it. The Stones would be just another group, it was important to be first. The Beatles did some more songs and later in the broadcast the Stones' spirits dropped further when they performed a Chuck Berry song. Mick heard this too and much debating was to take place later about whether the Beatles had professional arrangements or whether they were that good on their own account. The overall answer was a bit of each.

There was a feeling of anxiety in the air in the front room and I thought I would try to cheer everyone up a little. I casually opened the window a little way and took some dirty cups and plates from the table. I asked, "Anyone want these?" Before they could answer I threw them out of the window. They dropped all the way down into the front basement entrance and shattered into small pieces. At least they were laughing again.

Come the beginning of February the weather turned bad. It seemed extra cold back at the flat with snow outside, but that Saturday night the Ealing club decided to book the band for Tuesdays.

The first of the Tuesday gigs at Ealing did not bode well. I always regarded Ealing as the band's first home, their stronghold where the first followings were formed. This night it was virtually empty due to the poor weather, but it did provide an opportunity for a rare full-scale rehearsal.

The midweek gig at Ealing only lasted for three weeks and never became as popular as Saturday. I thought the Tuesday shows failed because they coincided with the extreme weather conditions, which made travel difficult. Only the regular hard-core supporters were there. Among these was "Eric the Mod," who would occasionally get up on stage with the band and sing two or three Chuck Berry numbers, giving Mick the opportunity to rest his voice.

Eric always looked self-conscious and unsure whether to move or not. Sometimes he would click his fingers as he sang or just tuck his thumbs in the waist of his trousers. Nevertheless, he looked cool with his lambswool pullover that matched his boyish looks and short mod hair style. Along with Pretty Mick, who probably had the first bouf-fant hairstyle around, and the energetic Rowan, Eric Clapton was an early member of the mod revolution.

WE WERE NEVER sure whether our landlord actually owned 102 Edith Grove, but we did know that he ran a dairy shop on the corner of Kings Road and the Grove. One of the things we did when really hungry was to get two shillings and sixpence together between us and go to the dairy for a fruit pie. The landlord and his wife were both from Wales and inevitably moaned about how the flat needed cleaning. I think they were supposed to come in every Friday and do this, but it seemed they had given up the battle. The fruit pies came ready made by a Welsh company called Morgan-Morgan, so that became the nickname for the landlord.

Black-currant and apple was our favorite flavor, and some days at moments when we were really hungry one of us would ask, "Anyone fancy a Morgan-Morgan?" Then after a trip to the dairy to buy one we would divide it up between us. If we had no money, the flat upstairs occupied by the Offers became the target. They were out all day, and we discovered where they used to leave the key, taking advantage of this to raid their flat on a regular basis. Mainly our quest was for milk, coffee, or bread but on a good day you could sometimes find an egg. Fortunately the larder where they kept their food stood above a sink outside the entrance to their apartment. Most of the food could be found here. We only went into the flat itself if the cupboard was completely bare—inside was where you could find luxury items such as toilet paper and Sellotape. It was almost a nightly routine to hear Mrs. Offer climbing the stairs then unlocking the door and screaming. Mr. Offer used to follow her in and immediately come under fire regarding the missing items. Sometimes he came down to complain and we would deny all knowledge. In the end I think he was just going through the motions to pacify his partner.

They never raided our kitchen though.

With the succession of late nights I had been struggling to arrive at work on time, arriving up to two hours late on occasions. I worked in the camera room with one other person and as business was pretty slack I was not particularly missed. So now I began to take whole days off work occasionally. My health-food kick had now been forgotten and replaced with the one or two meals of sausage, egg, and chips we could afford each week at the Ernie. Our hair was now even longer and beyond the point when people would have expected us to have it cut. It was now growing over our ears and down to our shirt collars. It was not a conscious decision by any of us to have long hair; it was just born out of lack of money, but we began to like it. Maybe the reason was because it offended, or was different—I did not know.

The Ernie became a sort of no man's land between us and the other regulars. Now that we had long hair, they were the Ernies and we were the "Nancy Boys." We sneered at them and they sneered back.

On one of the days I took off Keith and I lay in our beds after watching Mick leave to go to the LSE. Keith had just finished telling me the story of how he and Mick knew each other as kids and met up again years later on a train. I looked up at the poster on the wall that read "Rollin' Stones."

"Is it the Rollin' Stones or Mick Jagger and the Rollin' Stones?" I asked Keith.

"He'd probably like it to be Mick Jagger and the Rollin' Stones, but it ain't; it's just the Rollin' Stones."

"Everyone refers to it as Mick Jagger and the Rollin' Stones," I replied.

"It's like Cliff and the Shadows, everyone puts the singer's name first but we're just called the Rollin' Stones." There was no *g* on Rollin'.

It was about 10 o'clock and we decided to get up and make some coffee. I wandered up to the Offers' apartment to get some milk and anything else that might be going. But I could only find milk. The Offers were getting crafty, either hiding everything or not leaving anything spare hanging around.

I was washing, or rather just rinsing some cups under the cold tap and Keith wandered back in with his guitar.

"This kitchen's all shitted up again," I said. "Maybe we could get those tarts downstairs to clean it?"

"Judy did it a couple of times, but I think she probably wants Mick to give her one," Keith said as he fiddled some chords.

"Maybe we'll leave it then," I replied. "Why don't you play the Cash thing. I like that."

"Which one?" Keith asked.

"The 'Lonesome Whistle Blow' thing, or any one'll do," I said to him.

He played the "Lonesome Whistle Blow" thing, and the Cash riff was dead right. Finishing it off, he picked up his coffee and said, "I'm gonna get something to read and have a crap. Maybe we'll go up town afterwards."

I was in the bedroom having a shave and heard somebody come up to use the loo before finding it occupied and going back down the stairs. This happened about three times and then I heard Judy from downstairs banging on the toilet door.

"What are you doing in there, Keith?" she called out.

"Fuck off. I'm having a crap. What do think I'm doing?"

"You've been in there 20 minutes. I've got to go to work," she countered.

"Well, fuck off then," Keith replied from behind the closed door.

Judy disappeared a few minutes later, slamming the street door behind her.

For some reason Keith and I had taken to reading Dennis Wheatley novels. We liked the ones about black magic and his others with Gregory Salhurst as the main hero. I guessed that Keith was reading one of these books in the bog. I went in the front room— Brian had gone out—and put on "Goin' to New York" and some other records. After vacating the toilet Keith wandered in and then back out. I figured he was getting ready to go up to town. I played some more records and eventually wandered into the bedroom to see what he was doing. He had his back to me and was leaning halfway out the window.

"What are you doin', man?" I said.

"Pass me that wire over there," he replied without elaborating.

"What are you doin'?" I repeated, passing him the wire.

He reentered the bedroom with one end of the wire.

"Hang on, I'll show you in a minute." He disappeared back down to the toilet. Eventually he came back in carrying Brian's tape recorder.

"I've wired the bog up," he grinned.

He had hidden the small crystal microphone behind the cistern and ran the wires along the pipes then out of the toilet window. From there they came through the bedroom window and back to Brian's tape machine.

"I reckon we can do some recording now then," he said mischievously.

After that we spent the rest of the day ligging around and lying in wait for various victims to use the toilet. Eventually we had a collection of recordings of the other tenants in the house grunting and groaning away on the toilet, all unknowingly being taped in the process.

When Brian and Mick came back we had a long playback session and a good laugh hearing our victims straining away and flushing the bog. We left the microphone in the toilet for a few days until we had filled up the tape with the recordings. One afternoon we finally caught Judy coming out of the toilet and invited her in to listen to what she probably thought was going to be some music. Keith turned on the machine and played back for her the sounds of her "sitting." She ran out of the room screaming and down the stairs to tell the others, "They've been bloody recording us all going to the toilet for days." We then started the whole tape running from the beginning and played it full blast into the hallway for them all to listen to each other.

On the Saturday at lunchtime we were all in the front room, wearing our coats because the flat was so cold. It was a crisis meeting. With the Ealing gig due in a few hours, Mick announced that he did not think he would be able to perform. He had been spraying all sorts of things down his throat and taking various lozenges for the last 24 hours trying to rid himself of a sore throat but without success. He decided to take another trip to the chemist in the Kings Road, and as I felt I was suffering from something similar I decided to go with him to see what medicine was available.

The chemist was a small place in need of some extra lighting, and an old-fashioned bell attached to the door clanged every time someone entered or went out. When we walked in, there was a queue of people at the glass counter waiting to pick up prescriptions or remedies for their ailments. Standing in line I wondered why chemist shops always smelled of soap and antiseptic, then figured that medicine was probably made from both of them. Some of it really tasted vile as I recalled and you needed a Band Aid over your mouth to keep it down. I told Mick we needed to buy some of the red stuff as that tasted best. When our turn came at the counter the man informed us that we needed a prescription for the red medicine. We ended up buying between us some kind of spray and some more smelly black throat lozenges before making our way back. Oddly enough, this trek up the street on that dismal day may have fixed an image in Mick's mind. At this point, though, neither of us knew there would one day be a song called "You Can't Always Get What You Want," which would come close to depicting this minor event. Its verse would tell of how he "stood in line with Mr. Jimmy at the Chelsea drugstore."

"We'll have to do as many instrumentals as we can," said Brian. "I wonder if Ernie can sing," he added doubtfully. He was referring to Bill. The instrumental idea seemed optimistic as the band never played instrumentals. You won't get away with busking 12-bars all night, I thought.

"I'll give Clapton a ring, get him to come, and give us a hand with a few numbers then do what I can," said Mick. He was referring to

Eric the Mod. It seemed the only possible alternative this late in the day. He sprayed his throat some more and went out to phone Eric from the call box at the end of the street.

"I wish we could find a different bass player," said Brian "This one's a right fucking Ernie with his greasy hair."

"Why not get someone else?" I enquired.

"Yeah, we would," said Keith. "But he owns half the equipment."

As far as they were concerned, Bill was an Ernie who was in the band by default. They were put off by the fact that he was married, and to make things worse he had a daytime job. Also Bill looked a bit like a rocker, which he probably was, and he never appeared to share everyone else's sense of humor either. We used to try to do all sorts of things to shock him but he would just stand there deadpan as if nothing had happened. He would just look back at us with a straight face as if we were stupid. We could not find what made him tick. He carried this manner with him on stage, standing at the back dead quiet and looking as if he was watching everybody or had seen it all before. Sometimes when he turned up they would more or less ignore him and only speak if they had to. Brian and Keith also used to get pissed off at him because he always sat in the front of Stu's van. They used to come in and moan, "Ernie says he can't sit in the back of the van because it makes him sick." Maybe Bill was just shrewd.

Eric turned up and did a good few numbers that night, and the band managed to drag out the breaks for a bit of extra time as well. Listening to Mick you could not really tell he had a sore throat—he seemed to get through the evening pretty much as normal.

I spent the evening chatting up one of the girls in the audience. She said she wanted to run away from home, so I took her back to the flat and slept with her. During the next day, while I was at work, Brian chatted her up, and that night he slept with her. Keith remarked later when we were in our beds: "Typical fucking Jonesey. Phelge brings a bird back, and he's gotta go and pull it. What's the matter with him?"

I said I was not bothered. As it turned out Brian was tired of her the next day and dumped her back on me. She then slept with me for the next three nights and by then it did not seem such a good idea to have brought her back. We were all expecting the police to turn up at any moment—she had now been missing for five days.

When I came in on the Thursday I found Mick and Keith waiting for me like a deputation.

"Look," said Mick. "I know she's your bird and all that and we've got nothing against you having a bird here. The thing is she's run away from home, and there's probably people looking for her."

"Her parents may have the cops out looking for her as well," added Keith.

"Yeah, I was thinking about it," I said. "But she's frightened to go home because her parents never let her out. I can see she can't stay here. What do you reckon?"

"Shall I have a word with her?" said Mick. "See if she's got somewhere else to go?"

"Do you mind?" Keith asked me.

"No man, I was wondering what to do with her anyway. How to get out of it. Go ahead and let's see what she says," I said to Mick.

We all trundled into the front room. Mick did an excellent job of being sympathetic and caring. He gave her all this talk about her parents missing her and being upset. Finally he persuaded her to phone home, which she did. Her parents drove over from Ealing later that afternoon and knocked at the door and asked for their daughter. They did not pass any comments or cause any fuss and just waited on the doorstep. Maybe they were too taken aback by the state of the building to come inside. When the girl went down to meet them, they all seemed happy to see each other and after hugs all round they drove off together.

We were all relieved after she had gone, no one more than me. I spoke to her a couple of weeks later at the Ealing club, being careful not to get involved once again. She seemed happy, and said she was getting on really well with her parents since she had been back. It had worked out neatly for everyone.

It was around this time that Brian and Keith seemed to be developing a closer relationship, spending hours locked together in the front room. Mick was still at college and arriving back late at night; then he would be up and gone again before seeing much of any of us. A microphone connected to the tape recorder had been rigged up hanging from the electric light in the center of Brian's room. It hung down below the bulb about four feet on its flex so that it became level with someone's face if they stood next to it. The object of this was to test record their new act. They went on and on, night after night, performing a duet of an Everly Brothers ballad into the tape recorder and only stopping to make more coffee. Mick and I used to lie in the bedroom inwardly groaning for them to give it a rest. There was no chance. As each recording of the song ended, they would play it back and then decide to record it again. This continued all night, and they would still be doing it when Mick and I woke. After we left, they would eventually go to bed only to begin again the following night. The microphone was moved up and down into all sorts of different positions as they tried to get the balance between their voices and the guitars correct.

One night I had gone to bed at about midnight and must have fallen half asleep. I do not know what woke me but I suddenly felt aware of something and opened my eyes. It was two o'clock. Keith had crept in and turned on the light, and as I turned my head toward the door, there was his ass in front of my face. He had dropped his trousers and was bending over, just about to fart in my face. Deciding I had to react instantly I did the first thing that came into my head: I quickly leaned over and sunk my teeth into his ass and bit it. Keith let out a big yell and went scurrying through the door back to the front room. I could hear Brian laughing.

"What happened? What happened?" I heard Brian ask.

"He only woke up and bit a chunk out of my fucking ass," said Keith. Then they slammed the front room door and I heard them laughing.

Whenever Mick was around during this period he seemed genuinely pissed off. He began entering rooms without speaking to anyone, slamming doors behind him and becoming generally uncommunicative. It seemed difficult to get him involved in any type of conversation, and he wandered around the flat like that for a couple of days.

I asked Brian, "Mick seems a bit off. What's up with him?"

"It's because he's feeling left out," Brian explained. "He doesn't like it because I'm doing something with Keith. I knew it would upset him. Don't take any notice."

Keith and Brian continued their routine with the same song for about a week before they finally gave up. I never did find out if they got it right, and I didn't much care. I reckoned they eventually gave in through exhaustion or caffeine poisoning. They were never going to sound like the Everlys. Mick started talking again.

I had not particularly noticed that anyone was in sole command of the band at this point. Keith did not seem to give a toss as long as he could play somewhere. Brian acted as spokesman on occasions and wrote letters to the musical press on behalf of the band. Mostly the letters concerned themselves with making a case for the type of blues being played by black American artists. The listening public had only come across the word *blues* in song titles such as "Singin' the Blues" and "Mess of Blues." The jazz fraternity knew more about blues, but often the pieces they played just had the word *blues* pasted into the title. The New Orleans jazz favored by some bands was probably the closest thing to authentic blues, but it was still a long way from the raw Chicago-style blues Brian favored.

I put the spokesman role down to the fact that Brian could look serious if need be and was capable of sounding sincere and plausible with his soft-spoken voice. Mick would always keep tabs on everything and make suggestions as and when he felt the need. He never came across as especially wanting to run the band; rather he just wanted to make sure he knew what was going on. The band had so little work it was not as if there was a big bundle of major decisions to be made—if the Stones were offered a gig at this stage, they usually took it without debate. If anything ever arose that did need debating, Mick, Brian, and Keith always discussed it among them. Charlie was always very affable and just took everything in his stride, contented with the outcome whatever they decided. Stu was much the same as Charlie, although he had an added interest in having everything organized because he had the responsibility of transportation. On the rare occasion that he did argue about something he generally gave up in frustration—once Mick, Keith, and Brian had a fixed idea they were immovable. Bill was never consulted—he was still not really regarded as a permanent member and was told about decisions later.

The band was beginning to sound good now—more of a coherent unit than a few individuals who had gathered for a blow. It all seemed a question of balance. Having a few gigs at the same places on a fairly regular basis gave them the advantage of being able to get a better feel for the acoustics of the various venues. The Stones were gradually becoming more conscious of how they sounded overall, as opposed to how they had performed individually.

Compared to the small confined area of the Ealing club the Marquee was a big wide-open space. The few regular gigs there with the Cyril Davies band had given them the advantage of being able to set their equipment to suit the surroundings. This in turn meant they could concentrate more on the music and performance rather than have to waste half the evening making fine adjustments to everything as would have been necessary at a one-off gig. They were always asking me, "How did it sound?" or "Does it sound OK at the back?" I used to move to various points around each club and sometimes I wandered back up to the stage in between the numbers to suggest more of Keith, or Mick, or whatever. Sometimes they would move the volume up or down in acknowledgment; other times they took no notice. Like most bands they would get louder and more enthusiastic as the evening wore on.

There was not much to lug in or out in the way of equipment. The front line was made up of a pair of Vox speakers and an amp for the PA, plus a small 30- or 50-watt guitar amp each for Brian and Keith. Charlie's drum kit consisted of four cases, one of which contained stands and fittings. The biggest and heaviest item was Bill's enormous bass speaker that appeared homemade and seemed to dwarf everything. Along with the three guitars and an old holdall containing the mikes, maracas, harmonicas, various leads, and a plug-board, that was it—just about half a van load. Stu drove the van and usually Bill and Mick would sit alongside him in the front. Keith, Charlie, Brian, and I would all be cramped in the back with the gear. That's how the gigs were done.

MORGAN-MORGAN WAS A squat little middle-aged guy with balding hair. He always wore a tie with his dark-colored jacket, a blazer that housed a collection of different-colored pens in its top pocket. He turned up at weekends to collect the rent, which more often than not we wouldn't have, but he was never too pressing and always prepared to be lenient and collect two weeks' worth next time. He did not make much reference to the state of the flat unless his wife visited with him. Then from her it would be, "I want this place cleaned up by the next time I come or you're out." Or "Look at this mess; it's a disgrace! Look what you've done to this room. It's ruined!" The stock answer from Brian was, "We never got in 'til late. We'll have it sorted by Friday." On another occasion he even turned around and told her, "We've just done it. We've spent all day cleaning."

I was still working at the printers down in Fulham although my time of arrival was becoming erratic following all the late nights. Some days I never made it at all. Keith suggested I should pack it in and "get involved in some fiddle rather than work." I was earning £10 or £11 per week, and by the time I had paid my fares in addition to my share of the rent, I was not really any better off than the others. The remainder of my money was being eked out on food. I ran the thought of "some fiddle" through my brain. Keith meant making some easy money from your workplace without your boss knowing what was going on under his nose. Other options would have been selling stolen goods or conning people. There was not much market out there for printing plates, and I couldn't see anything around the flat worth selling. I looked around the room and figured I would have to pay someone to take any of the shit we possessed. I let Keith's suggestion pass.

Inevitably, each week we would borrow a few shillings from each other to get by on a daily basis. Keith's mother came to visit him at the flat occasionally and always seemed concerned at how we were all getting on.

"Are you looking after yourselves and getting enough to eat?" she would ask. Obviously her prime concern was Keith, who used to lie, "Yeah, everything's fine; we've got some work, don't worry."

She always brought with her a carrier bag of food that we would later share or eat all at once after she had left. In return we gave her a bag of shirts to take back to be washed. She was a nice lady, and it must have been a long trip for her from Dartford by public transport. I do not think she ever believed anything we told her though.

Keith and I found ourselves alone in the kitchen one morning and decided to try and clean up once more. We actually washed all the pans again and dumped the milk bottles and cans. Then we gathered all the dirty washing and stuffed it into a couple of plastic buckets of water and left them in the bathroom upstairs. It was not until three weeks later, after we had run out of shirts—we only wore one a week—that we remembered they were still up there. We emptied the buckets into the bath, hung the shirts up overnight to dry and put one of them on the next morning. Although the collars appeared a bit bent, the shirts seemed quite clean and did not look too bad considering we were wearing them without being ironed. We felt quite pleased with ourselves. The kitchen reverted back to its usual state of course following Brian's culinary expertise in frying purloined food. Along with the Yellow Humphrey and Scarlet Jenkins, we now had a Polka Dot Perkins and a Green Gilbert on the ceiling.

Apart from the landlord and Keith's mother there were few visitors. That is, apart from two girls who suddenly started turning up occasionally at one o'clock in the morning. They were twin sisters called Sandy and Sarah. (These names have been changed.) Usually it was Sandy who came on her own to see Mick and join him in bed for a couple of hours before leaving again. On other occasions her sister Sarah accompanied her and I too had female company. They were two well-built girls. They would slip out from their unsuspecting parents' house after everyone had retired to bed, then catch a taxi to Edith Grove. Then they would stay for as long as they could while still leaving time to get home before their parents rose the next morning.

Charlie and I had a common interest in modern jazz and drums. For something to do Charlie, Keith, and I took a trip one Saturday morning across to Bayswater to the big store called Whiteleys. I think Charlie primarily wanted to buy some clothes. He always seemed to dress in what became known as the "Ivy League" style long before it became fashionable. Wearing a sports jacket and tie suited him. He always looked neat, tidy, and clean, which was probably the advantage of living at home. Charlie's concession to joining the Stones was taking his tie off at gigs. He would never look right slopping about in jeans and I doubted if he had any.

Whiteleys had a sale on, so it was natural to go down and check out the record department and find out if there was anything worth buying. Sorting through the disarray of albums I finally settled on a copy of *Walkin'* by Miles Davis; it was going cheap as it did not have its original cover, just a plain brown cardboard sleeve. It had the title and artist's name written in pencil in one corner.

When we arrived back at the flat, Brian was strolling around the front room in a horrible hand-knitted black jumper he wore that was about three sizes too big. Charlie and I walked in with the record while Keith went to make coffee.

"What have you got there?" Brian immediately pounced on the record while I cleared the turntable on the gram of singles.

"Miles Davis? Where'd you get this?" He demanded. "It's got my writing on it."

"Over at Whiteleys," I told him.

"It is my writing. I used to work there in the record department. Could be one I did. It looks like my writing."

"Yeah, well, you read it and we'll play it," I said. He passed over the album and I stuck it on the player. It played as Charlie and I listened intently. Keith came in with some coffee.

"It's a good record," said Charlie, who named and described the other members of Davis's group.

"It sounds like a load of crap. Music for pseuds," said Keith.

"No, it's real music. Listen to those drums," said Charlie.

"Load of old bollocks," said Keith, leaving the room.

Charlie and I listened in peace to the first side, then turned the record over. Keith stuck his head back round the door and called out to Mick, "'Ere, look at these two, making out they're all hip diggin' this jazz shit." We ignored him.

"I can't work out what it is he's playing," said Charlie. "It doesn't sound right for a trumpet and it's not a sax. Sounds more like an alto."

Keith reentered.

"What does that sound like?" Charlie asked him. "He normally plays trumpet."

"It sounds like shit to me," replied Keith, referring to the whole record. "You two don't really like this."

"Maybe it is an alto," I said.

"Don't sound right for an alto either. The speed of that drumming—it's incredible," said Charlie, clearly impressed.

For some unknown reason I wandered over to the gram and tried to read the label as it was going round in a bid to find out the name of the track. Then I noticed the speed symbol on the record.

"Aw, fuck. It's still on 45 rpm. I forgot to alter the speed on the player," I cried out.

"Aaahh, you pair of turds," laughed Keith, running out the room. He then called out to Brian and Mick, "Hey, get a load of this. These two fucking pseuds have only been playing this record for the last half hour at the wrong speed and standing there saying how great it is."

Loud jeers from Mick and Brian floated into the front room.

"You pair of wankers. I told you it was shit," Keith said triumphantly.

I put the record back on at the right speed and started it again from the beginning.

"That's better. It sounds like a trumpet now," said Charlie.

"You two, Stan Gutz and Charlie Turd. It still sounds like shit," said Keith.

"Yeah, well, this music sounds good at either speed," I said to Keith in a bid not to be outdone.

Keith laughed at us and walked out. Charlie and I looked at each other and shook our heads in embarrassment.

The Ealing club was packed that night to a level, which must have been way beyond its legal capacity. It was virtually impossible to get close to the bar and totally impossible to get onto the dance area. Forget about getting down the front to be nearer to the band. People were trying to make their way up the narrow staircase to go outside for a breath of air, battling past the flow of others coming back down. The number of bodies crammed together caused the temperature to rise to an unbearable degree and the sweat just rolled off you, soaking your clothes. The atmosphere was fantastic. Everybody wanted more.

The promoter was an unpleasant and evil-looking Asian who was accompanied by a couple of equally obnoxious bouncers. Maybe they were relatives of his. He would station himself at a small table at the top of the stairs where he collected the entrance fees, exuding an air of rudeness and abruptness. The Rollin' Stones band and the escalating attendances each week were sheer pieces of luck for him. He was coining a small fortune and paying an unfair pittance in return to the boys, who were virtually starving. When he came to pay them at the end of the evening, he always claimed he had not taken much money in entrance fees, arguing that many people had managed to get in free. It was not difficult for the band to realize the true situation. They may have been foolish in playing for virtually nothing, but they were not that naïve.

This particular gig I felt somehow signified a change in the type of audience the Stones were attracting. Whereas before the Ealing Jazz Club had been exactly that—a jazz club—it was now more of a locale where young people met for a rave. It was becoming trendy. Gone were the real hard-core, laid-back intellectual types who associated blues only with jazz. They had been replaced by a new breed of fan who came to hear only R&B and had no preconceived ideas tied to jazz purism. This audience readily accepted that the Stones played authentic R&B and that electric guitars were part of the music. Along with them remained some people like myself who originally came to see Alexis and Cyril but preferred the Stones' style. There was also a third element—people who came just because the club was *the* place to be on a Saturday night. Oddly enough for a jazz club they had a wall-mounted jukebox selector and when the Stones took a breather, this pounded out records such as "Swiss Maid" by Del Shannon and Tommy Roe's "Sheila." The three elements merged together at Ealing and seemed to be creating a new culture.

I also thought it was the Stones' first great gig.

The routine each Saturday at the end of the evening was for Stu to park the van outside on the pavement, ready for the equipment or "gear'" as we called it to be humped up the stairs from the club. I usually gave Charlie a hand breaking down his drum kit as this always took longest to pack away. The fact that Ealing was just up the road from his home in Wembley meant Charlie could make his own way home by either bus or train. Stu would then drive us back to Edith Grove where some of the van's contents were unloaded before he took Bill home to Penge. There was generally a bit of chitchat regarding how everyone thought the gig had gone down or whether a solo had been a bit late coming in or whatever, but this time everyone seemed very pleased.

"Fuck all this," groaned Mick at the general situation.

I smiled. It was Sunday morning and we were all still lying in our beds, half hoping someone else would get up and make some coffee. Our beds were warm and no one wanted to move. Mick gave in first.

"I wish we had some fucking money," he groaned again. The rent was behind and due for collection that day. "I'll write a check for the rent and you can give me the money for your share," he said—he was the only one who had a bank account and a checkbook.

Mick stretched his left arm up toward the cabinet next to his bed and fumbled about on the shelf. Deciding he could not reach it properly, he sat up and swung his legs over the side of his bed and sat with his body drooping and his feet resting upon his clothes, which were heaped on the floor. He reached back to the shelf and moved some stuff around as if searching. "Fuck it," he said again as he gave up with the shelf. He kicked his clothes over and reached down and started going through his pockets until he found his checkbook. "I need a fucking pen now," he sighed and went back to the shelf, eventually finding one. I looked over at Keith and saw him grinning.

"I wish we could make a load of money and not have to fucking go through all this," Mick went on as he started to write the check.

"A million quid would be all right," said Keith. "That'd do," he added, looking at the ceiling as if he could see the money hanging there in used notes.

Mick finished writing and tore the check from the book, then looked at it and passed it to me. "Give that to Keith," he said.

I took the check, looked at it and laughed, then passed it on to Keith who held it open with both hands. Then he laughed, threw his head back and said, "If only it were real. Maybe one day . . . "

Mick had written the check out and signed it at the bottom. It read, "Pay The Rollin' Stones: £1 million."

Mick grinned, then sighed and wrote another check for the £16 rent. Unbeknown to all of us, Mick had written his first seven-figure check, which lay around the bedroom for several weeks until it eventually disappeared.

Brian was the only one who ever received mail. Mostly official-looking letters that started with the L.B.H. initials, plus a few more personal types where the address was handwritten. That week one of the personal letters came to life in the form of Pat Andrews and her baby, or should I say Brian's baby. Pat had arrived out of the blue to see Brian and to let him see the child. Perhaps she was hoping to get some money toward the child's care. It was probably all three reasons, although she was optimistic if she thought she'd ever get any money.

Having Pat and the baby there for a few days proved a big inconvenience for the rest of us and restricted our use of the flat. The door to the front room would be closed, but we would just walk in as normal, maybe wanting to play some records. Brian used to fly into a fit of anger shouting things like, "Fuck off out of here; you can't come in," or "You come in here again and I'll smash your fucking face in." So we ended up being confined to the kitchen and bedroom. Then we would be hanging around in the kitchen, smoking, and drinking coffee, when Brian would come down in a better mood and say, "Why don't you come up and listen to some records?"

Brian played with the baby on occasions but did not show any other signs of responsibility. I presumed Brian never gave Pat any money—it was more likely that he talked her out of what little she may have had. Whatever the arrangement, Pat left after a few days.

After Pat had gone, Brian was in the doldrums. He stayed locked in his room and did not want to be disturbed. The bedroom was OK as I had furnished it with a portable auto-change record player and we had a few singles stacked on it, mainly for playing at night. One evening I decided we needed some different records and went into the front room. Brian flew across the room to the door shouting, "I told you to keep the fuck out," and started swinging punches, so I hit him back. It was only a short scuffle, and no one was really hurt. Keith just stood watching with a rather dazed look on his face. Neither of us really knew what to make of it and felt weary with Brian, so we went out. It was raining and Keith had found a tatty old umbrella, which had the material beginning to hang off it.

We caught a bus into town and wandered around a few clubs and pubs. About midnight we were walking in the rain down London's exclusive Park Lane and came to the Hilton Hotel.

"Come on, let's go in," he said, collapsing the umbrella and making for the entrance. I just followed behind him, wondering why. A big guy in a uniform and top hat looked at us as if we were shit but he opened the door for us out of habit before he could regain his wits. By then we had strolled past and up to the reception desk. Another guy in a uniform sat there also looking taken aback and I could see him thinking, "If the doorman's let them in, it must be OK . . . "

The receptionist opened his mouth to speak just as Keith raised the soaking umbrella in the air and banged it on the reception desk. Bang! Bang! Bang!—he used it to emphasize every word he spoke as water splashed over the desk and the man behind it.

"I say, my man. We'd like a room for the night," demanded Keith. The clerk behind the desk paled, then replied, "Yes sir!"

Keith banged the umbrella again. "Well, how much is it?" he shouted.

The guy quoted a ridiculous Hilton price we had never heard of.

"We don't want a piece of cheap shit like that," said Keith, sounding hurt. "We'll go and look for something decent elsewhere." He turned around and marched back to the door. "Open the door then," he demanded of the first guy, who duly obliged with a bewildered look on his face. Outside on the pavement we both collapsed into fits of laughter and hailed a cab back to the flat.

Next day when I came back from work I climbed the stairs and saw the front room door remained closed, so I headed toward the bedroom. The fact the door was closed did not really mean much, but I guessed Brian was still skulking in the room.

Brian opened the door as I was going past. I looked at him and he said, "Can I have a word? Look Phelge, I'm really sorry about last night. I don't want to fall out over it and create a bad atmosphere."

I could see he wanted to smile but was not sure. I thought, "Fuck you, Brian," but said, "It's OK, man, let's forget it." He smiled and we forgot it.

Another afternoon I came back early and found Keith alone, lounging on the sofa with a book. Brian had mentioned a girl he'd met at the Ricky Tick club, a venue in Windsor where the band played occasional Friday night gigs. Her name was Linda Lawrence and I figured he had probably gone down to see her in Reading.

"What are you doing?" I asked Keith. Obviously he was reading a book—what I really meant was "What shall we do?" He understood anyway.

"I was just thinking about going up the Wang Ho in me sampan," he replied. I grinned—he was obviously reading a Gregory Salhurst story.

"Yeah, well, I'll come with ya, gonna make some coffee first though," I said, wandering off to the kitchen. It was all messed up again with dirty dishes, cartons, and empty bottles everywhere. I made the coffee and went back into the front room. Keith was now writing, so I lit a fag then sat on Brian's bed. I looked at the sheets—there was blood on them, probably from when he had been humping the runaway girl, who had been a virgin before she arrived at Edith Grove. I pulled the cover over the stained sheets.

Keith finished his writing then signed the letter. Passing it over for me to read he said, "It's a letter to BBC Television." He grinned. I started to read the letter, of which the gist was:

Dear Mr. BBC,

How would you like me to come down to your studios for an audition? I can prance around the studio pulling funny faces while shouting "Fuck off!" I can also gob all over the walls and the windows. Then I can prance around a bit more and gob on the floor. I am very talented and can gob on anything. Please let me know when it will be convenient to come.

Signed

The Masked Nanker X

"Hey man, now I know your real name," I said grinning.

He looked at me, smiled and said, "You're the only one who does."

We both went back down to the kitchen to make some more coffee. Brian had been into making porridge for himself in the mornings and eating it straight from the saucepan before dumping the pan and remaining porridge straight into the sink. Next day he would find a different pan and do the same again. Then it would be fried bread in the frying pan keeping the same fat until it had all turned thick and brown and did not move anymore. So as usual the sink was all shitted up. Somehow all the rest of the cups and mugs seemed to be buried at the bottom of a pile of greasy pans and dirty saucepans yet again.

Keith filled the kettle and put it on the old black gas cooker, itself covered in brown grease, as I opened the window. I walked over to the sink and asked him, "You fancy cleaning up again?" I knew he didn't really, but the look on his face said he might give a hand. I picked up a couple of pans then turned around and walked back to the window and threw them straight out. He laughed, then said, "What are ya doin'?"

"Fucking cleaning this place up," I replied. "Give me a hand. I'm not washing up again."

Keith grabbed a couple of pans and they followed the previous ones out of the window and down into the garden. We took turns emptying the sink—out went all the saucepans, the two frying pans, and all the saucepan lids, followed by the knives, forks, and spoons. Each piece made a nice clanking noise as it landed on top of something else. We looked out of the window down to the garden below. All the pans and cutlery were neatly spread across the grass.

A couple of days later we came home together and found all the pots and pans, as well as the cutlery, neatly arranged on the small kitchen table. They looked gleaming and clean, almost like new. We looked at them. "Looks like the landlord's wife's been in," said Keith. I agreed but did not understand why we had not received a bit of moaning aimed at us.

A few minutes later Judy from downstairs came up and entered the kitchen. "I picked up all your pans and cleaned 'em for you," she said. "What did you throw them all in the garden for?"

"Because they were dirty," replied Keith.

"Keith," she said. "You can't just throw them out the window if they're dirty. You have to wash them."

"We thought it was gonna rain and that would clean them," I told her.

She pulled a face that told us she thought we were hopeless. We just stared at her and smiled.

"Well, now you've cleaned 'em," said Keith, "Why don't you wash the cups and make some fucking coffee?"

Judy put the kettle on, then stacked all the clean pans in the cupboard of the ancient-looking dresser, which stood adjacent to the sink. Keith and I were taking as much advantage as we could of her. I liked her as a person and she was always friendly, no matter how we behaved. She made some coffee, sat down at the table, lit a cigarette, and told us she would be moving out from her flat next week and going home to Sheffield.

IT WAS FREEZING cold in the flat, and outside there was still snow on the ground. To add to our misery there was no food, apart from an occasional loaf of bread or a block of cheese we might have bought or purloined. The band's workload was once again falling, and the future looked bleak. With the rent now almost three weeks overdue, Mrs. Morgan-Morgan was threatening us with eviction. All that we needed now to complete the scene was an out-of-work, down-at-heel film producer from Russia. So the resourceful Brian found one—Giorgio Gomelski.

My first impression of Giorgio was, "Here's another bum who fancies himself as a bit of an artist." A big guy with a long beard and an idealistic air, his only saving grace was the black corduroy coat that was not dissimilar to mine, only bigger. To complete his bizarre image Giorgio was into jazz and ran the hall at the back of the Station Hotel in Richmond as a jazz club. This was probably what had attracted Brian toward him—the chance to scrounge some much-needed work for the Stones.

Giorgio visited the flat accompanied by a person who was either his wife or girlfriend—I was never sure which. She wore a fur jacket, black trousers, and high boots. She seemed to take particular care walking round the front room, as if trying to avoid touching anything while at the same time checking to see what she might be putting her feet in. I was going to ask her if she fancied cleaning the kitchen but decided to not to. I also wondered if she would like to hear the toilet tapes, but again I decided against it.

Brian enthused about the band and their music, prompting a promise from Giorgio to come down to Sutton and listen to them at the Red Lion, which he duly did. I always felt there was something about the Red Lion that made everything feel ordinary. The band never seemed to gel properly, never really managed to get into full flow. There was always a reasonable-sized crowd of followers in attendance, but something was lacking every time. Whereas in the other clubs I would make suggestions about the sound, I gave up bothering to do that at the Red Lion. Perhaps the general acoustics of the building just never lent themselves toward music, or maybe all the bodies killed the sound waves and left the music sounding undynamic and flat.

Giorgio and his woman stood together listening at the back of the crowd. With his long black coat, dark beard, and a half of beer in his hand he seemed to tower above everybody. He looked as if he was scrutinizing other members of the audience like a rebel leader seeking suitable recruits. Brian came over during a break, putting on a smile and his best friendly voice to welcome him. Giorgio chatted with Brian again, enthusing over the music, which seemed to be the sort he liked. Then he surprised everyone by setting up a gig for the very next evening.

It was another room at the back of another pub. This time it was the Manor House in North London. The back room was named the Harringay Jazz Club. But even the news of an extra show didn't raise the mood in the van on the way back to the flat from Sutton. Hardly a word was said—everyone was silent with his own thoughts. Maybe it was the cold, or just tiredness, or the weary realization that the band's hopes of progressing seemed futile. Here we were, uncomfortable and cramped, in the back of a cold van on the way back to our freezing cold, food-free home. It had not been the best gig that night and the idea of making it as a band seemed a trip to nowhere. Everyone seemed to feel imprisoned in a nightmare of his own making.

I had spent the best part of my childhood in North London and knew the location of the Manor House pub as it stood next to a tube station of the same name. It was a building more like a hotel than a regular pub, and inside there was more of a hotel "feel" to the place.

I guided Stu across London and we parked the van on the pavement as usual before carrying the equipment into the new venue. It seemed a strange gig after playing in places that were purely clubs. The Manor House was just a regular bar, given over to music on one or two nights per week, when it would become a club. What I would call a pub-club, it was really just a place for people to meet. It was a clean, carpeted place with polished tables and curtains at the windows that matched the lamp shades. It could definitely have made it as a hotel lounge. Double doors in one corner led into a rectangular room. There was a highly polished, shiny bar on the right and immediately opposite the doorway was a slightly raised platform that acted as the stage. This meant the band was stuck in one corner, facing the door, in the area where most of the tables stood. The PA speakers needed to be pointed toward the main audience, rather than straight ahead of the stage as usual, and this made it a little awkward for Mick to hear himself.

I stood at the bar drinking a beer, wondering what to make of the place. People were coming in and it seemed likely they had never heard of R&B. Their attendance was more due to the fact that this was their "local." I looked around at them all standing there and tried to decide if they were expecting to hear country and western or rock and roll, or maybe even jazz. The people looked at the band sorting themselves out on the stage, and you could tell from their faces they were ready to sneer at these weirdos.

Keith put his fag down and nodded to Brian, then played the intro. Mick hit them straight off with a Chuck Berry number. Not much reaction followed the first number, and Brian looked around as the audience managed some muted applause. I could see Keith's face wearing a look that said, "Fuck you. Here's some more."

The Stones' Manor House debut was a partial success: Mick worked well with the vocals and the band won over a fair percentage of the audience. It was not a great gig, but a satisfying one. Having gone into a new club in an alien area for the first time, they had given a solid performance and earned a few new fans and another weekly gig. In weeks to come the place would become mobbed.

With Harringay added every Thursday, the band now had four regular slots each week, the others being Ealing every Saturday and Tuesday plus the Ricky Tick on Fridays. This meant each member was now earning about £8 per week, less band expenses. This left just about enough for rent and cigarettes plus an occasional meal at the Ernie. We would continue to steal milk from upstairs though—it was a matter of principle.

Knowing how much fun the boys had listening to the Perry Como version of "Route 66," I had managed to find another delightful treat for them. At a market stall in nearby Fulham I found a rare old 78 rpm record of Perry Como singing "I Wonder Who's Kissing Her Now" with the Ted Weems orchestra. As far as I knew it was his first recording, dating from the late 1930s. The Como album the boys had listened to when I first arrived at the flat carried a sleeve note about him appearing with Ted Weems at the Palmer House in Chicago in spring 1936. I wondered if he had sung the song on the 78 in the big blues town.

As our player only worked at two speeds, 33 and 45, I had to find a way of playing it. At the lithographic printers where I worked we used flat sheets of film for photographing art work and I brought an unwanted sheet of this back to the flat with the record. Brian, Keith, and Mick were up in the bedroom chatting when I arrived back at the flat so I went straight into the kitchen and delved through one of the cupboards until I found a large saucepan lid. I rolled the sheet of film so that it was cone-shaped, trying to make it resemble a gramophone horn similar to the one in the famous "His Master's Voice" posters featuring the dog listening to the gramophone.

Climbing the steps up to the bedroom, I held the saucepan lid upside down by the black knob in the middle and balanced the record on top. As the knob was loose I was able to spin the lid around at a reasonable speed like a turntable. After entering the bedroom I placed the fine edge of the film at the bottom of the cone into the record's groove. It worked quite well and Perry Como came forth from the cone singing.

"What do you think of this?" I asked as the record began to slow. Their blank faces turned into laughter as I speeded it up again and carried it around the room.

"Where'd you get that," laughed Brian.

"Down the market. It's his first record. Good, ain't it," I replied, listening to the ancient, scratchy music—it sounded pretty awful.

Keith stood there with his hands thrust deep down in his pockets, looking at me quizzically and saying nothing. He was either admiring my ingenuity or thought I was totally raving mad. Maybe Perry Como was beginning to grow on him at last.

Some nights Mick would not arrive back at the flat until about midnight. He would come in and dive straight into bed, having maybe spent the evening somewhere else with other LSE students. On other occasions he never came back at all and I presumed he had gone home to see his family in Dartford.

Keith and I had grown into the habit of going to bed around midnight. We would stick a pile of singles on the record player and lay there listening to them and making comments. It was always the same selection of records, including "Donna" by Ritchie Valens, Jerry Lee's "Ballad of Billy Joe," Ketty Lester's "Love Letters," "You Better Move On" by Arthur Alexander, and Jimmy Reed's "Goin' by the River." A selection of 45s we described as "Guv'nor," a word we used in approval of anything we liked. After all the records had played, one of us would get up and turn the records over and we would listen to all the B sides. By the time we had finished playing both sides it would be well past one o'clock; then we would get up and go out. It became a habit. One of us would say in a nankering voice, "Who fancies a trip to the pie stall then?" Having gone through the routine of getting undressed and into bed, we then got up again and dressed.

Lighting some cigarettes we made our way down to Chelsea Embankment at the bottom of the Grove. That time of night it was devoid of other pedestrians, and the only life consisted of a few passing cars. There seemed to be something attractive about being there late at night. The deserted pavement and the old-fashioned streetlamps on the embankment walls, their lights reflecting back off the river, created a special atmosphere. Even the closed funfair standing on the opposite side of the river seemed to be enjoying the stillness. We just strolled along smoking and talking about nothing in particular, looking at the boats moored along the edge of the Thames and thinking how it would be cool to live on one.

Usually it took two cigarettes each until we found ourselves having walked the distance to Chelsea Bridge. Across the bridge on the left was a stall, which sold minor refreshments. The stall was a wooden construction mounted on wheels and the upper part of one side opened to form a counter and canopy. It was always open through the night and a place where cab and lorry drivers would make their way to for a break or snack. We became regulars there, too. The guy who ran it used to serve hot meat pies and large tin mugs of tea, a very basic menu. Resting our mugs of tea on the wall of the bridge we would cover the hot pies in brown sauce and then eat them with our fingers from the grease-proof paper. When our late night banquet was over, we would stroll back to the flat and go to bed for real.

When the front door crashed open and banged against the wall I looked down the stairs and saw Keith, wearing a scarf around the neck of his leather coat, come charging into the hallway. Mick and Brian followed in behind him. Between them they were carrying a large bucket and rolls of paper. "We've been out with Giorgio sticking posters up all over town for Richmond," explained Brian. "And he's put an advert in *Melody Maker*."

Richmond had arrived. A couple of weeks earlier, following the booking at the Harringay club, Giorgio had told the band a vacancy was occurring at the Richmond club and offered them the gig, which they had accepted. Going around London sticking up posters on a cold winter's night was the first piece of active promotion the band had ever done. Because of this and Giorgio's extraordinarily wordy advert in the weekly music paper, they all looked forward to the coming Sunday's gig.

There were some yellow posters left over with black writing on them. A couple of days later I suggested to Keith, "We should stick a couple of these on the pillars outside the front door, just so we know where we live."

We took the posters and the bucket of glue downstairs onto the front steps and on each pillar we pasted one of the oblong yellow posters, worded simply in black, "The Rolling Stones." They were now officially The Rolling Stones with a *g*. The posters were to remain on the pillars for several years, while the *g* would stay forever.

The hall at the rear of the Station Hotel looked big and sparse. The ceiling must have been 20 feet high above the bare wooden boards of the main floor and your footsteps echoed around the building as you walked—it sounded as if you were being followed. With all the lights on it looked even bigger than its 80 by 60 foot size. Like all the club and pub halls it looked in need of some new paint.

We came in through the rear entrance, each carrying a piece of equipment over to the three-foot-high stage, and went casually about the task of setting up each item. I gave Charlie my usual help with his kit and left Mick and Brian sorting out all the cables for the PA, which was placed on some tables either side. Despite Giorgio's advertising in *Melody Maker* and the poster campaign there was a disappointing turnout. Only a mere handful of people had bothered to come. The Stones finally kicked the gig into action when it became apparent there would not be more people arriving. I put the poor turnout down to the fact that the previous band who played the club on Sundays could not have pulled much of a regular crowd. The few people who did make it that night were mainly the real die-hard followers like Clapton, Pretty Mick, Rowan, a few girls, and my old friend Fengey, who I chatted with over a beer.

A few people danced as the band gradually warmed up with Rowan as usual seeming to need the most space, which was not a problem here. Giorgio turned off the main lights after a while and the place was quite dark, with only the stage lit. The darkened hall now had a bit of atmosphere—the high ceiling was not visible, and the place seemed less like a barn.

After a longish break the band played their second session and most members of the audience were dancing at some point, which at least helped to make it look lively. For me it was OK as I enjoyed the freedom of being able to move around easily with a beer in my hand while listening to the music. A couple of times the boys asked how it sounded from the back, but the small audience size meant the sound was able to travel and the hall's acoustics were good.

I thought it rather ironic that Bill looked the worst-equipped with his big homemade bass cabinet, while Brian and Keith looked quite professional as they each used one of Bill's guitar amplifiers. After an average and uninspiring evening the first Richmond gig ended around 10:30 P.M. and we went through the routine of packing away the equipment and carrying it out to the van. On the way back to Edith Grove we stopped for a meal at the Wimpy Bar next to Earls Court tube station.

We were all in our beds with the light still on, talking about who had come to Richmond.

"I see your mate was there, the one you used to hang out with. I used to see you down the Ealing club and say to Mick, 'There's that little beat again.' What was all that beatnik crap you were into with the beard and pipe?" Keith asked me.

Mick sat up in his bed resting on his elbows and laughing. He looked across at me and asked, "Where did you go to before you came to Ealing?"

"I used to go modern jazz places," I replied. "Like the Bulls Head in Barnes."

"What the fuck do you see in modern jazz?" he asked.

"I like it. It's OK," I told him.

"Yeah, but what do you see in it? All the people at those places don't know what they're really listening to. What do you like about it anyway?" Mick continued.

"I think it looks cool. I like to watch the drummer." I visualized Mike Hugg playing drums with Manfred Mann back at the modern jazz club.

"Fucking Chrissakes," said Mick and fell back laughing. Then, sitting up again but still laughing, he said: "Now I've heard fucking everything. The visual effect of modern jazz, ha ha ha." He and Keith both laughed.

"Well," I mused, "You've got a fucking drummer that plays jazz."

They both continued to laugh. "Not no fucking more he don't," said Keith.

That week Brian's new girlfriend, Linda, came to visit him at the flat and they kept themselves locked away in the front room. Mick and I also had another late night visit from the twins, Sandy and Sarah, who stayed until about five in the morning. Mrs. Morgan-Morgan came to the flat, saw the state of it, and told us to get out, even though it looked no worse than when she last visited. Brian told her, "We'll have it all cleaned up by next week and pay the rent as well." We also continued to eat at the Ernie when we could and go through our "How's ya job" routine. Our hair continued to grow too.

The Ricky Tick club down in Windsor was about the only venue I never went to. By the time I returned from the printers in Fulham, the boys would already have left. One Friday evening I had planned to sit around playing some records and reading some Wheatley until they came back, but found the flat in darkness. We never replaced blown lightbulbs, and the one in the lounge had been the only bulb left that worked. In the kitchen we relied on some candles for lighting. I came up the stairs to the front room in the dark and, threw the light switch. The lounge one was dead too. "Fuck all this," I thought, and decided to raid the Offers' flat before they came home from work.

Their place was quite neat and tidy, no dust and the furniture all polished, dark wood shelves full of neatly stacked books and classical records, a clean carpet with rugs scattered round, and a couple of table lamps—just the things I needed. I removed the bulbs from the two lamps and "borrowed" the one from the room's central light fitting. I had a lie on their comfortable-looking bed, then relocked the door and returned to our flat.

I made some coffee after hiding two of the bulbs and putting the other in the front room. I then sat down and started reading. I realized afterward I should have put our duff bulbs back in the Offers' lamps upstairs. I was thinking about doing this, but then it was too late—clumping up the stairs came Mr. and Mrs. Offer, so I carried on reading and waited.

The Offers finally made it up to their apartment, unlocked their door, and threw the light switch. Nothing. I heard Mr. Offer say, "Oh dear, the bulb's gone," meaning it had died. I thought "It's gone all right," and waited some more. Then he tried the first table lamp and said, "The lamp's gone too . . ." Then he tried the second lamp—again nothing. That's when he must have looked inside the lamp shade. "There's no bulb here." Silence, then, "There's no bulbs anywhere!" That's when Mr. Offer went hysterical.

"Now they've stolen all our fucking lightbulbs." He was shouting. "That fucking does it. I'm not fucking having any more of this. Those bastards. That's it."

He came flying down the stairs still ranting, "This is their fucking lot this time."

He kicked the door open, rushed in, and stood there foaming as he looked around the room.

"Where are they?" he barked loudly.

"Doing a gig in Windsor," I replied congenially, assuming he meant the Stones and not the bulbs.

"They've stolen our fucking lightbulbs."

"I wouldn't know," I said. "There was no one here when I came home."

"Look," he said. "I know it's not you. You're a normal guy who's out at work all day. It's the others. They've stolen all our bloody lightbulbs. I don't know how you can stand living with them."

"Well, we've only got this one," I replied, referring to the lightbulb. "There's none anywhere else. We use candles all the time—do you want to borrow one?"

He stood speechless, trying to contain his rage and glaring around the room as if he thought the guys were hiding somewhere. He looked like thunder.

He finally recovered. "It must be them."

"I don't know, I've been at work all day. We've only had one bulb for weeks." Trying to throw him off further I continued, "Nick came up from downstairs when I came in—he wanted to borrow a bulb. I told him as well—we've only got this one." I thought I would point him downstairs.

"Nick wouldn't steal our bulbs but the bloody Stones would. They steal our food too," Mr. Offer said, still annoyed.

"Maybe downstairs have one you can borrow now." I thought he was beginning to look a bit unsure.

"I'll lend you a candle," I said helpfully, trying not to push him too far.

"I'll let it go this time," he finally warned. "I know it's not you, but I'm not having any more of this. So make sure you tell them that next time I'll complain to the landlord."

"OK, I'll tell 'em," I replied meekly, like a scolded kid.

"I'm sorry about bursting in on you like that," said Mr. Offer.

"That's OK," I said. "It frightened me at first."

I grinned at the door after he had closed it. Later I heard him going out and wondered where he was going to find a shop selling lightbulbs at that time of night.

THE STONES' DECISION to leave the Ealing club was not a difficult one when you examined the reasons behind it. The club was packed full every time, but the band was hardly earning any money from the gig. The promoter still claimed poverty, blaming people who sneaked in for free, although how these fans ever crept by him and his two eagle-eyed henchmen I never knew. The Stones felt confident about Richmond—the new gig was still being actively promoted. They would not be any worse off than before. Whatever Richmond paid would replace the Ealing money, and they still had a weekend gig.

I did feel sad to see them give up Ealing. It was a good gig in terms of atmosphere and I liked the club and the people who went there. The band had been "resident" there for months now and I could recall first seeing Mick getting up on stage looking nervous and shy as he sang. I remembered how awkward he had looked with his elbows locked tight against his body and his hands waving. All amateur singers did that, never keeping their elbows free for arm movements and ending up looking like someone drowning. All in all I would miss the Ealing shows, the final one being among the more memorable nights.

The band was well into the first set and people were dancing as I stood at the corner of the bar drinking. Linda Lawrence was dancing with a friend immediately in front of the stage, close to where Brian was playing, when in walked Pat Andrews with the baby. I winced at the prospect of a confrontation between the two women in Brian's life, but was also amused by the irony of the situation.

Up on stage Mick must have seen her coming too—he started laughing in the middle of a song. He turned toward Keith who also caught on and began to laugh. Brian looked mortified and cast his eyes down upon his guitar, trying hard to concentrate. When the song ended I did not really see what happened—all the people were still on the dance floor—but after a couple of minutes Pat came back to the bar area and sat at a table with the baby on her knee. Shortly afterward an upset-looking Linda left the club with her friend. I never did actually find out how Brian managed to wriggle out of his predicament. As far as I could tell, neither of the girls appeared to know who the other one was, and that saved his skin. That night we carried the equipment out of the Ealing club for the last time.

Giorgio had managed to get the band booked into Studio 51, better known as the Ken Colyer Jazz Club, for a Sunday afternoon gig. The club was close to Leicester Square station and the lack of rush-hour traffic on a Sunday meant it was only a short journey from Chelsea.

It seemed strange leaving for a gig in the daytime. Charlie had arrived at the flat wearing a smart tan-colored sports jacket with a waistcoat and tie. He looked more like a squire who had driven up from his country estate than a drummer from Wembley. We amused ourselves by poking fun at his new clothes in our nankering mode until Stu arrived with Bill in the van.

One of the things we had grown used to before leaving for a gig was a last-minute search for Brian's bottleneck, the short piece of tubular metal that fitted over one of his fingers, which he used for playing slide guitar. Whenever we were almost ready he would discover it was missing and I found it difficult to understand why he could not keep tabs on such a vital piece of his equipment. Keeping it in a regular place where it would be easy to find did not seem to me a daunting task. It invariably meant a complete search of the front room before we left, which included turning his bed over and searching through clothes and down the sides of the armchair cushions. Most times we would never find it and he would wait until we arrived at the gig, then search for a bottle. After finding one with a suitable size neck he would break it, hoping the neck came away in one piece.

Many times he played an entire gig using what was literally a glass bottleneck. Other times when he did find it or buy a new metal bottleneck he would leave it behind at the first gig. But this time—maybe because it was daylight—he found it under the bed and we drove into London.

The club was a well-known venue for traditional jazz that had been very popular in the late '50s and early '60s, when artists like Acker Bilk and Kenny Ball had records in the charts. The entrance was down a narrow stairway that had a booth on the left at the bottom where you paid your entrance fee. Beyond that was a cloakroom, which also acted as a small snack bar. Having paid your admission you then turned right into the club area, which was just another rectangular hall, similar in size to the Ealing club. The Stones would play for two hours here, then go on to Richmond. It was what I termed a "stand-and-watch" club—nobody seemed to dance. A few people would be lucky enough to get one of the wooden chairs in front of the stage; the others would sit on the floor or just stand around.

The act that followed the Stones was the Kid Martyn Ragtime Band, and sometimes they would be sitting there patiently watching and waiting. There was no ill feeling; they were just waiting for the Stones to finish so they could get on stage and play—like most musicians they would rather have been playing than watching. The Kid Martyn band consisted of people who I termed "weekend hippies"—bankers, advertising executives, and other such business people. Some of them thought the Stones were crap and viewed the playing of electric guitars in a jazz club as a sacrilege, even more so if played by a group of arrogant, disrespectful, laughing morons. Nothing much had changed, but we were beginning to like the effect we had on those people. The audience was a mixture of Stones followers and jazz enthusiasts who watched with a certain amount of curiosity. The Stones seemed to work at a casual and relaxed pace throughout the gig, almost as if they were rehearsing for later that evening.

The same day, back at Richmond for the second week, a few more people arrived though not in huge numbers. You were still aware of all the space around you—I likened it to the feeling you get when you are the first guest to arrive at a party. Although you felt self-conscious about being one of the few people on the dance floor; at the same time you had the smug feeling that you were where the action was taking place, as if you were a member of an elite group.

Outside our little world other things were beginning to happen too. The Beatles were topping the charts with "Please Please Me" and getting big media coverage. They had broken into the charts, which had previously been dominated by American artists and a few antiseptic British rock stars who wanted to be family entertainers. A few old-time singers from the '50s still featured in the charts as well, alongside one or two easy-listening jazz records.

Carnaby Street in London was making its first noises in the fashion world with trendy clothes for young people. The majority of teenagers were still going to ballrooms to hear pop music played by orchestras with singers, or the occasional rock and roll group. Traditional jazz bands were still appearing at these venues, but the audiences wore mod-style clothes, showing how things were beginning to change. Until now these places had been dominated by people who came from the Teddy Boy or rocker era and wore long jackets, drainpipe trousers, and suede shoes. The mod types were having their hair styled and no longer used Brylcreem to grease it in place. Short jackets, woollen sweaters, and straight or flared trousers were the order of the day. Fights used to regularly break out between the opposing camps following a trading of insults. The Stones' hard-core fans consisted entirely of mods and students, and one wondered what the rockers would make of the band.

During the following week Judy and Nick left the flat below ours and some new occupants took possession. We were returning from one of the midweek gigs and made our usual noisy entrance into the Edith Grove hallway, slamming the street door behind us. A guy with a beard, wearing glasses and a suit, was standing in the lighted entrance to the downstairs flat. He was holding a trombone. We thought that it was quite funny to see a jazz musician, of all things, living there. I assumed he played traditional jazz as he was the epitome of the type of musician we had seen around the clubs.

Obviously our new neighbor needed a name, and I decided to call him Triffid. I would find out later his real name was Ian Gilchrist and that he was a journalist, but to us he would be called Triffid from then on. In later weeks Brian or Keith would say, "Hi Triff," to him if they ever saw him in the hallway, sometimes even, "Thanks Triff" if he opened the door to let them in at three o'clock in the morning. I am sure the poor guy must have wondered what they were talking about.

Our first official meeting with Triff was on a Sunday morning following a late trip back from Guildford the night before from the Wooden Bridge Club. How the gig came into existence I did not know—it was nearly 40 miles outside London. This was the farthest the Stones had ever traveled to a gig, and we made it back about 3:00 A.M.

I was lying in bed feeling warm and could not decide if I was still asleep or awake. My body felt like it wanted to be awake, but my eyes didn't want to open, so I just lay there. As far as I knew, Mick and Keith were still sleeping and there were no sounds from Brian in the front room. I must have been like this for about half an hour when I heard footsteps advancing up the stairs. I presumed at first it was one of the Offers on the way back to the flat above. The footsteps continued up past the toilet and stopped outside our door. I waited for the door to open but instead somebody knocked. I figured it was probably the landlord calling for the rent and stayed quiet. A few moments passed and whoever was there knocked again. Still not bothering to acknowledge, I lay there waiting for the person to go away, assuming they would eventually leave. Then came a third knock on the door, subsequently followed by a fourth. I had no intention of opening the door, but suddenly Mick sat up and threw all his bedclothes back and down onto the floor. He leapt out of bed, totally naked, and marched angrily to the door. Turning the handle he threw the door violently open. It came back and banged against the left side of my bed and I was unable to see who was there. Then I heard a voice say, "Hello, I'm from downstairs. I wonder if you can tell me if the landlord's been round for the rent yet?"

This was followed by a loaded silence, which seemed to last ages. Finally Mick took a deep breath and shouted: "Fuck . . . off!" He emphasized the gap between the two words and slammed the door shut as hard as he could—it made a mighty bang in the face of the caller. Mick then turned around and picked up his bedclothes and climbed back onto his bed, pulled the covers over himself and flopped back onto the pillow. I listened to the footsteps retreating slowly back down the stairway.

Keith and I both burst out laughing and when we finally stopped Keith asked, "Who was that?"

"Fucking Triffid," replied Mick in a tone of disgust at having been made to get out of bed for no good reason. Keith and I laughed again and I asked Mick what Triffid had wanted, in case I had not heard him right first time.

"He wanted to know if the rent was due, for fuck's sake," said Mick.

Keith and I laughed again, picturing the situation once more. A polite, respectable guy, knocking on a door, which then violently opened to reveal a totally nude person standing there telling him to fuck off. That image, plus the mounting squalor of the flat and the continued shortage of food and money, made it hard to take seriously anyone worrying about paying the rent.

Eventually we left our beds around lunch time and everyone went through the usual routine of shaving with my electric razor, which we plugged into the bedroom's only wall socket by way of an adaptor plug. Luckily Keith and I had clean shirts—thanks to our laundry routine of sticking them in a bucket in the bathroom, then hanging them on the indoor line above the bath until they were dry enough to wear. When Charlie arrived, followed by Stu and Bill, we set out for the two Sunday shows.

The audience at each club was just a little bigger, mainly because some supporters from Ealing had found out where the Stones were now playing and had made their way to the respective clubs. The two gigs were much the same as the week before: the stand-and-watchers at the Ken Colyer and the dancers at Richmond. The band was still using the same equipment as at the Marquee, the odd harmonica being the only thing replaced after its predecessors' reeds wore out. The band was also still doing a full program of R&B material, so nothing had changed there either.

The next night was a big one. The Rolling Stones were going to make their first recording. Apparently they had met a recording engineer named Glyn Johns at one of the gigs and made an arrangement with him for a recording session in a studio somewhere in London's West End. Mick, Keith, and Brian finally got back to the flat at around midnight. They were not exactly bubbling over with excitement, but they seemed happy and pleased with themselves. Now came the nerve-racking wait for the record.

The studio-cut acetate was due for collection in a few days. They were dying to hear how they actually sounded as a band for the first time. This would tell them how good they were compared to their heroes, whose musical style they were trying to emulate and develop.

With the excitement over for the evening, Mick left us and went off to his bed. Brian then joined Keith and me on another late-night walk along the riverside to our Chelsea pie stall haunt.

A couple of nights later I came back to Edith Grove and none of them were there. Expecting to find them eating in the Ernie I went there to join them, but again they could not be found. After having a meal of sausages, egg, and chips, I returned to the flat and hung around the front room on my own, fooling around on Keith's old cello guitar, which he always left lying around.

It was about 10 o'clock when the three of them came waltzing through the door. They all seemed jubilant with big smiles on their faces. Brian, who was absolutely beaming, waved the record in the air as he cried out with excitement, "We've got it; we've got the record." It was a big moment for him, especially after months of desperation.

They now had something tangible to reward their musical beliefs and justify all the suffering. The record itself was about the size of a 10-inch album and was in a plain white cover. Brian decided to play it on a small portable record player that he had acquired from somewhere and quickly set this up for use. We all crowded around the player, everyone still wearing coats, as Brian carefully placed the record on the turntable and lifted the needle onto the edge of the record.

We stood there totally transfixed until the record finally burst into life. Not a word was said as each of us just concentrated on listening. We all stared at the record too, watching it spin round as if we were witnessing a miracle. I only heard the overall sound of the band, but no doubt Brian, Mick, and Keith listened only to themselves, each one of them secretly evaluating his own part and how it sounded. At the end they all appeared reasonably pleased and after a few comments opted to play it again. We then listened to all five tracks for a second time, then Brian asked me how I thought it sounded—"great," I replied. Not that I would have told the truth if I hadn't liked it, but I really thought it sounded good. The Bo Diddley tracks sounded like Bo Diddley records with Mick singing, and the Jimmy Reed track, "Bright Lights, Big City" was spot on too. The other songs featured on the record along with Bo's "Road Runner" and "Diddley Daddy" were the Muddy Waters's song "I Want to Be Loved" and another Reed track entitled "Honey What's Wrong." Maybe the recording standard of the actual record was a little low and the acetate cutting was not quite the same quality as a pressed-vinyl record, but the Stones themselves sounded as good as anyone else. They then decided to listen to it again, but this time they played it one track at a time and then began to analyze it. This is when they started to pick holes in it—things the average person would not have noticed.

Brian said he could hear things he thought were not right. "I don't think my guitar sounds right on this bit," and then to Keith, "Your guitar's too loud," and then it just went on. "I don't think that bit's quite right" and "They haven't balanced the sound correctly; Mick's too loud on this one."

Then Keith said, "What about the bass? You can't hear it. Always the same in England; they never put any fucking bass on anything; it's like they're frightened to turn it up."

"I never noticed that," I said to Keith.

"You listen to the radio. There's never any fucking bass on anything," he claimed.

Brian agreed and they decided to take the record back to the studio the next day and get it recut, this time having the bass level up loud. I thought it was all right as it was, and I think Mick seemed quite pleased with it too—he sounded good and you could hear the vocals up front. I asked how much it had all cost and Brian said, "About 90 quid." Whether that was expensive or not for making a record I had no idea.

They did take it back to the studio, but whether they ever had it recut I never knew. It turned out that somebody at the studio was willing to take the tracks and make approaches to various record companies on the band's behalf. Everyone waited expectantly. It was a good record, and there should not be a problem. Somebody would surely want to give them a break.

The pillars outside the street door with the posters on still announced loudly that this was the official residence of the Rolling Stones, but no one took any notice. Even the few teenage girls who lived in the Grove and spent time hanging around in the street never paid any attention to the band when they saw us loading up the van. They probably didn't notice Brian either as he walked past them so many times during the next few days on his way to the phone box at the top of the Grove. He must have phoned his contact at the studio at least twice a day for news of interest in the record, and whenever he returned it was always negative. Everyone waited for positive news, although we had the weekend gigs and other distractions to while away the time.

Between us we had gotten to know a few of the girls who were beginning to come on the scene, but at this stage they were more casual acquaintances, none of which had evolved into full relationships. Brian was seeing Linda Lawrence on a fairly sporadic basis as she lived so far out of town. He would see her at the Friday gig and once or twice she came to visit the flat.

Mick had also met a girl at the Friday gig in Windsor—she lived in the area and she started to come down to Richmond with her friend on Sunday evenings to watch the band. Her name was Chrissie Shrimpton and her relationship with Mick would develop gradually from there. I had met a girl at one of the final Ealing gigs, but only met up with her at weekends. Charlie had started seeing an old girlfriend named Shirley, and Bill of course was married and still lived in Penge.

The odd man out was Keith, who either had not met anyone or just remained totally uninterested when it came to women. I thought it was more of the latter, because Keith's only interest lay in playing guitar, and for his satisfaction this had to be at a gig. With him the attitude was almost like, "Who wants to be hanging around with a bird when you can be playing?" Out of all the band members, I think he was the most single-minded regarding music. To him it was his life and nothing else mattered. "We're a band, so we gotta play," came across as being his motto in life. If the other members of the Rolling Stones had called it a day and decided to go home, they would have done so without Keith. He would have been on stage with the next band, and the one after that if necessary. He played guitar and that was it. You could sense there was nothing else he was ever going to do, no matter what came next.

To be admitted back into the Edith Grove premises you were usually reliant upon giving two hard bangs on the old-fashioned door knocker. The two bangs indicating you wanted the middle floor. If no one from the flat answered you usually just kept banging away until someone else came and opened the door. We only had the one street door key among us, and it was seldom anyone knew exactly where it was. Whoever had it last probably put it down somewhere but could never remember where. Eventually it would turn up after being left hidden in somebody's pocket.

As it was a Friday the band had gone to the Ricky Tick club and I had been to visit some relatives in Hammersmith. From there I went to a local pub for a couple of drinks then came back to the flat and went to bed. The thing you learned fast at Edith Grove was that if the Rolling Stones were not home you did not get into bed and expect to sleep. If you lived downstairs you would probably have to get up to let them in. There would be no point in lying there waiting for them to stop banging or hoping they were going to go away. If, like me, you lived with them, their next objective once they had come charging in would be to wake you up, just for fun. If you were very lucky they would not decide to play any Chuck Berry records.

On this particular Friday night I was just lying in bed half asleep, expecting to be woken up when they arrived back. Either Keith, Mick, or Brian must have had the key as I heard them open the door. It was not actually the opening of the door I heard, but the way it crashed and vibrated as one of them kicked it back against the wall. Whoever led the way in then caught the door on the rebound and kicked it back onto the wall for a second time, the noise echoing along the hallway and up the stairs. That was the regular entrance ceremony to announce they were back. Hearing this I decided to take the initiative and leapt out of bed wearing just my underpants. I turned on the light and went out onto the landing. I was intending to stand at the top of the stairs and nanker at them as they climbed, but then decided to make it look even more ridiculous. I imagined it would be a good laugh if I had no clothes on at all, so I took off my black underpants. Then I found they would have been in the way for nankering if I kept them in my hand. I decided to put them on my head and pull them over my face which I thought would be an even cooler and more absurd thing to do. This all happened in a matter of seconds, as I had to get to the strategic position at the head of the stairs before them.

They were still milling about in the hallway with the guitars knock-ing against the wall as they moved toward the stairs. I stood there with the underpants on my head and my hands on my face, nankering down at them. As they were occupied trying to see what was happening in the darkness below I started to make one of our nankering call-noises toward them. It was a high-pitched "Oo-oo-oo-oo-oo." The three of them stopped in their tracks at the bottom of the stairs.

"Ha ha ha, look at him," laughed Keith after the initial surprise. "He's only got his underpants on his head."

Brian burst out laughing as well, then said in the darkness, "Mick, look at Phelge with his underpants."

Mick, who was just slightly behind the others, looked up and laughed. I guessed then they thought that was the end of it. I waited and then just as Keith put his foot on the first step I started to gob down on him, but the first attempt missed and he jumped back.

Keith looked up the stairway and said, "You bastard," so I gobbed down at him again.

"What's up?" Brian asked, unable to see properly in the dark.

"He's only gobbing down the stairs at us now," Keith replied.

"Oh no, he's not is he?" said Brian. The "oh" was long and drawn. This time I gobbed hard toward Brian so he could be sure what was happening.

"Watch out, ha ha ha, he is. Oh no watch it, Keith!" Brian laughed as he moved back toward Mick. A guitar or something fell over in the dark.

Mick gave a bemused groan, "Oh for fuck's sake, Phelge." He sounded resigned to staying down in the hallway all night.

In between the gobbing on them I was still making the "oo-oo-oo-oo" noises. The idea was to keep them trapped there as long as possible. Every time they came forward I gobbed down on them and they leapt back. I wondered if the people downstairs knew what was happening, but they never came out. Finally, after I gobbed down at them a few more times—my mouth and throat were getting a bit dry—Keith timed it so he could rush up the stairs in between shots and reach the landing. When he reached me he was laughing and said, "Fucking baggies on your head, ha ha ha. Too fucking much!" I laughed back at him as the others came past behind him, Mick shaking his head and laughing as he looked at the "baggies."

"You're fucking mad," said Brian, and I made as if to gob on him again and his body jumped.

"Aaaah, don't . . ." he cried out and then we both laughed. I thought to myself, "That all went down quite well really," then went for a piss in the toilet.

Once again Giorgio had placed one of his strangely worded yet atten-tion-grabbing adverts for the Richmond gig in *Melody Maker*. Brian would get the paper each week and go straight to the gig guide at the back to find the ad. He would shout out, "Look what Giorgio's written this week," and took great pleasure in reading out loud to us the unorthodox language used to describe the band. As far as I knew no one considered how much the adverts had cost, or who was paying for them. Presumably the money came from the enterprising Giorgio's own pocket—it seemed to me the adverts were primarily aimed at inspiring people to go to his club, where the Rolling Stones were the attraction, and that any publicity for the Stones was of secondary importance. Whatever his intention, people were going.

On the Sunday following yet another zany advert, the Studio 51 club had a few more stand-and-watchers and appeared to be filling up, although it was only a small club. Richmond, by contrast, boasted a significant number of extra dancers but was still far below half full. Though different, both venues were showing encouraging signs of becoming regular attractions for the band and successful ventures for the promoters.

Richmond, being a town by the River Thames next to a Royal Park on the outskirts of London, was always noted as having plenty of affluent residents. Many of the shops in the town were akin to those found in London's expensive Bond Street area, and with its riverside dwellings with boats moored alongside, it was never a district to be poor. For the fans who were beginning to attend the club, and those who would come later, the town had the advantage of being nicely accessible by "tube"—London's underground railway system—or by bus. What the local residents would later make of their town becoming a R&B mecca was hard to imagine. After that evening's gig we adjourned to a small restaurant up by Richmond Bridge. There was no pie stall for Keith and me in this area.

If the nankering on the stairs episode had not held much interest for our neighbors downstairs, Keith and I had an even better idea with which to entertain them once we got back from Richmond late that Sunday night. Again we were in the kitchen waiting for the kettle to boil to make coffee. There was no sign of life from downstairs, and it was reasonable to assume everyone was in bed sleeping—the next morning was a work day. I went over to the wooden kitchen cabinet and looked through the contents and decided to utilize the frying pan. Pulling it out and holding it in one hand I asked Keith, "Is there any string knocking around here anywhere?"

Keith looked down at the pan and asked, "What for?"

"So we can haunt the bastards downstairs," I replied. I could see Keith's eyes light up at the thought of a bit of mischief. "If we lower the frying pan out of the window we can swing it so it bangs against their window and make them think it's a ghost or something."

Keith caught on and went upstairs to look for something suitable.

I slid the window upward and looked down to see how long the cable needed to be. Keith came back in the kitchen with a length of flex. The frying pan had a hole in the end of the handle that could be used to hang it on a hook, so we threaded the flex through it and tied a knot. We then leaned across the small kitchen table and lowered it out of the window down toward the flat below. I thought it made a decent sort of booming sound as it scraped against the brickwork on its way down. Keith had hold of the flex and I gave it a tug so that it swung backward and forward across the window below. The pan started to twist around on the string and kept catching the brickwork each time it swung to and fro. This helped to create even more noise, but there was no obvious response from the people below.

Brian came into the kitchen, saw us both hanging out the window and asked what we were doing.

"Take a look," Keith told him over his shoulder. "We're haunting Triff."

Brian came over and stuck his head out the window too, looked down and saw the dangling frying pan and then laughed out loud when he realized what was happening. I could see the pan was traveling across the window OK, but we could not get it to hit the glass as the window lay recessed back slightly. We needed to get it moving at a different angle so it would have more of the desired effect.

"We need to get it swinging outwards so that it bangs on the glass," I told Keith. This was a little harder than I first thought, so we both had to get hold of the cable and swing it back and away from the building. It went out a few feet, then swung back in and banged nicely onto the glass. Each time it landed it rattled against the window and almost came to a stop—we both had to make a big effort to get the momentum going again.

I tried to conjure up in my mind a picture of the scene inside the bedroom below. Were they all cowering beneath the bedclothes terrified, only occasionally sticking their heads out to see if the ghost was in the room? Perhaps they had climbed out their beds and drawn the curtains and looked at the window and seen nothing. Then suddenly an evil frying pan would come floating out of the darkness attacking their window. I wondered if they would all run and jump back in their beds, hoping it did not get in the room.

"You'll break the glass," said Brian. I thought that was a good idea and wished I had thought of it first, although Brian had not meant it as a suggestion. Keith picked up on it too and straight away the plan developed a bit further.

"Swing it harder," said Keith. "See if we can get it to smash through the window."

I imagined I could see the pan shattering its way through the glass into the room like some flying phenomenon, wreaking havoc before disappearing into the night. We tried even harder to get it to swing out further—it was never enough to give the pan sufficient momentum to smash the glass, but it was making plenty of noise each time it landed. Then someone below finally got out of bed and came down the hallway to the foot of the stairs and called out pleadingly, "What's going on up there? We are trying to get some sleep."

The three of us just laughed more at the sound of the distraught voice, beseeching us to stop. Whoever it was retreated as Keith slowly reeled the frying pan back. Satisfied we had been successful at embellishing our image further we made some coffee and went off to play some records. It seemed a good end to the day.

While the horseplay at Edith Grove and the weekend gigs were distractions, the boys had remained hopeful that someone would at least show some interest in the record. Brian continued to pursue his contact for news with daily phone calls. Most of the likely record companies had now been approached, and it was becoming apparent there would be no breakthrough on this front. Brian, despite his early criticism, continued to play the recording over and over again.

The band felt disappointed by the reaction—or the lack of it—to their record, but perhaps not really surprised. The people who called the shots at these record companies were called A&R men. The letters stood for artiste and repertoire. These were the people who made the decisions on new talent and material. Brian and Keith's attitude was that they were all mostly "a bunch of wankers" who knew little about music or trends—they reckoned that it came down to a question of who you knew. To a certain extent they were right and there seemed a prevailing attitude of "Well, so-and-so's been writing and recording songs for 30 years and knows what a hit is." Or "He's a friend of so-and-so who discovered him . . ." Even if you only listened to the radio you were aware of this lack of adventure—many times you would hear a new young artist who'd been forced to record with some old-hat orchestra that always played the same type of music. It was very much a closed shop, even before the record people knew what the Stones looked like, which would have undoubtedly proved an added obstacle. Whether the brief episode with the record companies was responsible for the next incident I never knew. Maybe it was a retaliatory gesture by the boys to get back at them, although I doubted it.

It was pouring down with rain outside as I came back to the flat at about two o'clock in the afternoon and climbed the stairs. It was all quiet and I assumed everyone was out. When I entered the bedroom, Keith, Brian, and Mick had the window wide open and were looking at something outside. They turned as I opened the door and looked at me, then turned to each other with knowing grins on their faces.

"What are you looking at?" I asked. The three of them looked pre-occupied.

"Just looking out the window," replied Brian with a big smug grin. Keith and Mick caught each other's eye and smiled.

I knew that looking out the window was not a hobby of theirs and guessed there must have been something to attract their attention. I wandered around the end of the beds over to the window, where Brian moved over slightly and I looked out with them. The view appeared normal, the backs of the houses in the next street apparently all there was to see.

"It's pissing with rain out there," I said, having just come in. They laughed. Still noticing nothing unusual, I looked down into the garden and saw nothing but grass. My gaze wandered over to the garden of the house next door.

"Hey, look," I said to all of them. "Someone has chucked some records out in the garden next door."

"Oh, yeah," said Mick, grinning widely.

Lying in the middle of next door's grass were two records that I thought were old 78s glistening in the rain.

"Wonder what they are," I said, not really interested. Brian looked blankly at Keith, who shrugged.

Still looking down at them my eyes wandered off to the right and there was a larger record, which was broken completely in half, although the two pieces lay next to each other.

"There's an old 78 over there," I said. "The others must be 45s— the green one looks like a Cliff Richard record. It's a Columbia label."

Mick looked at me and still said nothing, I looked back at the records, wondering about the one with the red label, and then slowly it dawned.

"Hey, they're my fucking records down there, the red one's my 'Three Stars,'" I shouted, shocked at seeing them down there. "And my Perry Como 78, how did they? . . . You bastards."

Brian and Keith burst out laughing and pushed themselves back from the edge of the window.

"Ha ha ha. He's spotted 'em," Brian laughed out loud and the three of them scampered quickly out of the room, their mocking laughter echoing in my ears. I looked down at the rare Perry Como 78 and thought, "Assholes, it's fucked." Cliff Richard's "Travellin' Light" looked as if it had been purposely bent too before being thrown out in the rain. "Bastards," I thought again as I looked at Ruby Wright's version of "Three Stars." I knew that one was rare too—it had been banned two days after being released because the BBC considered its references to the deaths of three pop stars distasteful. I looked down again. "Bastards."

I never bothered to retrieve the records—that would have looked weak to them. Within a few days all the discs had disappeared.

Keith lay flopped out amongst a pile of dirty clothes on the sofa in the front room reading a newspaper. His feet were crossed, his boots resting comfortably on one of Brian's shirts. We were just hanging around with nothing particular to do—this was quite often the case some days when we were up early, or at least a time regarded by us as early. The paper must have been one we found hanging around on one of the tables at the Ernie as we never bothered to buy them. As with most popular daily papers it had a society-cum-gossip page and something caught Keith's eye and made him laugh.

"Hey, look at this," he called across the room. I went over and looked over his shoulder as he held the paper up for me to see.

"What?" I asked, scanning the page.

"This picture down here," he said and pointed to a photo in the corner. I looked at the picture and read the caption that ran, "Austin Noseworthy and his feathered white cock." The picture was of someone holding a white bird. We both burst out laughing at the implication of the caption.

"Hey, Austin Noseworthy's a real cool name. Couldn't make something like that up if you tried," I told him. "Austin Noseworthy. Ha ha ha!"

He laughed and said, "Austin Noseworthy and his white cock. Ha ha ha. Let's cut it out and stick it up."

We carefully cut out the picture and used some tape to stick it on the wall above the mantelpiece as if it were a piece of art. It was the only picture in the room. I carefully drew a frame around it with a red ball-point pen. We both stood back and grinned some more at it. If only it hadn't been somebody's real name—it was the sort of outlandish name we'd have liked to have used—ideal for taking the piss in a posh hotel or somewhere similar.

"C'mon, let's get a bus and go up town," said Keith as he lit a fag.

"Yeah, OK. What do you fancy doin' then?" I asked him.

"I gotta make a payment on me guitar, man, to start with," he replied. "Let's go there first and wander around."

We went to the top of the Grove and caught the number 11 bus into the West End, traveling on the top deck as usual. We always sat in the front if we could, as this gave a full view of all that was going on down below in the Kings Road and Sloane Square. The journey took about 25 minutes—depending on traffic—and we would leave the bus near Trafalgar Square. From there we would walk to the guitar shop in Shaftesbury Avenue called Sound City. The manager was a big, kindly looking man named Bob Adams who knew all the musicians and had earned their respect. He always seemed pleased to see the lads and would offer friendly words of encouragement. He came across rather like a friendly uncle and many of the top bands went to the shop, including the now-famous Beatles. A couple of doors along from Sound City the company had another shop called Drum City, a place dedicated purely to percussion. In the months to come Charlie would get himself one of the brand-new metallic blue Slingerland kits displayed there. Keith chatted about guitars with Bob as he marked his payment book, then checked out a few Fender Telecasters; perhaps he was thinking of changing to one later.

From there we visited a few record stores, stopped for a coffee, and generally wandered around the shops, gradually making our way through Piccadilly and back toward the river. Part of the routine was to walk back toward Chelsea until we got bored, at which point we would jump on the next bus. On this occasion we decided to walk down the Mall toward Buckingham Palace, and in the process I received my first real indication we were beginning to stand out from other people's idea of normality.

As we walked along the side of the Mall next to St James's Park, we noticed quite a few groups of tourists visiting the area. Keith and I strolled past a guy who was standing around as if waiting to meet someone. He wore a navy blue two-piece suit with brown suede shoes and a white shirt. He also had curled greasy hair and looked like an ageing Elvis fan who had grown a bit tubby through drinking beer. As we passed he called out in a northern accent, "Nancy Boys!"—an insinuation that we were homosexual. It was probably because we had longer-than-average hair and wore unconventional coats, mine buttoned to the collar and Keith's made of leather. The guy probably thought we were going to just take the insult and walk off, but Keith turned on him.

"What's your fuckin' problem?" Keith asked him in a loud aggressive voice.

"Get your hair cut, Nancy Boys," said the northerner. He pronounced Nancy as Noncy.

"You big fat turd!" said Keith contemptuously and moved toward him. Other passers-by were turning to look.

"Ya come down t' Lun-don from north for day," Keith continued, mimicking the man's broad accent. More people started to look. "What ya doin'? Get bus t' come see sights 'ave ya'? No black puddin' down here, lad."

I joined in, "You big greasy fat wanker. Fuck off back up north and get a beer to put in your brain."

The guy looked around and saw all the people watching. Baiting a couple of effeminate-looking guys had suddenly escalated beyond his control. He was not expecting to get involved in a fight. He looked away.

"Come down t' Lun-don f' day t' find Noncy Boy then?" Keith continued to chide him.

"Fucking asshole," said Keith in his normal voice and we walked off feeling pleased with ourselves at embarrassing our prejudiced opponent in front of all the other people.

"He won't open his mouth again in a fucking hurry," said Keith as we headed for the bus stop.

I WAS STANDING in the kitchen doorway when I heard the letterbox clank as the postman made his delivery at the front door. Although I was not expecting any mail, I went down the stairs on the off chance. I picked up the handful of letters and sorted through them—there were a couple for Brian that I took back upstairs. Mick and Keith were in the process of getting dressed and I wandered past the bedroom into the lounge where Brian was searching the floor close to his bed.

"I can't find my inhaler," he called over his shoulder while down on his hands and knees.

"You looked in your coat?" I suggested. He sometimes put it in his pocket if he was going out. It was almost as if it were a game he made up and enjoyed playing: go to the chemist, buy an inhaler then bring it back and forget where you have hidden it. Then see if you have an asthma attack and die of panic before you can find it. I guess it made a change from hunt the bottleneck.

"I've found it; it was under the bed," he said, testing the inhaler's rubber bulb and spraying some of the contents into his mouth. Sometimes he had bad asthma attacks but other times, such as this, I thought he used it out of habit, almost as a form of reassurance.

"There's a couple of letters for you, L.B.H.," I said, placing them on the bed beside me as I sat down. He squirted the inhaler into his mouth again, placed it on the mantelpiece and picked up the letters. He studied his name and address on each envelope, contemplating who they were from. Deciding they might possibly have been tax forms or something similar he put them down unopened next to his inhaler. I thought I would ask him again about the *H* as I did every time he received mail with his initials on. It was a sort of routine now to go through the motions in a bid to prize his hidden name from him.

"C'mon, tell me what the *H* stands for?" I asked, although I knew he would not say.

"Don't start all that again," he said, smiling. "I'm not telling you."

"I bet it's Herbert and you're embarrassed," I said innocently.

"Yeah? Well, it's not, so there!" He turned his nose up. I smiled at him and tried to think of another possible name that I hadn't already guessed.

"Herbert or Howard, they're Welsh." I didn't have a clue what the real name was—it was just a game.

"I'll tell you," he said quietly. "Promise not to tell anyone else."

"OK," I said expectantly. Was he really going to tell me?

"If I tell you I don't want the others to know," he reiterated. "And don't burst out laughing."

"Well, I won't tell them, Brian," I said like a trusted friend. "It can't be that bad that I'll laugh."

He smiled and said, "You'd better not. I've never told anyone before."

"I won't tell anyone else," I said, shaking my head.

He looked at me and said very quietly, "It's Hopkin."

I immediately burst out laughing and rolled back on the bed. "Hopkin?" I laughed.

"See, I knew that you'd laugh," he said, now slightly annoyed.

I rose to my feet, still laughing, and ran to the door, opening it and calling out at the top of my voice, "It's Hopkin! The *H* is for Hopkin!" I went into the bedroom to make sure Keith and Mick had heard. "It's Hopkin. The *H* in Brian's name stands for Hopkin."

Mick and Keith both said the name almost simultaneously and started to laugh with me. Brian came storming into the doorway waving his finger at me. "You bastard!" he shouted and I moved until the bed was between us. "You bastard, I'm never talking to you again. I told you to keep your mouth shut." He stormed back into the lounge and slammed the door so that it shook on its hinges.

"Anyone seen Hopkin today?" I said to Keith, emphasizing the name.

"Hopkin?" said Keith so that Brian was sure to hear. "I think Hopkin went out."

"Hopkin's gone out?" I asked.

"I think Hopkin went to the shop for a Morgan-Morgan," said Keith laughing.

"You mean Hopkin Jones?"

We continued with our meaningless conversation using the name Hopkin at every opportunity. After a few minutes Brian put a record on to drown our gibes. After giving him time to calm down, I opened the door and went back into the lounge. Brian was standing by the record player. He looked at me all sullenly and said, "Fuck off."

"C'mon, man, cheer up," I said. "I think it's a cool name. Hopkin Jones sounds great."

"It sounds fucking stupid," he replied.

"No, it doesn't. You should use it," I said sincerely. I genuinely thought it was a cool name that people would remember because it was unusual. I continued trying to talk him into it. "It's a great name to use for the band anyway. There's already a Lightnin' Hopkins, so it's blues-related and it's your real name."

"I don't like it so don't call me that again," he said, looking at the next record he wanted to play.

"How about Elmo Hopkin then?" I ventured. He smiled, and we left it there.

The band's fortunes continued to trundle along throughout March. They were now getting an average of five gigs a week at different venues and the financial outlook, although not great, was slightly better. The failure of the record had been virtually accepted and the bill for the studio was never mentioned. The audience size was beginning to increase at each place too. The Manor House crowd was now fully receptive to R&B music and had now grown used to the sight of the Stones. Fans who came to Studio 51 on Sundays were starting to make their way across to Richmond for the evening session as well. Stu turned down many requests from followers who wanted a lift in the van—there was no space for anyone else. Nevertheless, using the tube they all made it over to Richmond on time.

The word was starting to spread and the Station Hotel was gradually getting fuller each week, helped by students from a nearby college. The band was now drawing a fair-sized crowd to keep the promoter happy—I think it would have been fair to say his club had never been more popular. The other thing I began to notice was that all the people who came seemed to be very fashion-conscious. They all seemed to wear smart new trendy clothes along with well-groomed hairstyles. The Rolling Stones, except for Charlie, were just about the worst-dressed people in the building. As far as I could remember, the Stones had always worn the same clothes every day, apart from an occasional clean shirt. They certainly didn't share the apparent affluence of their audience, but this didn't get in the way of another good Richmond evening, after which we returned to the flat to wreak more havoc.

Earlier in the week Keith and I had received a complaint from one of the next-door neighbors. Surprisingly it was not about noise but a piece of iron. Our street door adjoined that of the neighboring house. Between the two flights of steps there had probably been some railings in the past, but all that was left now was an iron bar running across between the pillar and the wall. While we were waiting for someone to answer the door we would invariably sit on this bar. Everyone did this.

Although it was about half an inch thick and three inches wide— quite a sturdy piece of ironmongery—it had begun to bend slightly in the middle. Keith and I had been sitting on the bar, waiting for the door to be opened, when a man who lived next door came out and complained.

"Look at this bar—it's getting bent. I don't want to see you sitting on there again."

Just as he finished speaking our door opened, we grinned at each other and vanished inside. I think it was the first time there had been any contact with the people next door, so it seemed a bit mystifying that he should complain about this bar. It did not appear to serve any purpose and it was not as if it was new or anything.

Arriving back from Richmond in high spirits at about 1:30 A.M., we woke someone up to open the door and took the guitars from the van. After putting them in the hallway, I turned to Brian and Keith.

"Hang on, give me a hand with this bar, let's see if we can get it off."

Keith did not need asking twice and gave me a hand to work it backward and forward while Brian watched bemused.

"Phelge, what are you doing? What do you want that for?" Brian asked. When he wasn't involved in music he could be a bit slow.

"I need this bar—you'll see in a minute," I replied.

Keith and I finally wrenched the bar free from its fixing points. It was heavier than I thought it would be and about five feet long.

I asked Keith to grab one end of the bar while I took the other and we gradually fed it through the letterbox of the house next door. When it was almost through we gave it a final big push and sent it flying on its way with a great crash down the hallway of the neighbors' house. The noise seemed to echo down the street.

"Stick your bar up your ass!" I shouted out toward a bedroom window.

We all disappeared inside and had difficulty getting the guitars upstairs we were in such hysterics. We never heard anything from the man next door again, and the bar never reappeared. When Charlie and Stu next came round they both asked what had happened to the bar by the door. Charlie laughed at the outrageousness of what we told him, Stu shook his head in sorrow once more. "C'mon, let's go," he sighed.

Toward the end of March, Giorgio started to make noises about managing the band. I was first aware of this when Brian declined my invitation to the Ernie one evening, saying he, Keith, and Mick were going to Giorgio's for a meeting and would probably get something to eat while they were there. Later that evening after they had returned Brian mentioned to me that Giorgio wanted to act as the band's manager and that they were thinking about it. The tone that Brian spoke in sounded very unenthusiastic and halfhearted. He answered my questions on the subject without any interest. "I don't know, I'm not really sure," was all he said.

I knew that Giorgio could become infectiously enthusiastic once he had formed an idea. I could picture him waving his hands about and talking nonstop, pushing all obstacles aside in his excitable European manner. But he didn't seem to have convinced them. My opinion was that it could have been a proverbial case of the blind leading the blind. Although Giorgio could describe a scenario with great flair, the Stones really needed someone who could fit the pieces together to make them pop stars. Apart from knowing they would need a record released, no one had a clue about promoting the band. Giorgio's experience came across as just booking a band for his club—he seemingly had no more contacts in the music business than the band themselves. Money and organization were also needed and without these I could not see Giorgio's plan—assuming he had a plan—as a sound one. However they continued to talk.

We had found an effective new way of disposing of the rubbish. By this stage it was not unusual to throw a cup out of the first floor window if it had been left around on the table and fungus had formed inside it. It seemed a natural progression for any rubbish, including tin cans, Morgan-Morgan wrappers, empty cartons, and stale food, to take the express route. It was all sent raining down into the basement entrance where the rubbish bins stood. At times there would be a huge pile there and whoever picked it up, we neither knew nor cared. Whether anyone lived down below we never knew either. I never saw anyone ever go in or come out from that part of the building.

The Welsh landlady still used to make the odd unannounced

flying inspection with her "If it's not cleaned up by Friday I want you boys out" routine. She used to sweep out the downstairs hallway but never cleaned beyond that. What the rental terms were I never found out, although obviously it did not include items like clean sheets. They were never changed at all. The ones on my bed, apart from being as dirty as anyone else's, were also torn. Both sheets had gone threadbare and holes had appeared. When I got into bed my feet would invariably catch on the worn sheets and tear them some more. One night after coming back from the Red Lion I finally became exasperated with them and climbed out of bed. Throwing all the other covers off the bed I gave the sheets a good tug and removed them.

"What're you doin' now?" Keith wanted to know. He sounded amused.

I gathered the sheets and made a loose bundle of them. "These sheets are fucking useless," I replied. "May as well not have any. They're all virtually torn in half."

Putting the sheets down I walked over and slid the window open. Keith was lying in his bed smoking a cigarette and sat up as I moved around.

"I think I'll chuck 'em out," I informed him and gathered them back up from the floor. I was carrying the bundle over to the window when my eye caught the glow of Keith's cigarette.

"Hey man, we may as well set fire to them," I said. "Save anyone from bringing them back again."

"Set fire to them?" Keith said, grinning.

I thought about it for a moment and said, "Yeah, we can make out the house is on fire and get them all out of bed downstairs."

Mick had turned round in his bed and sat halfway up, watching what was happening. "You probably will set fire to the house," he laughed.

"I've got some matches here," said Keith, shaking the box so they rattled. He came over and knelt on the end of his bed by the window and removed a match from the box in readiness.

I held the sheets up on the window sill, ready to be dropped in case something went wrong and we really did set the house on fire. Keith stuck a match and held it against the material but its flame died. Mick laughed at us again.

"Hang on. I'll light another one," Keith said and he opened the box and tried again.

He held the second match against one of the sheets and after a few seconds it began to burn, then he did the same in a second place and that caught too. The flames took hold quicker than I had expected and I had to release the sheets. I threw them forward as far as I could, hoping they would float down slowly. Keith and I stuck our heads out the window to watch the sheets descend, shouting out, "Fire! Fire! The house is on fire!" We could both hear Mick laughing behind us as we saw the flaming sheets dropping to the ground.

We continued to laugh as we watched them burn and then suddenly a light was switched on somewhere downstairs, illuminating part of the garden. We had succeeded in waking someone up again. Pulling our heads back into the room Keith slammed the bedroom window closed and we went back into our beds.

"We'll have to tell Morgan-Morgan's wife how we saved the building," said Keith.

The main reason I never went with the band to the gigs at Windsor each Friday was that it was a bad day to take off work. It was pay day. I spent most of those evenings alone, hanging around the flat. The routine was that I would usually go to bed around midnight and the boys would arrive home at around 2:00 A.M. unless they became involved in some escapade on the way back. Going to bed before their return was a gamble—either they would go to bed immediately or stay up and blast out music.

This week, knowing how much they'd enjoyed themselves when I nankered and gobbed over them previously, I decided they might like a similar performance. I went to bed expecting to fall asleep, but figured if I was still awake I would entertain them once more. When they came in, I was still awake.

It was their usual thoughtful entrance, incorporating a test of the street door's hinges by booting it back against the wall. The door shuddered and the noise of banging guitar cases and loud voices once more filled the hallway. I took up my strategic position again at the top of the stairs, naked with my underpants over my head.

There was no point in pulling the exact same gag twice, as I knew they would get bored. As they approached the stairs, from beneath my "baggies" I nankered down at them once more. To give them warning, between some flying phlegm, I gave out the nanker "eek eek eek" noise. They all stopped in the hallway and peered up.

"He's only up there with his baggies on his fuckin' head again and gobbin'," Keith called out to the others.

Brian came and looked then laughed. "Ah, watch it! He's gonna gob on us again. Who's going first?"

I eeked at them once more. Mick was trapped behind the guitars and stood looking up open-mouthed at me. Assuming I was not going to be so boring to as to gob on him again, Keith came forward to put a foot on the first stair. I took one hand from my face and grabbed my dick.

As Keith advanced I began to piss toward him. The spray arched through the air and splashed somewhere near his feet and he dropped his guitar in the dark and scurried back.

"He's fuckin' pissing on us now," he called out to the others.

"What? He's not is he?" asked Brian.

I floated another stream of piss down the stairs in answer to Brian's question.

"Watch out, fuckin' get back," said Keith. "He almost got me."

Brian laughed. "Ah, Phelge, you fuckin' horrible bastard. Don't!"

"He's fuckin' insane!" said Mick. I was enjoying myself now, so I sent them down some more piss.

"Look at those baggies on his head," laughed Keith. "Fuckin' ridiculous."

"C'mon, Phelge," said Mick, wanting to come upstairs but standing well back.

"I think he's finished now," Brian said, coming forward.

I was running out of "ammunition," but holding a little back. I sent another squirt down as he tried his luck on the first step.

"Ah, no he hasn't, get back," shrieked Brian. Keith laughed as Brian almost received a direct hit.

They all stood at the bottom of the stairs, out of range and laughing, knowing I could not carry on much longer. I started descending the stairs towards them.

"Look out, he's coming down," laughed Keith.

"Quick, Mick, get out the way," Brian squealed, trying to step over the gear.

They all moved back some more as I approached. A third of the way down the stairs I let go with my last reserves and gave them a final spray. The three of them cried out in horror before laughter took over once more.

"You dirty bastard," shouted Keith.

I turned and fled back up the stairs as they picked up the guitars and came chasing after me. I ran into the bedroom and jumped back into bed. They followed me in still laughing.

"Too fuckin' much," said Keith.

The last Sunday in March saw the largest crowd to date in Richmond. Again the Studio 51 afternoon session had been almost full and many of that audience again made the trek across the river. On this occasion it was difficult to even walk around the very edges of the dance floor as the band played. If you wanted to buy a drink in the bar outside the club area you needed to wait until after the interval session had ended to stand a chance of being served. When you joined the dancers on the floor there was little room to move—if you saw space you stepped into it. You also got hot. Corduroy clothes were now very fashionable and the finely turned-out audience wore them in abundance. The smartly dressed mods liked to show off their latest clothes and the "in thing" was to dance with your coat on. You may have been sweating but you looked cool.

The dance routine had become very restricted and most of the time you would stay in one place just moving your knees and arms. Some of the more extrovert people waved their arms high in the air in time with the music. The dance was to become known later as The Shake. For the last set of the evening the Stones played music that captured the mood of the audience in a way they never had before. It had become magical in that darkened hall. The more the band rose to the audience's escalating fever the more the crowd responded. The noise from people stamping their feet with the beat of the final Diddley numbers was deafening and you could not help wanting to join them. You began to run out of energy but the band drove on and you did not want it to end. Where once before the band had sounded merely good, now you realized how great the Stones were. When Giorgio finally turned the lights back on after that fantastic closing finale, you just stood there with a feeling of awe, wondering if you would ever witness something as incredible again.

With the lights back on and most of the crowd gone, the hall took on its feeling of bareness again. Mick and the others were still on the stage, beginning to disconnect the equipment. They knew the band had done something special that night and there were smiles all round. For it to have happened in the presence of their largest-ever audience was an extra bonus. Unplugging all the cables and putting the guitars away seemed to take longer that night. It was as if the spell still remained and no one wanted to hurry from the building.

As fate would have it, there was only one gig—at the Red Lion—scheduled for the week after the Richmond triumph. Keith, Brian, and I spent a couple of evenings wandering around London's clubs just checking out what was going on and watching other bands.

On Thursday they disappeared for another meeting with the effervescent Giorgio. I was starting to think they were showing interest in his management proposals as an excuse to visit him for a free meal. When they came back they still didn't seem sold on the idea.

Saturday April 6 was another night off—the first time they had not played on a Saturday for months. Pat Andrews had come with the baby to visit Brian again and that evening we all went to the West End to wander around. Getting close to midnight we decided to go for a meal in a Soho restaurant. Taking our places at a table in the downstairs section I thought we were going to have problems due to our images again. The place was completely full of Scottish soccer supporters who had come down to Wembley to see Scotland beat England two to one.

The Scottish football fanatics had a reputation for heavy drinking and getting involved in skirmishes with the "auld enemy." With Mick, Brian, Keith, and myself looking the way we did, I assumed we were going to be the butt of the usual comments that would then get out of hand. Most of the Scotsmen had long finished eating and remained at their tables continuing to down as much alcohol as they could. Brian sat at one end of the table with Pat and was making a great fuss of his baby throughout the meal, picking the child up to soothe it several times.

When we had finished eating, one of the Scotsmen, who could barely talk, staggered over to our table. I looked up and seeing how big he was I thought to myself, "Here it comes." He made his way unsteadily to where Brian sat with the baby and towered over them. He was the archetypal Scottish football fan in long tartan scarf and matching beret. Suddenly he bent over toward Brian and thrust his hand out to the baby.

"Who's the wee bonnie bairn then?" he said to the baby in his deep voice with broad accent. "Is this your dad?" The baby held on to the man's finger.

Brian started baby talking. "Go on, tell him who your daddy is."

"Is it boy bairn or girl bairn?" said the Scotsman.

"You're a little boy bairn, aren't you?" Brian said in his baby-type voice.

"He's a great wee-looking little lad," said the man shaking the baby's hand.

"You're a big boy, aren't you?" said Brian, almost cooing.

"Are ye the wee bairn's mum?" said the big man to Pat. "He's a real wee bonnie boy."

"That's your mum, isn't it?" Brian said. "Say hello." The baby started to cry.

"He wants his mammy now. Give him to his mammy." The Scotsman seemed heartbroken.

"You want to go and see your mammy?" asked Brian and then handed the baby across to Pat.

"How old's the bairn?" the man asked. Pat told him the baby's name—Julian—and his age.

I had no idea whether Mick and Keith had been expecting any aggravation, but we now sat there creased up with laughter at the whole situation.

The Scotsman turned and called to his friends across the restaurant, "See the wee bairn over here? He's a jolly fella. Let's have a collection from you lads for the wee bairn."

All the Scotsmen started putting their hands in their pockets for loose coins and placing them on their tables and the big man went over and collected them. As the Scottish were frequently the subject of jokes regarding their being penny-pinching, I was amazed and thought to myself, "Gee, the baby will be able to pay for the meal."

The big man came back with all the coins and gave them to Pat. "Buy something for the baby; it's been real nice meeting you," he said. Between them they had given the baby more than two pounds—a larger sum than each Stone sometimes earned for an evening's work in a club.

AFTER THE SATURDAY night out it was back to work again at Richmond. This Sunday turned out to be similar to the previous one only with more people. It was getting heavily crowded inside the club, so much so that during the last part of the evening some people unstacked a few tables and started to dance on top of them. I was in the middle of the floor and as I looked across toward the door I saw them gyrating two to a table. It added even more excitement to the atmosphere. As the temperature had risen in the hall due to all the bodies packed inside it also looked a good method of getting a little extra breathing space. Giorgio was waving his arms about encouraging more people to do the same, and it certainly added to another spectacular evening for the Stones.

At the end of the evening a reporter from a local newspaper made himself known and took some photographs of the band for the coming week's edition. To complete his story he asked for the name of the club, but the truth was it did not really have one. No one had considered that; it was always simply referred to as "Richmond." Wanting to be helpful to the reporter, someone put the name "Crawdaddy" forward. It was a pure spur of the moment impulse—the word came from one of the Stones' last song titles of the evening—and the venue was known as the Crawdaddy from then on.

The second of the successful Richmond nights was followed by another slack week for work. This time there was no gig at all until the following Sunday, and this meant it was back to the breadline again as far as our diets were concerned. Brian was back in the kitchen making porridge for himself—nobody else liked it. He accompanied

it with the occasional egg or a fried slice of bread. He would slop it
around in horrible thick grease in the blackened pan, then ask if you
fancied some, even though there was not much to go round. Other
times he would just say there was only enough for one and then
proceed to scoff the lot. Keith and I would invariably say no if he
offered, preferring to buy some bread or a Morgan-Morgan. We used
to cut the pie across the center and have half each, then wash it down
with coffee.

I was sitting in one of the armchairs—this one had its interior poking
from one of the arms—when the Welsh Gestapo burst in unexpect-
edly one afternoon. Brian happened to be wandering around the room
in search of something and Linda was in his bed. The door burst open
and in burst Mrs. Morgan-Morgan with another woman who looked
as if she might have been her sister. As well as looking similar, they
also shared the same opinion of the state of the flat, which was particularly messy that day.

"Oh my God!" said Mrs. Morgan-Morgan. "Look at the state of
this room."

"It's disgraceful," said her friend in support. "They're wrecking
the house; you'll have nothing left."

"You've ruined all the furniture; the table's all marked and
scratched," shouted the landlady.

"I wouldn't put up with this; it's disgraceful. Look what they're
doing," added the sidekick.

They were well into their double act and I looked across at
Brian—he did not seem bothered. Then they saw Linda.

The landlady screamed: "Oh my God, they've only got a girl in
the bed. Look at it; look at it."

The other one gasped. "There's a girl in here as well? Whatever
next? You can't have this," she shrieked.

"You're not supposed to have girls in here," the landlady shouted.
"I'm not having you bring girls back here."

"It's my sister," said Brian. "She's visiting."

"Oh, he's lying, sister indeed!" said the support lady. She had probably noticed Brian had blond hair while Linda's was near black.

"I want all you boys out of here by this weekend," the landlady screeched. "You all get out. Girls in here? Get out straight away."

The distraction of Linda meant that at least she was no longer worrying about the state of the room.

"I want you all out of here. I shall tell my husband you've got girls in here," the landlady threatened. I noticed that Linda was now "girls."

Then they stomped off into the bedroom. They were probably looking for more girls, but it was empty. Keith had gone to the toilet and shut the door, probably to read. Pretty soon there was more shouting coming from the bedroom.

"The sheets are missing off this bed. They've stolen my sheets." The landlady marched back into the front room. "What have you boys done with the sheets from that bed?"

"I think someone downstairs stole them," I said. It was all I could think of—I thought the flaming sheets story might have been too much for them at that point.

"You make sure you're all out by the weekend," said the landlady as she left, slamming the door behind her.

I never knew what to make of it all. The building was badly in need of repair, but it was not as if we were ripping it to pieces—it was just basically very untidy. All the fuss about the girl made me wonder what things were like in Wales. Perhaps they were all religious and spent their time in church. We knew nothing would happen over the girl incident—whenever Mr. Morgan-Morgan came he never bothered to look around closely, he just collected the money then left.

Keith and I also spent a couple more nights doing the rounds of the clubs. Because the band was known to most of the door staff we never had to pay to get inside, thus making it possible to visit several clubs in one night. If it was a club that had a drinks license, we would sometimes go to the bar for a beer, but it was not a major consideration as we never really drank that much.

We walked into the Marquee fairly early one evening before the music had started. All the lights were on and people were just standing around chatting. We saw Clapton and Pretty Mick in conversation with someone and we strolled across the dance floor to where they were standing. Eric was talking about blues. I was not particularly paying attention to the conversation, instead looking around the club to see who else was there, until Eric brought up the subject of some people he knew and a band. He then went on to say that he was playing with a group now and again. I tuned back in to the conversation.

"Who's this band you're singing with?" I asked. It was more out of politeness than interest.

"I'm not the singer," replied Eric, looking serious.

That puzzled me. "So what are you doing?"

"Playing guitar," he answered, shrugging his shoulders.

It surprised me—I thought he was just a singer. "I didn't know you played guitar at all."

"Yeah, a bit, I've been messing around on some blues stuff for a while, nothing serious. A bit of classical too," Eric informed everyone.

"Where are you playing?" I asked, thinking we might go and watch sometime.

"We're not. We're only really messing around at the moment to see how it goes. It's just a get-together with a few friends." he said.

I nodded and we turned our attention back to the others who were talking about Richmond and asking Keith where the Stones were playing next week. After that we left them and decided to go elsewhere as not much was happening. Maybe it was country music night.

"I never knew Clapton played guitar," I said to Keith as we climbed the stairs. "I've known him all this time and only ever seen him singing."

"It's different playing on stage to playing in your bedroom," Keith replied. I got the impression that Keith had never seen him play either.

Another club we started to visit that had not been open long was the Scene. It was in a basement in Ham Yard, opposite the Windmill

Theatre, and it was the first place I had ever seen that had an ultra-violet light positioned over the entrance. If you were wearing anything white it appeared to be luminous. If you wore black, as we did, it high-lighted every flake of dust on your clothes. It was a good way to find out if you had dandruff.

Once you went into the club it was very dim. The walls and ceiling were painted matte black to enhance the effect of darkness. On the right-hand side stood a very small booth that housed the DJ, and on the far side there was a dimly lit snack bar.

Keith liked visiting the Scene, mainly because of the records. The disc jockey was Guy Stevens and he had a superb collection of R&B singles. The booth had a door and a glass window and we would go inside and talk to Guy. Three people made it really cramped but talking was easy as it was quite well soundproofed. It seemed Guy was an authority on most blues artists and had a good supply line for records from the States. If any new records made their way onto the American market Guy would have them a few days later. The records played at the Scene were all R&B music. It was the only club we knew that played only recorded music, but later they would begin to book bands.

At the end of that week money was as tight as ever and the boys were glad to get back to the two Sunday gigs, which were now the only regular work they had. The Studio 51 club was now packed in the afternoon and I was beginning to dislike it. For some reason it felt as if the band was in a goldfish bowl. People still sat on the chairs across the front of the stage while others stood crowded behind them. Everybody just wanted to watch. It was as if they were waiting patiently for the warm-up men to finish and the main act to come on.

The place had a club atmosphere but it seemed to be more of an appreciation society where people just listened. It was almost as if every-one was expecting something else to happen other than a band playing, as if they were standing about aimlessly on a railway platform. I imag-ined the stage complete with the band on it suddenly moving out of sight, a train pulling up and everyone getting aboard. Perhaps it was just too early in the day.

That night at Richmond started off very ordinarily. We arrived and unloaded the van, then set up the equipment. People were now starting to turn up earlier and would be waiting for the band to arrive. Giorgio gave Brian a copy of the local paper with the write-up from the previous week. All of us wanted to read it. Brian was so pleased, he would have forced us to read it anyway. Once we had read it, Brian read it again out loud to make sure we understood every word. He was very happy.

The article was short but it captured well the progress of the band and finished with some promising comments about their prospects. The Stones were now in print through their own merit rather than a paid advert.

The club was practically full by the start and surely would not hold that many more people. The Stones, whether or not inspired by the press write-up, were in full swing in by the middle of the first set.

Then in walked the Beatles.

I saw Giorgio fuss them past his entrance table into the hall and they then stood at the left-hand side of the stage and watched the Stones. One by one the Stones saw them too as they played, then very soon the word spread around the hall, "The Beatles are here."

People were straining to get a glimpse of the Fab Four and Mick must have been aware of the distraction as he sang. Brian just beamed over the top of his guitar, and Keith's face seemed to light up for a moment too.

The Beatles were then invited up onto the stage. As cheers and applause greeted them, John Lennon waved back, and then the other Beatles took their hands from their pockets and waved, too. They stood there looking neatly groomed in their long black coats, reminding me of the Everly Brothers at the Palladium. Apart from the fact that there were four Beatles they could have come from the very same mold.

During the final part of the evening the Stones played a superb version of "I'm Movin' On" as the Beatles watched and occasionally signed autographs. They didn't seem in a hurry to rush off, which suggested they approved of the Stones' music.

After the Stones had finished playing, arrangements were made for the Beatles to visit the flat in Edith Grove. This time there was no hanging around as we packed the equipment into the van. With this done quickly and efficiently Stu drove at top speed back to Chelsea.

Almost as soon as Stu had parked the van the Beatles and several of their entourage pulled up behind in two cars and we all trooped up the stairs into the front room. Apart from myself, the six Stones and four Beatles, there were another four people. The room now held a total of 15 people, all of whom seemed to be talking at once.

Mick stood in the middle of the room talking to John while Paul leaned against the table listening to Brian. I saw Paul glance casually around the room to gain an impression of his surroundings. His eyes ran slowly over the furniture, walls, and ceiling. He did not seem unduly perturbed by anything—the look on his face said, "I've been here before."

Ringo looked at a chair and then decided to sit on its arm as if imagining something could happen to his coat. He sat and talked with Bill and Charlie as Keith stood with Stu talking to George.

The Beatles carried with them the air of a big professional outfit. All the members of their entourage were smartly dressed in the same dark-colored overcoats as the band, giving the appearance of one big team. I stood and talked with a couple of them, one of whom asked if he could get a drink. I gave him directions to find the kitchen and he left the room. He came back after a couple of minutes and said, "I think I'll leave it and get something later."

I looked at him and smiled then replied, "I thought you would." He smiled nicely back. He definitely looked like a clean hotel man to me.

It was difficult to keep track of all that was being said. Occasionally Mick or John would mention an artist or song and say, "I like that. We used to do it." The conversations were really about finding out what the other group liked or listened to. Everyone was trying to find out as much as possible in a short space of time. Eventually Mick put a Jimmy Reed album on for John to hear.

Lennon stood and listened with hands in pockets as Jimmy Reed sang "I'll Change My Style." I don't think he had heard Reed before and after a few minutes he looked at Mick and said, "What's this? I think it's crap." Mick looked surprised for a moment, unable to understand why John did not like it. If he liked the other blues material, why not Jimmy Reed? They debated it for a while and then other records came up for review.

The Beatles team was getting restless and wanted to leave, particularly the man who'd asked for the drink. The meeting began to break up and eventually Stu drove the remaining Beatles, George and Ringo, back to their London hotel. The first encounter with the chart-topping group had gone well, although the Fab Four were streets ahead of the unknown Stones at the time.

The next morning Brian and Keith were up early and dashed into town to meet the Beatles again at their hotel. When they came back a few hours later, I asked Brian if he and Keith had seen them.

"Yeah, we went in and saw them," said Brian. "There were loads of girls waiting outside and wanting to get in. All screaming for the Beatles. You should have seen Paul. He had nothing to shave with and got a tube of toothpaste and squirted it on his face."

"Toothpaste?" I asked.

"Yeah, green stuff, spread it all over his face," said Keith laughing. "They invited us to meet them at the Albert Hall on Thursday as well."

When Thursday evening came Mick set off along with Brian and Keith to the Albert Hall in Kensington near Hyde Park. I hung around the flat as Brian had said they did not know how they were going to get in. They returned close to midnight, really excited.

"Did you get in to see them?" I asked.

"We met up with the roadies outside and just walked in carrying some guitars. No one knows who anyone is anyway," Keith explained.

"Yeah, it was dead simple," continued Brian. "All the Ernie doormen don't have clue of who the band is. They probably thought *we* were the Beatles. There were all these girls screaming at us thinking we were them as we went in. It was fantastic." Brian had been more impressed by this than anything else. He never even mentioned the Beatles' music.

The weekend after the Beatles encounters, Giorgio had come up with a film-making idea for the Stones. To me it sounded like a mad spur-of-the-moment scheme—I wondered if Giorgio actually had any equipment. If he was going to invest some money in the band it would have seemed a better idea to have bought some new stage equipment.

The Stones set off to meet Giorgio and spent the weekend helping with the project. Arriving on Sunday at the Crawdaddy Club, as it was now officially called, Giorgio was carrying a large, professional-looking camera. It must have been heavy but Giorgio had no trouble running around with it. It looked impressive and I guessed maybe he did know what he was doing after all. He certainly looked and acted like a chaotic film director. Apparently the finale for the film was to record the audience coming into the club and maybe some of the gig. Whether he did this or not I never knew—the place was just too packed.

The club was so full it was verging on ridiculous. You could not move at all. More people were dancing on tables than ever before. On the dance floor you were so cramped, even turning around was almost impossible. I felt that if the lights were turned on you would be able to see people hanging from the ceiling too. People still danced in their coats though, it was just not the "thing" to take them off. Eventually I went outside to get some air. Giorgio had a rota system working at the door, only letting people in as others left. He made an exception for me and when I returned inside the club I stood close to the door with Chrissie Shrimpton. It was the only place you could breathe a draught of fresh air.

Fresh from the coverage in the local press, the Stones were half expecting another journalist. Giorgio had phoned a reporter for *Record*

Mirror, one of the major music papers, trying to get him to visit Richmond. Previously the band had been neglected by the music press, and no one would have been surprised if this had happened again, but this time the journalist turned up. His name was Peter Jones and he spent some time talking with the band and watching them play.

On the way home from Richmond the best that the Stones were hoping for was a write-up in the music press. But unbeknown to everybody Peter Jones was to set in motion a chain of events that had a more unexpected conclusion.

Everyone had more or less forgotten about Brian's letter to the BBC. A couple of follow-up calls had been fobbed off, then out of the blue a reply arrived inviting the band to come to an audition. The main problem was that Charlie and Bill were working and neither of them could take time away from their jobs. Brian, Mick, and Keith made last-minute arrangements for Ricky Brown and Carlo Little from Cyril Davies's group to deputize as their rhythm section. When the band returned from the audition they had some hopes of getting a booking on the BBC's *Jazz Club* program, although they had the feeling the people at the studio hadn't cared for them very much. Again it was their appearance, coupled with the electric guitars that linked them to rock and roll.

The day after the audition the Stones received a booking to play at the Eel Pie Island Hotel for the first time. Despite its name the building had probably not been used as a hotel since the war. It now functioned as an almost derelict dance hall and was one of my favorite places. Everyone referred to the venue as Eel Pie Island—it was on an islet in the Thames and access from "mainland" Twickenham was by means of a concrete footbridge.

I had never been there with a band before, only as a spectator, and never realized the hassle involved in getting the equipment to the venue—we couldn't get the van over the bridge, which was a short, arched construction, hardly wide enough for two people to walk side by side. Once over the bridge you then had to walk down a long, twisting path for a hundred yards or so until you reached the venue. The amplifiers would seem extra heavy by this time. Then after the band finished, you had to struggle back again in the pitch darkness.

The hotel always looked eerie as you approached it, especially so in the dark. It seemed to suddenly loom out of nowhere and always made me feel I was approaching a haunted mansion. The entire place had an aura of immense character. When you finally entered, it was enormous. It was like stepping back in time to some huge state ballroom or banqueting hall. Although it was run-down, you could imagine its past splendor.

There were two stages, one placed at each end of the hall. On special nights like the one I had spent there on New Year's Eve, different bands appeared on each stage. As one group of musicians stopped for a break, the other at the opposite end would begin again so that the music was nonstop. The hotel also had another very special feature. Separating the two stages at each end of the hall was a sprung wooden dance floor. It had been created so that the center of the floor was arched slightly higher than its edges. When you walked across the boards it would put a bounce in your step and the effect when you danced was almost like being on a trampoline. To complete the atmosphere a gallery supported by pillars ran all the way around the upper part of the building and from there you could look down on the dance floor. Through the railings around the edge of the gallery, you could see doorways that presumably led to the old guest rooms. The Eel Pie was another mecca for New Orleans-style jazz, which was now gradually giving way to blues music.

The island was a very popular venue among the student generation, and the Stones again attracted an excellent turnout. After humping the gear out and over the bridge then into the van we had to unload it all again back at Edith Grove.

Stu needed the van emptied so that it could be worked on the next day at the garage. We struggled again as we carried the amplifiers up the stairs to the flat. We piled everything up by the doorway inside Brian's room, where there never appeared as much of it as in the back of the van.

With that task completed Mick and I wandered off to the kitchen to boil the kettle.

The next thing Mick and I heard was Bo Diddley, about 50 watts of him at full blast to be exact. Keith and Brian had converted a guitar lead and rigged up the radiogram into the stage PA system, which now had its speakers pointing happily out into the hallway. This might have cost Bo a few of his fans in the Chelsea area—it was 1:30 A.M.—but Brian and Keith thought it sounded great and played the whole album flat out. People for miles around must have heard it, but if they complained at all we were never aware.

The next evening Brian was fooling around on Bill's bass guitar, playing Jimmy Reed music. He never said so, but maybe the Beatles were still on his mind.

"If we got rid of Ernie I could play bass," he stated, mulling it over. It seemed feasible as he could play almost anything. He thought about it some more and continued playing.

"It means I would have to get a bass and an amp from somewhere," Brian said flatly.

"And a decent guitar amp," said Keith, reminding him they were using Bill's amps for gigs.

"It means you'll have to play the Bo Diddley stuff if I play bass on it," Brian replied.

I stood next to Brian and wondered if he was thinking about making the band a four-piece unit. He seemed to go off the idea as quickly as he thought of it.

"I don't know, I wish we could find a different bass player," he said sighing, then got up and put the bass away.

Later that night Keith and I went down to the pie stall as Sandy had turned up to see Mick and we had decided to leave them to it. We were strolling along the embankment and stopped to lean against the wall for a smoke. We stood and looked at the empty funfair across the water, just chatting. It was as if Keith always knew how it would turn out eventually. He looked out across the river saying, "I reckon we're gonna be big one day. We might be little uns now, but one day I reckon we'll be big uns. I can see it. Get a big house in Barbados and a yacht. I reckon we'll make it."

I looked at him and replied, "It'd be great, man. Just cruising around the Caribbean with loads of dough. The band's getting popular—it could happen."

"Yeah, I reckon it's all starting," he said, still gazing across the river.

Mostly when they all talked of success it was with the idea that it might last two or three years and that they should make the most of it while it lasted. Could Keith see beyond that? I did not know. We walked back.

Entering the house we decided to give Sandy a taste of our humor. Stomping up the stairs Keith attempted to put on a serious adult voice. "Sandy, Sandy," he shouted. "What are you doing here? Why aren't you home in bloody bed? Sandy, where the bloody hell are you?"

Rushing movements came from within the bedroom. It was the sound of panic.

"Mick, Mick, it's my dad; he's here. Where's my clothes? Oh my God, Mick. Find my clothes!" Sandy cried in vain.

We burst into the bedroom and Sandy screamed. She was hopping about alongside Mick's bed, hastily trying to get some clothes on and cover herself up. We stood in the doorway grinning. Mick just lay there. "Oh, for fuck's sake!" he groaned.

11

ANDREW LOOG OLDHAM looked totally confused. We were sitting at a table near the back of a restaurant close to Richmond Bridge. People from the Crawdaddy were coming over and talking to Mick and Keith, while a couple of the other Stones had gone off to chat at different tables. Every time someone came to our table Andrew would ask, "Who is this; is he in the band?" Then we laughed at his bewilderment.

When the Crawdaddy emptied at its 10:30 P.M. closing time, the hundreds of fans would fill the small cafés and coffee bars in the area. The club had been just as crowded as the week before, with even more people queuing outside. I had noticed Andrew earlier but only because of the out-of-place character he was with. The man in glasses and conventional clothing resembled a schoolteacher and stood close to where the Beatles had been two weeks earlier. I was expecting at any moment he was going to tell everybody to, "Stop this nonsense and get back to work." Andrew appeared as a child-in-tow of a parent except he almost looked like one of us. A couple of days ago he could have been tall and thin, but now he looked lean as if he had since had a couple of meals. He wore a long dark coat that accentuated his short fair hair. His casual well-made clothes almost had him "made" as a mod, but somehow he did not look as if he'd come to party, more like a young plainclothes policeman. During the interval the pair of them had spoken with Brian and Mick. The other man was not Andrew's dad. He was Eric Easton.

The two of them were at the club as a result of Andrew having an accidental meeting with Peter Jones, the journalist who had been present the week before. When the Stones had finished playing, Eric returned to his Acton home and Andrew joined us for a meal. As Stu parked the van outside the restaurant I asked Brian who the guy was. He replied, "He might be interested in managing the band."

Everybody was in high spirits and mentally stimulated by the way each Crawdaddy gig now seemed to be more successful than the previous one. The only person missing that night was Giorgio, who had gone to Switzerland.

At the table Andrew was still trying to acquaint himself with exactly who was in the band and at the same time trying to remember everyone's name. He came across as a friendly person who would quickly join in anything for a laugh. To begin with he was struggling to keep track with the sense of humor around the table.

"Is he in the band?" Andrew asked yet again as Charlie came back and took his seat. "Is this one of you?" he asked, pointing to Bill. "How many of you are actually in this band?"

"There's six of us all together," said Mick.

"Six or seven? I thought there were seven. There's actually six in the band? You, you, you . . . " he counted, pointing at each person.

As he said that something clicked in my mind, and I looked at him and thought, "He's going to say the band is too big for a pop group; there are too many members compared to other bands. He is not going to be interested."

When Andrew had satisfied himself with the configuration of the Stones he began to relax but still appeared bemused by everyone around him. Brian did some nanker faces while ordering the meal and the general sense of humor and attitude seemed to throw Andrew off balance a little. While we ate he began to outline some of his previous background. No, he was not in fact a manager but a publicist and had worked with Brian Epstein on behalf of the Beatles. He had also achieved some good results in the press for British pop star Mark Wynter, including some front-page photos. Andrew made jokes too, smiled a lot, and seemed to gradually become at ease with the situation around the table. The band members seemed to like him, and everyone hit it off. When we eventually left the restaurant, Andrew

arranged that Brian would give him a call the next day. The consensus
on the way home in the van was that Andrew was OK, but after the
reaction to their demo record, the Stones would not have been disappointed had they never heard from him again.

The next day Brian again made a trip to the red phone box at the top
of Edith Grove, this time to phone Andrew. Upon his return he gave
out the news that Eric Easton would like a meeting regarding possible
management. At this stage it was only regarded as exploratory by the
band and they would go just to see what Eric and Andrew had to say.
The pair had not previously been associated. Andrew was well aware
that his forte would be the publicity and marketing of the Stones. He
had been around other artists' managers who ran the day-to-day business side and had approached Eric, who was known as a reputable
show-business manager, to fill this role. Eric would be the one who had
contacts for bookings. He even had an office, whereas Andrew did not.

The meeting with Eric Easton must have been somewhat different
to those with Giorgio Gomelski. To start with I could not imagine
Eric sitting behind a desk in his somber clothes waving his hands
around in the air and becoming more and more excited. Whereas
Giorgio would put things across as being wild dreams that could come
true, Eric would appear as a stern headmaster talking realistically.
Whatever the differences of approach between the two, Eric had the
advantage: Giorgio was a friend who had helped the band out, whereas
Eric was an established show-business manager with a track record
and a working organization. He already had several well-known per-
sonalities as clients and obviously had all the right contacts.

Brian came back and told Mick and Keith about the meeting. He
described Eric as "a real old fuddy-duddy," but admitted that he
seemed to know what he was talking about. At this point all three were
hesitant, but it was their first and only offer from someone who was
already in the business. After much debate they arranged to see Eric
in London three days later on Wednesday, May 1.

Before they left the flat for the afternoon appointment in Regent
Street, Brian worked out a routine he wanted to go through. Mick

and Keith were to wait outside somewhere and Brian would go in and talk with Eric. Brian seemed a little unsure at the prospect of dealing with a businessman and thought this arrangement would allow him the option to escape. Should the talks not be going as he wanted or if he felt badgered to sign something, he could use the need to get Mick and Keith's approval as an excuse to delay things.

However the meeting went, Brian did go out to put the details forward to Mick and Keith, who sat ensconced in a nearby tea house. Brian laid out the details of the deal over several coffees and cigarettes. The contract with Eric Easton was finally signed later that day.

Bill, Charlie, and Stu arrived at Edith Grove for the evening's work and heard the news of the day's events. Everyone glowed with excitement at the prospects that lay ahead. With the addition of a manager they were now a fully professional band, although it could be argued that Mick, Keith, and Brian were pros already as the band was their only source of income. Bill, Charlie, and Stu still maintained their full-time day jobs.

That night the band played again at Eel Pie Island and the fast-moving Andrew attended only his second Stones gig. Although I was present as well I never heard his bad news until the following day.

I was in the lounge when Brian and Keith entered the room, both looking terse. Seeing their faces, I asked Keith, "What's up?"

"We have to tell Stu he's out of the band," said Keith, who looked very unhappy.

"You're kidding?" I replied, shocked. "Why?"

"Andrew doesn't think he can do anything with the way he looks," Keith said. I knew of course what that meant and visualized Stu's face with its prominent chin. Stu dressed differently as well.

"What are you going to tell him?" I asked. Surely they were not going to tell Stu that directly. It looked difficult.

"We don't know yet," said Brian. "We don't know how he's going to take it or how to tell him."

"Andrew said that Stu could stay on as road manager or some-thing," said Keith. "It's just the image thing."

James Phelge

"What's gonna happen if he doesn't?" I asked both of them. I couldn't see Stu taking to this idea, and if he left they would lose his van too.

"We'll have to see what he says," answered Brian, but he sounded as if his mind was made up—the Rolling Stones would go on without Stu.

"When are you going to tell him?"

"We'll have to do it tomorrow before the gig," said Keith. "When everyone is here."

I remembered back to the previous Sunday and the thought that had crossed my mind when Andrew had been trying to count the members of the band. Was it something to do with that? Most groups had three or four members, and the Stones were well above average in that respect. Would a large band have less chance of making it to the top than a smaller one? Without Stu there would still be five members of the Stones, which did not conform to most people's notion that groups consisted of four people at most. Maybe Andrew would have preferred the Stones to have been the same size as the Beatles.

When I arrived back at the house on Friday evening, Stu's van stood already parked outside at the curb. I imagined that a big bust-up would be taking place upstairs with much arguing. Perhaps some members of the band would take sides over the issue. Maybe Stu would tell Brian to "stick" his band and drive off in the van. I knew there would be an atmosphere but wasn't sure what it would be like. When I made it upstairs and entered the front room the meeting had almost ended.

Stu was standing over by Brian's bed and the other Stones were around the settee except for Brian who was by the radiogram and nearest to Stu.

Keith turned to me over his left shoulder as I came in and said, "Stu's agreed to stay on as road manager for us."

I smiled and said, "Great," but felt embarrassed. I thought Keith should have put it another way—it did not seem fair to let Stu know that I had known about the situation before he had. Keith did it more as a natural reaction of relief, but Stu gave me a look that seemed to say, "So you were in on it too!" It was not a good time for anyone.

Obviously they had told Stu who had reluctantly accepted the job as road manager in order to stay with the band. He stood with his hands in his pockets and looked crestfallen at the turn of events. Everyone was trying hard to act cheerful—the boys knew how upset Stu would be feeling. Brian then began to promise things.

"You'll still be able to play with us on occasions," said Brian. "We'll work something out, won't we, boys?" The others made conciliatory noises in agreement.

Then Brian said to Stu, "Don't worry about it; we'll see you all right; we'll make sure you get a sixth of everything." With that he put his arm around Stu's shoulder and hugged him.

There was no doubt it had been an emotionally strenuous time for everyone. Stu did not want to be dropped from the band but he also didn't want to stand in the way of any success that might come to the others. With that in mind he made way and accepted the road manager position. For their part the others did not want him out of the band although the thought that preoccupied everyone was that the band would only have the one chance to make it. The short period of two or three years was still uppermost in everyone's minds.

With Andrew's instructions carried out and Stu agreeing to stay, the five remaining members of the band were relieved that it had worked out reasonably amicably and left to get ready for the gig. I felt they left the room quickly, more to get relief from the awkward situation than anything else. I remained with Stu in the room. I felt bad and did not know what to say other than the few words that came into my mind.

"I'm sorry to hear about this, Stu." I offered genuinely.

He took his hands from his pockets and turned his palms limply outward as a token of hopelessness.

"I expected something like this might happen." He sounded upset and said it so sadly. I looked at him and thought he was going to cry— if I had not been in the room, I felt sure he would have done so.

The following day felt important as the Stones were going to do their first gig under Eric and Andrew's management. Mick, Keith, and Brian all left the flat early to go into town to meet up with Andrew, who had arranged to buy them some clothes. They returned around midday along with Charlie and Bill and an array of paper carrier bags from the morning's shopping spree.

If it was an attempt by Andrew to smarten them up, dressing them in black polo-neck sweaters with black jeans, it failed. I thought it made all of them look worse than if they wore their normal clothing. Maybe it was because everyone was so thin, or the sweaters were too big, but they seemed ill-fitting, and I thought the whole effect made them look like zombies. The best articles were the Cuban-heeled boots with their stylish soft leather tops and high wooden heels. Very soon they would become the latest rage and people would queue for hours outside Anello & Davide in Covent Garden to buy a pair. The shop only made a certain amount of these boots per week.

The gig was a Charity Gala organized by a Sunday newspaper and was just around the corner from Edith Grove in nearby Battersea Park. It was the same park that contained the funfair that Keith and I had looked at across the river on our early-morning strolls. We could have walked from the flat and across Albert Bridge for the gig that afternoon.

On our way down the stairs to get into the van, we saw Triffid standing close to the open doorway inside the downstairs flat. By now we knew he was a journalist and when Keith saw him he said to me, "Hey, Triffid's writing something on us; that's what you should do—write a book about us and get in on it. It's all happening." I smiled and thought, "Wish I could write a book," but never took it seriously. We then made our way down the front steps with the guitars and crammed ourselves into the back of the van once more as Stu drove us the short distance to the park.

It was a sunny afternoon for early May but a little windy as we made our way through the gates into the park. We took directions over to an area by a children's paddling pool where the band was due to play a short set.

I was surprised at the number of people that were already in the park that afternoon with their families. As was still the rule, most of the men stood around in their best suits and ties and reminded me of the guy from up north who Keith and I had run into in The Mall. He would have fitted in perfectly on this day in the park. What was even more surprising was that we did not receive any catcalls regarding our hair or dress, although people did stare at us curiously as we went about setting up the gear. Although whatever the crowd thought didn't bother us, it did make you feel conspicuous to be among such a large crowd of suited people. There were no regular Stones fans for the public to identify us with, so perhaps they thought the dress and the hair was an intentional part of the act—five guys in fancy dress who were going to play guitars.

As soon as the Stones began they sounded like shit—if you could hear them at all. They stood close to the edge of the pool so anyone who stood around would have a good view. The water in front seemed to provide a clear space for the sound to travel over, but it didn't work out like that. I went through the usual routine of wandering around to report on the sound. When I got to the opposite end of the pool, which could not have been more than 30 yards away, the band was inaudible. The amplification was not powerful enough for outside work and with the added wind the sound just vanished into the air. Then I thought how funny it was, seeing hundreds of people standing around listening to a band they could not hear. As they were unable to hear any music, the only remaining attraction was to look at these five weirdly dressed eccentrics playing guitars. I went back toward where the boys were playing—the music was only barely audible if you were within about 15 yards of the band or if you were standing directly behind them. Undaunted, Mick and the boys played on to the bemused crowd.

The key criterion for male pop stars to gain female fans, apart from being good-looking, was to be available, in other words, single. It was part of the attraction that each girl had a chance of romance with her idol. Luckily there were not too many female fans there that afternoon, as halfway through the set, complete with pram and baby, Pat Andrews came marching through the crowd. From Pat's point of view I guess it was a nice day to take the baby for a walk and to see Brian at the same time, but for the band, on their first professional booking, to have someone's "wife and kid" show up looked nothing short of disastrous. While the band was playing, Pat and the baby weren't noticed, but I wondered how people were going to react when the gig ended.

The band finished and received a mixed reception from the holiday-type crowd, some polite reluctant applause amid a sea of staring faces that seemed to be more bewildered than entertained. I suspect the majority of people probably entertained themselves more with derogatory remarks about the Stones' long hair and physical appearance. All the men seemed to be standing around in small groups with glasses of beer in their hands, laughing as we packed up the equipment. Brian was now with Pat and holding the baby as everyone looked on. I had expected him to tell her to keep out of the way on this occasion and was surprised it never occurred to him that his actions might prove damaging if any members of the press were around. The rest of the band did not appear too pleased but there was nothing that could be done. Finally Andrew arrived on the scene and spoke briefly with Brian, and shortly afterward Pat left with the baby in the pram. We left in the van and made our way out of the park and back to Edith Grove, passing Pat on the way—she was heading back there too.

The following evening at another jam-packed Richmond gig a man from Decca Records arrived to listen to the Stones. The man was already on the way to music folklore as "The Man Who Turned Down The Beatles." His name was Dick Rowe, Decca's head A&R man. Andrew had invited Rowe to see the band and the type of audience that they attracted. It was a shrewd move by Andrew following Rowe's episode with the Beatles. Andrew no doubt knew that Rowe probably did not want to become even more famous as "The Man Who

Turned Down The Beatles and The Stones." For whatever reasons, the meeting this evening would ensure that the Rolling Stones had a recording contract with the Decca label.

I do not know if anyone else ever thought of it at the time, but a question that crossed my mind was whether Rowe had already turned the Stones down when their recordings by Glyn Johns were being offered around some weeks earlier. Another ironic aspect of the situation was that the management and record company deals had both been effectively clinched in Giorgio's own club during his absence. Brian never did tell Giorgio and left him to find out through hearsay about the band's new managers. The whole episode must have seemed like a slap in the face to Giorgio.

The next day Andrew arrived at the flat and was talking in earnest with Brian about the recordings the band had made with Johns. He wanted to know if any other recordings were lying idle elsewhere. Brian assured him, quite truthfully, that there were none. Andrew then simply paid the outstanding amount the band owed to the studio and secured possession of the tapes. What happened to them after that was never revealed.

A day or two later Eric Easton's first problem with the Rolling Stones occurred, although it would seem very minor by comparison with what was to eventually follow later in the band's career. Brian, Mick, and Keith were lounging around in the bedroom while I was in the front lounge when I happened to look out of the window down into the street below. A black gleaming Jaguar car had just pulled up outside the house and climbing from the car was the promoter of the Ealing club venue and his two heavies. All three wore dark suits and black overcoats and looked unhappy. They looked at the posters glued on the pillars and then cast their eyes up toward the flat. Then they raced up the steps from the pavement and banged impatiently on the street door.

I stuck my head around the bedroom door and told the others who was arriving. Someone below let the three "visitors" into the house, and they came racing noisily up the stairs and barged into the front room. I had already guessed why they were here and stood leaning against the table as they entered. The slimy-looking Asian promoter was about to speak, then suddenly his face changed expression as the state of his surroundings sunk in slowly. The front room had an effect on everyone who entered it for the first time. I waited for him to come to terms with it and regain his composure. Then when he had done that and was about to speak, I gobbed on the sofa and said, "Hello, do you want to sit down?"

His eyes went down to the sofa and then back to me and I could see him thinking. It did not look like he wanted to play friends. He looked at me all beady-eyed then rasped out, "Where's the Stones?"

"Stones?" I enquired.

"Mick and the Rolling Stones," he said by way of explanation.

"Oh, those Stones," I replied. "They're still in bed. I thought you were talking about jewelry."

"Where's the bedroom?" he asked irritably.

"Out the door and turn left."

The three of them turned on their heels and marched off into the bedroom where Mick, Keith, and Brian were expecting them. I had delayed the visitors just a little to give my friends some thinking space. They too had probably worked out why the Ealing guy was here, and it was not to invite them to a banquet.

"Hello Mick, hello boys," he said, suddenly all smarmy and friendly. "I want you to come and play back at the club on Saturday."

"We'd love to," said Brian. "But we have a manager now and you'll have to speak with him."

The promoter ignored Brian's answer and continued, "I want you to come back this Saturday; we can talk about extra money."

"It's all changed now," said Brian. "We don't decide anything; we just play. The manager does all the bookings."

The promoter turned to Mick. "What's he talking about, Mick? Manager? Come and play at the club on Saturday."

"It's like Brian said; we'd love to, but we have a manager now and you'll have to fix it up with him," said Mick, backing up Brian's answer.

"Who is this fucking manager?" The Ealing man was sounding angry and frustrated.

"His name is Eric Easton and he arranges all our work for us now," said Brian. "Ring him and if Eric says it's OK, we'll play."

"What is all this manager shit? We don't need no fucking manager. Come on, Brian, play Saturday," appealed the promoter.

"We can't. We've signed a contract and can only play places that he books for us. You'll have to speak to Eric Easton," Brian explained.

"Eric fucking Easton, who is he?" shouted the Asian. "We don't need no manager. This is all shit. Are you going to play the club on Saturday?"

Keith spoke next, "They've already told you; if you want us to play you'll have to phone Eric Easton. We can't play anywhere unless he says."

"Can't play anywhere unless he says," sneered the promoter. I then heard him start threatening the boys and saying he'd stop them playing anywhere else. There was a lot more shouting and argument before Keith brought the meeting to a climax.

"Aw, fuck off out of it," he said.

The promoter shouted angrily, "If you don't turn up on Saturday you'll be fucking finished and this Eric Easton too. I'll see to it that the Rolling Stones will never play again. You better fucking be there or we'll be back."

The Stones never bothered to say anything else, letting the Ealing promoter have the last word before he stormed out of the room. There was no point in prolonging an argument over a gig they were not going to play. The promoter and his helpers disappeared down the stairway ranting and slammed the street door behind them. I looked down from the window and watched them drive off, then went into the bedroom and told the others that they had gone. They were smiling.

"I think you upset him. Better phone up and say you're sorry; can you have your gig back?" I suggested.

"Fucking wanker," said Keith as he started to get dressed. "Coming round here threatening us. Didn't want to pay us before, did he?"

No one seemed that bothered or concerned about what had just happened. Brian was lying on my bed. "Is there any milk? I fancy some coffee," he said. Then in his nankering voice, "Oi' reckon we should steal some milk, have some coffee, then go up town and see Eric."

I traveled the short distance across town to Hammersmith to visit a friend for the afternoon, leaving the others to make their way up to the office in Regent Street. They had decided that they better inform Eric of what had taken place earlier. By coincidence I returned to the flat at almost exactly the same time as Brian and Keith, Mick having stayed in town. I asked Keith and Brian what Eric had said.

"You should have heard Eric on the phone. He was real knock-out. He rang the guy up and scared the shit out of him," said Brian who proceeded to imitate Eric on the phone to the Ealing promoter. He raised his left hand up to his face as if holding a phone and said in a serious tone, "Now, listen to me, Mr. Whatever your name is, if I hear any more nonsense from you or your ilk, I'll have the bloody lot of you deported out of the country back to where you came from."

"Eric said he'd have him deported?" I asked.

"Yeah," replied Keith. "Oi' reckon we've heard the last of him all right."

Whatever Eric had said must have been effective—we never did hear from the promoter again. The last link between the Ealing club and the Rolling Stones had now been severed.

MICK SAT ON the arm of the chair in the front room singing the words to Chuck Berry's "Come On" yet again. I was getting fed up with listening to it. Keith lounged in his usual place on the sofa while he and Brian played guitar. It must have been the umpteenth time they had run through it. They kept going over it, occasionally trying the song at slightly different tempos. Out of the vast number of records that cluttered around the radiogram I thought it was just about the worst track they could have picked. How or why they had decided upon this as their first single I did not know. They never asked me what I thought of it and I never offered an opinion. When I did ask why they chose that song, Keith told me, "Andrew thinks it's got a sort of commercial sound."

Within the first week of being signed by Andrew and Eric they had the record deal with Decca, who arranged a recording session for the coming weekend. This was to be the session for their first single release and "Come On" was to be the song. Although it had been an eventful couple of weeks nothing had changed physically apart from Stu's removal from the lineup. Gigs remained few in number and money was short. Bill and Charlie continued in their regular jobs, and Mick still attended college. Brian and Keith just lay around.

What had changed was everybody's overall outlook. After all the previous disappointments there now appeared some hope for the band's immediate future. In Andrew they had someone from the music business who was on their side and with whom they could identify. The other half of the management duo, Eric, was an establishment figure who could be taken seriously on their behalf. The recording session was the icing on the cake.

On the Friday evening they went to Olympic studios to record "Come On," using the arrangement worked out in the front room of the flat. The song for the other side of the record was "I Want to Be Loved," which they had rehearsed in the same manner as the A side. When the session was over and the mixing complete, Andrew would take the tapes to Decca for release.

While they were at the studio I went across to visit my relatives in nearby Hammersmith who were storing a few possessions on my behalf. One of the items was a painting of a man's head and shoulders silhouetted against an orange-and-white-flecked circular background. It was an artifact from my Mumbles the Beatnik days, painted by a friend of mine who fancied himself an artist. It could never have been described as one of the world's art wonders, but it was a picture. More importantly, I knew the Stones would not like it and for that reason took it back to the flat and hung it on the wall over Mick's bed. The other items I returned with were an air pistol and some pellets. I had no particular use in mind for the pistol, but just thought it could be the source of some amusement at a future date.

No one spotted the picture when the guys returned from the recording studio until the next morning when we were lying in bed. Keith woke up and spotted it after about 10 minutes.

"Who put that fuckin' picture up there?" he asked, laughing.

I looked over at it and replied, "I did; a friend of mine painted it. I thought you'd like it."

"It's fuckin' awful," he said, as if my tastes were hopeless.

Mick raised himself up briefly to see the picture and flopped back on his bed laughing.

"It's out of perspective to start with," continued Keith.

I looked at it again. "It does look a bit lopsided," I said. "But it's supposed to be like that."

"Supposed to be like that," scoffed Keith. "It looks like a wonky gorilla."

Mick laughed out louder at Keith's jesting. He then sat up and looked at it again before flopping back again and asking, "What's it supposed to be?"

"If you look at it hard enough you'll see the meaning," I replied, smiling to myself as I got just the reaction I'd expected.

"Fuckin' meaning!" groaned Mick. "Go on; what is it, then?"

"Depends how you see it," I replied, remembering my treacle tin. "It's fairly obvious. It's about how man will always survive against all odds."

Mick laughed again. "Man's survival, Ha ha ha. Load of crap."

"Well you can see it if you look properly," I continued. "The background is obviously a nuclear explosion lighting the sky and the guy has been burnt beyond recognition and is being carried off the edge of the picture by the blast. But like the sun behind the fallout he's going to survive when nothing else around him will. That's what it means. The white fleck bits are debris."

"What it means," said Keith, "is that whoever did it can't fuckin' paint."

Mick laughed again. "I bet he's another one of these people who listens to modern jazz too. Go on, tell me."

"He might do," I replied. "He's quite intelligent. He plays bongos as well."

My final remark had them both rolling in hysterics.

Sunday night at the Crawdaddy featured a surprise visit to the gig by our downstairs neighbor Triffid. He was hanging around and looking out-of-place among the mainly mod audience. Later he never commented to any of us whether he thought the band was good or bad, although it must have astonished him to see hundreds of people raving away to the annoying vagabond hooligans who lived in the flat above his.

The next day a letter arrived for Brian from the BBC regarding the audition the band had attended a few weeks before but had long since forgotten. It confirmed in polite BBC language the feeling the boys had sensed toward them while in the studio, saying their performance was not suitable. The letter further went on to say that Brian should phone the BBC's booking manager who would give a more detailed explanation. Brian laughed at the letter and was not going to bother making the phone call now they had signed with a manager. But the letter was worded in a way that hinted the BBC might be offering some helpful advice, so curiosity took over and Brian decided to ring them, if only for fun.

The BBC did indeed have a suggestion and when Brian returned from the phone box he laid it out. I was in the lounge with Mick when Brian came back into the room. Brian repeated the gist of his phone conversation and quoted the BBC man's crunch line, "We could possibly use the band, but we can't do much with the singer, he sounds too black."

We all fell about laughing and Mick could not believe it. He laughed but was almost speechless and kept repeating the phrase, "Sounds too black!" Keith heard us laughing and asked what the fuss was about.

"They said Mick sounds too black; they think he's black," said Brian, still laughing. We were all amused at the ridiculous statement from the BBC, although in many respects it was a compliment to Mick.

Andrew announced that Decca did not like the quality of the recordings and wanted the songs completely redone. This led to some hastily made arrangements for the Stones. This time however the recording took place in Decca's own studio with a staff engineer. The released version of the single would eventually be the one recorded from this second session.

Despite having a management team and a record in the offing the Stones were still only playing the three or four weekly gigs they had secured on their own account. The following Friday, a week after the first recording session for "Come On," they were playing again in Guildford. I stayed at the flat and eventually went to bed resigned to being woken up as usual when they came home. This time it was about five o'clock in the morning when Keith bounced into the bedroom, turning on the light and banging his guitar case around. Fortunately they went straight to bed instead of playing records.

The next day I walked to the local shops at the end of the street to buy cigarettes and milk. Upon returning to the house I noticed that one of the panes of glass in the street door was broken. The top half of the pane was still in place but the bottom half was completely missing. I put my hand through the hole and opened the door from the inside and went up to the kitchen. The others were already in there.

"Someone smashed the glass on the front door," I said as I placed the milk on the draining board.

Brian was smiling. "Keith did that. No one would let us in so he stuck his guitar case through it."

"Triffid thought he was being clever and didn't want to let us in when we got back last night," said Keith. "We kept banging and in the end I just shoved the case through the window so we could open the door."

Whether that incident or one of the following events over the next few days proved to be the proverbial final straw we would never be sure, but the fun-loving Triffid and his friends were about to run out on us. Perhaps escape was the only alternative left for them.

The Rolling Stones were, despite their name, gathering moss. Whereas two or three months before it was just the immediate band and myself, there was now a small gang of friends. Mick by this stage had a regular girlfriend, Chrissie Shrimpton, who in turn would invariably be accompanied by her friend Lizzie. I was dating a girl I'd met at the Ealing club, albeit only once or twice a week, and Brian was seeing both Pat and Linda Lawrence, with the latter receiving the most attention. It was no longer uncommon for everyone involved to be at the Stones' gigs or even squeeze together to fit into Stu's van. Keith still remained aloof from girls and undeterred from his musical course in any way. Sometimes both Mick and Brian would spend time at their respective girlfriend's home. That was the case the following Tuesday, when Keith and I were alone at the flat when "The Toilet Door Fiasco" took place.

We had spent another evening wandering around the jazz clubs in the West End until the early hours, then finishing the night off with our ritual at the Chelsea pie stall. By the time we had eaten yet another steak and kidney pie covered in brown sauce and strolled back along the embankment to the flat it was 5:00 A.M. Keith's ingenuity involving the front door meant we had no cause to wake anyone else in the building to gain access. We decided to have a last coffee and cigarette before going to bed and spent another hour in the kitchen.

"Do you realize everyone else will be getting up as we're going to bed?" I said, more as conversation than a question.

"Yeah, and as soon as we do they'll all be trundling up to the bog and pulling the chain," Keith replied.

I tried to visualize everyone coming up to use the toilet. "They wouldn't if they couldn't get in it. Like if the door was permanently locked."

We were both running the situation over in our minds, thinking of the possibilities. All those people getting up to go to work and the first thing they want to do in the morning is use the toilet. With the door locked tight as if someone was already in there they could not. This could create havoc for everyone concerned.

We stepped out of the kitchen to look at the possibility of locking the door from the outside. I studied it but there did not seem a feasible method.

"We could nail it up," I suggested.

"What are ya' gonna use for nails?" Keith asked, pointing out a key flaw in my plan.

"Maybe we could tie it to the window," I said, thinking aloud. Keith had wired it up from that direction before when he had installed the microphone.

"Or bolt it from the inside and get out the window?" he offered.

We stood silently for a few moments and considered this, but neither of us fancied the idea of having to scramble through windows with a three-story drop below.

Then I had a brain wave. "I know; get a screwdriver."

"Screwdriver?" He sounded puzzled.

"Yeah, we take the door off its hinges and hide it somewhere."

Keith liked that idea. He could see it would work just as well as locking the door. No one would want to sit on the toilet if there was no door to protect them from being seen by anyone else passing by on the stairway or wanting to use it themselves.

I started on the bottom hinge, scraping the old paint from the heads of the screws to make them easier to remove. A few minutes later we had removed all of them and the door dropped down and rested on the floor.

"Let's take it upstairs and put it in the bedroom," Keith said.

Between us we carried the door up the three steps and angled it into the bedroom and propped it against the wall at the foot of Mick's bed. Then we got undressed and climbed into our respective beds and waited. By now neither of us felt tired any longer in spite of having been up all night and we lay there smoking as daylight crept through the curtains. We guessed it would be around 30 minutes before the first victim arrived at the doorless toilet.

I would have bet that the person likely to be upset the most, Mrs. Offer, would be the first to arrive. I had a feeling it was going to be her, but I would have lost my money this time.

Just after six o'clock we heard someone open a door from the flat below, then some footsteps making their way up the stairs. They stopped on reaching the landing. The silence meant that someone was standing there staring into the toilet and getting their head round the problem and the consequences of using the toilet whilst the door was missing. The person eventually decided against taking any risks and we heard steps retreating slowly back down the stairs.

A few minutes later we heard movement from the Offers flat above and someone making his or her way down. Was it him or her? We heard the person pass our bedroom door and descend the last few steps to the landing.

There was a moment's loaded silence before all hell broke loose.

It was not the sort of scream that started slowly, then built up to a pitch. It was a high-pitched shriek at full volume that rang out through the neighborhood. Then Mrs. Offer shouted, "They've taken the bloody door!"

There were now doors banging everywhere. Mr. Offer called down concerned from the landing above, "What's wrong, darling? Are you all right?"

"They've taken the door. The toilet door's missing, the bastards."

Mr. Offer came flying noisily down the stairs. "Are you all right? Darling, what's wrong?"

"Look, there's no door on the toilet anymore, can't you see? They've taken the fucking door," she shouted angrily.

Mr. Offer continued down the stairs two at a time to the toilet to see for himself. "The bastards, the bastards, they're not getting away with this," he raged as Keith and I cringed in hysterics, trying not to make a sound.

"Right, don't worry, darling," said Mr. Offer, taking charge. "Go back up stairs and get dressed. I'll go and fetch the landlord now."

"I can't get bloody dressed yet," she wailed. "I'm gonna be late for work."

"Don't worry, don't worry. This'll be the last time. I'll have them thrown out on the street." Mr. Offer shepherded her back up the stairs, trying to placate her. "They're not getting away with this." They went into their flat and slammed the door closed.

Keith and I looked across at each other, laughing with immense satisfaction at the results of our work. The reaction of Mrs. Offer had been better than any we had hoped for. She had completely freaked out and Mr. Offer had leapt enthusiastically into the situation, his rage adding more energy to the drama we had instigated. It felt as if we were controlling two puppets and I marveled again at the effects of confronting people with unexpected and preposterous situations. It was another one of those "Nobody does that" situations that threw other people totally off balance.

Mr. Offer must have dressed quicker than Superman because he came hurtling back down the stairs within seconds. We heard him pass our door in full flight and run down the remaining stairs to the hallway, telling someone below he was off to fetch the landlord. Then the street door slammed closed behind him and the house was silent again.

Keith and I grinned at each other. "Too much! Offer's gone crazy," he said.

I looked at the toilet door standing against the wall. "What are we gonna do with the door?" I said. "Hey, why don't we put it back before Offer arrives with the landlord?"

Keith sat up and replied, "That'd really drive him mad, getting the landlord over and everything's normal. Let's do it."

We both leapt from our beds and started the process of putting the door back on to its frame. The key was to have the job completed before the landlord arrived. From the state he was in I imagined that Mr. Offer must have run the short distance to the landlord's dairy at the top of the street and screamed out his complaint as fast as he could. There would not be much time.

I held the door roughly in place as Keith went about reinserting the screws back into the hinges. We carried the whole operation out as silently and quickly as we could. The door fitted back perfectly in place as if it had never been removed. Apart from some scratches on the screwheads there was no sign of anything having been touched. We pushed the door closed then made our way back into our bedroom and waited for the sequel.

There was no panic this time as the front door opened and two sets of footsteps came calmly up the stairs. Mr. Offer was babbling: ". . . and my wife is going to be late for work . . . along with everyone else . . . this has really upset her . . . they stole all our lightbulbs the other week as well . . . now it's the toilet door."

As they reached the landing it all fell silent once more. They must have been standing there looking at the replaced door. Everything would have looked normal to the landlord of course but the door must have appeared like an apparition to Mr. Offer as he came to the head of the stairs and saw it back in place.

"They've put it back!" Mr. Offer said, slowly letting his breath out. "It was definitely missing before."

The landlord said nothing.

"This is the sort of thing they're always doing to us," continued Offer. He was beginning to see himself in an embarrassing predicament and sounded deflated. "It's all out of hand, I want them thrown out."

The landlord came up to our bedroom door, but finding it closed he never came into the room. With not much else to be done he turned to Offer and said, "I'll come over and see them later."

Mr. Offer bade him thank you and good-bye, then made his way back up to his flat. "I'm back, darling, the landlord's going to . . ." His voice trailed away as his apartment door closed behind him.

Keith and I had listened intently to the whole episode, sniggering at the turn of events. The landlord, disturbed during a busy period at his shop, quickly made his exit from the building as he was eager to get back. The toilet door could not have been uppermost in his mind—he never did come back to mention the incident again.

We were obviously out of favor with the Offers and they made this apparent by removing the key to their flat from its hiding place. They also began being extra cautious. They made absolutely sure not to leave anything that remotely resembled food in a position where it could go missing. As they now seemed tired of subsidising our pilfering, later that day Keith and I turned our attention to the flat below.

In our routine search for milk, having seen that the Offers' larder on their landing was bare, we decided to try our luck in the flat downstairs. When Judy had been there the flat would invariably be occupied most of the day, but since Triffid had taken over, it stood empty during working hours. Keith and I decided to make our way downstairs.

To our surprise we found the entrance door to the flat unlocked. I turned the handle and we walked straight in and stood in the middle of the room. It was a much nicer flat than ours, or maybe this was how ours should have looked. The place was still fairly dismal and in need of painting, but like the Offers' place on the top floor it was neat and tidy. It looked as though Triffid and his companions took care to keep the place clean.

They had two armchairs that were actually not broken sitting at each end of a rug in the middle of a clean floor. There did not seem to be anything in need of dusting and everything appeared to be in its place. A walnut dining table stood to one side and the top surface shone with polish beneath a rust-colored tablecloth set diagonally upon it. In the exact center of the table, standing like a lone soldier on guard, stood an unopened bottle of beer.

We wandered around the flat and into the kitchen at the back, where everything again was tidy although there was no sign of food. The place had an utterly boring air about it: nothing to do in it, nothing to eat, and no milk. I stood there with my hands in the pockets of my coat and perused the room, then my eyes went back to the bottle of beer on the table. It seemed to be screaming for me to pick it up and eventually I did so and read the label on the side of the bottle.

"Triffid's left us a bottle of light ale," I said to Keith.

He looked nonplussed. "That's about all there is," he replied.

"Mmm . . . well . . . shall we drink it?" I asked him.

"I dunno if I fancy a beer right now," Keith replied.

I wondered if Triffid would be upset if he came home and found the bottle empty, or would he think he had drunk it himself and then forgotten about it? I chewed it over and made a decision.

"I reckon we should drink it, have half each. No point in a bottle of beer being wasted on Triffid," I said.

"Well, I reckon I could drink a beer then," said Keith. "Pity to waste it, I s'pose."

I was going to hold the bottle cap against the edge of the table and bang it downward to remove it, but then I changed my mind.

"If we take the cap off carefully so that it doesn't look as if it's been touched, we can refill the bottle then put it back unnoticed," I said to Keith.

"May as well just drink it," he replied. "It's gonna be gone either way."

"No, let's refill it afterward and put it back. We need an opener."

Keith wandered back to the kitchen and after a few moments came back with a small metal opener and passed it to me. I carefully started to prize up one side of the cap a little then turned the bottle around to do the same on the opposite side.

"Need to get it off without bending it," I said.

Keith stood there patiently watching as I worked on the cap, which eventually came away from the rim of the bottle unmarked.

"There we are," I said and took a swig of light ale from the bottle and passed it to Keith.

"Nice of Triffid to buy us a drink," he said, holding the bottle up in tribute to its owner. He downed a mouthful and then we took turns swigging the beer until there was nothing left.

"I guess we better refill it for him now," I said and undid the zip on the front of my trousers.

Keith pulled a face that seemed to say, "Oh, no," as he realized what was going to happen next. "What are you gonna do?" he asked, although I think he knew.

"Better refill Triff's bottle for him," I said. "He may complain if he comes home and finds it empty."

Keith stood there grimacing as I peed into the top of the bottle until it was full again. Having finished I put the bottle on the table and pressed the metal cap back on top, then placed the bottle in its original position.

"It looks brand new, like it's never been touched at all," I said, admiring my handiwork as Keith stood there smirking.

"Just hope we don't come back in here and drink it ourselves by mistake," Keith said, groaning at the thought of it as we made our way out of the door and back upstairs.

At the end of that week Triffid and his companions moved out of Edith Grove and I never saw any of them again. Whatever happened to the beer we never heard, but presumed that no one ever drank it. I did wonder if Triffid may have returned the beer to the place where he bought it and complained. That would have been a scene I would have liked to witness.

13

AFTER THE COLD winter we had just gone through—1963 was one of the worst ever—the weather in May was sunny and warm. The flat itself seemed a different place to live. The big bare windows, which had stared with depressing darkness at you through the preceding months, now allowed the front room to shed some of its gloom and appear almost big and bright. We actually began to open the windows occasionally for the purpose of letting air in rather than just throwing rubbish down into the front basement. The daylight now extended into the early evening, indicating that summer was near. This, coupled with the optimism surrounding the band as they awaited the release of their record, made for a good atmosphere. It was during this period I discovered the "Immaculate Dollies."

As I lay in bed one morning, gradually waking up and intermittently flickering my eyes open, I became aware of how bright the day seemed. I sat up momentarily in bed to look out of the window and then sagged back onto my pillow. Still not fully awake, I thought to myself, "Did I see that?" After a few moments I sat up again to take another look.

In the house directly across from ours, on the same level as our bedroom, was an open window with a naked woman with enormous breasts sitting in front of it. It was not just a naked woman; it was gorgeous, young, naked woman with blond hair—she looked about our age. Then as I watched her she was joined by another with dark hair, equally as nice and just as undressed. I went over to Keith's bed, nudged him, and then sat looking across at them.

"Hey man, look at these two birds," I said enthusiastically. "Both naked."

Keith threw his covers off and crawled down to the end of the bed and put his head next to mine and looked. There was only the blond girl there now, combing her hair.

"She's well stacked, nice," Keith said, pushing me along to make more room at the window. "I reckon she's a piece of all right."

"You ought to see the other one," I replied.

"Who's this?" said a voice from behind. I turned and saw Mick watching us.

"There's two immaculate dollies with big tits in the flat over there. Look!" I said.

"Immaculate dollies," laughed Mick. "Let's see." He got out of bed and came over and stood next to the wardrobe and looked out the window, just as the second girl came into view. He stood there and watched them both as they passed to and fro across their room. The way that the blond-haired girl sat sideways in front of the window suggested she was at a dressing table.

"The dark one's nice," agreed Keith.

"Yeah, but it would be hard to choose," said Mick, looking across intently.

"I think I'll go and tell Hopkin, if he's awake." I couldn't image Brian not wanting to see them either so I went out and stuck my head around his door. He looked up from his bed and said, "Hello."

"There's a couple of birds across the back displaying their tits if you want to see," I informed him quickly and went back to the bedroom. Brian followed me seconds later and made his way to the window. His face immediately lit up when he saw the blond girl.

"Ah, look at her, fantastic!" he gasped. "I thought you said there were two."

"The other one's gone off somewhere," said Keith.

"Ah," Brian said again as the second girl reappeared. "Have they been living there all the time?"

"Dunno," said Mick. "Must 'ave." Maybe he was wondering how he could meet them. I knew I was. None of us knew the answer to

Brian's question. We had never seen them before but then again they would not have had a window wide open in the winter. We continued to watch them as they began to dress, a striptease in reverse. When the two girls had finished dressing we all lost interest, even though they did still look just as attractive in clothes. We would keep a check on their window regularly from then on for another free show.

As the others returned to their beds I looked down at the garden and saw that someone had been doing some general tidying up. I guessed that it was the new occupants of the flat below who had moved in a short while after Triffid had left. It seemed that a couple of guys lived there, but we were not sure or particularly interested. One of them called Tony had introduced himself in the hallway below. Compared to us he was clean-cut with an Elvis hairstyle and probably in his mid-20s. He seemed friendly enough, though we would find out later he could get aggressive. Fortunately for us he never left any beer lying around—he was definitely not the kind of guy who would have been pleased had there been a repeat of the light ale incident.

Giorgio must have known by now that he was not going to be the manager of the Rolling Stones. On his return from abroad they had gone to visit him one evening with Andrew in tow. I asked Brian later if he had told Giorgio who Andrew was—Brian said he'd probably figured it out for himself. It was not a clear answer, but I assumed it meant no. I felt it seemed typical of Brian to opt out of any responsibility at the last minute. Perhaps Pat and the baby were another case in point.

Publicity was Andrew's speciality and to achieve maximum effect he needed some photographs of the band. He duly arranged to call at the flat one morning with a photographer for a session to be shot on location in Chelsea.

Turning left at the bottom of Edith Grove you immediately entered the Cheyne Walk area of Chelsea Embankment. This was where Keith and I had looked at the houseboats moored by the river and thought how cool it would be to live on one. It was probably just as well that we didn't—I often imagined us waking up on our houseboat at the mouth of the Thames after a late-night prank had backfired. We would have flown the skull and crossbones flag, and probably ended up sinking.

Most of the barges had originally been working vessels on the river but only existed now as converted accommodations. Many had been fitted with street-type front doors and windows complete with lace curtains. They looked as if they had not moved in years and I wondered if in fact any of them were still capable of sailing. The one we admired most was named "James Piper" and we always leaned against the embankment wall close to its mooring. It was this particular jetty that was chosen as the location for the photographic shoot.

In the bedroom the boys spent considerable time rummaging through the few clothes we owned and trying them on to check out their suitability in the wardrobe mirror. There was not a wide choice and Keith asked if he could borrow my black corduroy coat. I agreed to lend it to him. After putting the coat on he slung a dark scarf loosely around his neck as the finishing touch. Brian had a gray tweed herringbone jacket and decided to wear that along with a tie, while Mick opted for a plain sweater. Charlie was the best-dressed as usual—his clothes actually looked as if they came from a shop rather than a junk sale. Bill also stood out—he was now sporting a combed-forward hairstyle and new gray jacket that made him look a bit like one of the Beatles. In spite of their efforts to dress up, the band looked a somewhat disheveled bunch as they strolled down to the location.

I watched them for an hour or more as the photographer went through his routine using several different cameras and many rolls of film. Some of the pictures taken that day with Albert Bridge as a backdrop would be published for years to come.

None of us had any reason to make contact with the new group of people who had moved into Triffid's old flat downstairs. The first real instance was a Sunday evening upon our return from another overcrowded Richmond gig. Mick had gone straight from the gig to stay with Chrissie, and Brian went off somewhere with Linda. Stu dropped Keith and me back at Edith Grove, and we wandered up the darkened stairway leaving the street door wide open behind us. We went straight into the kitchen to make coffee. The window by the small table was open wide on its sash from earlier in the day and it looked like a gaping black hole. Keith put the small tin kettle on the cooker and picked a pan out from the sink, which was now full again.

"Time for a clean up again," he said. He wandered over to the window and threw the pan out. It floated away into the darkness, followed a few seconds later by a clang as it landed somewhere below.

"OK, why not?" I shrugged as Keith repeated the gesture, this time with a handful of dirty plates. I started to give him a hand by throwing out some bottles and whatever else was lying around on the table and the draining board next to the sink. Eventually the sink was empty and all that remained were the two cups for our coffees. Neither of us had any intention of actually cleaning the sink—disposing of the offending greased-up utensils was enough.

Keith was getting on with making the coffees when somewhere below a door banged open and we heard footsteps running along the hall, growing gradually louder as they turned and advanced quickly up the stairs. Then came a voice.

"Hey! What the fuck's goin' on up there?"

I looked out of the kitchen door toward the stairway. To begin with all I could see was a white shirt emerging from the gloom, until it got nearer when I saw it contained Tony. I turned my head and gazed blandly back at Keith who was equally unconcerned and continued with the coffee.

Tony got larger and bounded into the kitchen. I could see he looked agitated, angry even. His fists were tightly balled by his sides.

"Hey, what the fuck's goin' on up here?"

"Nothing much," I said in greeting.

"Oh, hello, Tony," said Keith. "What's up?"

"You guys been here all the time?" he asked.

Keith shrugged. "Yeah, why?"

Tony's shoulders flexed and he looked as if he was ready to hit someone any second. He came straight to the point. "What's the idea of throwing all the plates an' that into the garden, then?"

I took my coffee from Keith and kept a face of mock concentration as I tried to think of an answer for him. Then Keith spoke.

"Plates? Oh . . . that," he said.

"Well, what are they doing in the garden?" Tony demanded. Then I realized that he must have been the one who had tidied the garden.

"Oh, yeah, sorry about that, man," said Keith, not sounding sorry at all. "We can't do anything about it."

Tony looked confused and his face darkened. "What do you mean? Can't do anything about it?"

"Yeah, I'm sorry, Tony," said Keith. "It happens all the time. There's this bloke who lives up the road who keeps coming up here and throwing all our stuff out the window and we can't stop him."

I looked at Keith in amazement but tried not to show it as I looked back to Tony for his reply.

"Do what?" he said, baffled at this explanation.

"There's this big bloke who lives up the road somewhere," repeated Keith. "He just comes in when he feels like it and throws all our stuff out the window. We can't stop him because we're scared of him."

It sounded ridiculous to me and I looked at Tony to see whether he'd bought it.

"If I get hold of him I'll punch his head in," said Tony. "I've just cleared the garden up so I can sit out there. Next time he comes up here give me a shout and I'll sort him out for you."

This time I looked at Tony in amazement. He believed it!

"Ah, thanks, Tone," said Keith in relief. "You've only just missed him; he's left the door open. We've been wondering what to do about it; we've only got two cups left now."

"It's all right, Keith. Just give me a shout next time he comes here. You might be scared of him, but I'm not. I wish you knew where he lived," Tony said.

"That's great, Tone, but we don't. I'll come and get you straight away next time he's here. Maybe you can sort him out for us? He's made our life a misery up here for ages." Keith was making a good job of sounding upset.

"Yeah, I will, don't worry about it. I'll bring your plates back tomorrow—I'm going to bed right now. Goodnight!" Tony turned and made his way out.

"Goodnight, Tone. Thanks," we called after him.

Keith drew hard on his fag, his face covered in a big smug grin, as we waited for the sounds of Tony to recede back into his flat. Then we burst into laughter.

With the Stones' recording of "Come On" completed, Decca Records had arranged to rush-release it at the beginning of June. In the meantime the band carried on playing their regular weekly club gigs, which were still all the work they had. By comparison the Beatles, now known to almost the whole nation, were topping the charts again with their latest record "From Me to You." To add to the unknown Stones' frustrations even further, the Beatles also had friends with hit records in the charts alongside them. Beatles' manager Brian Epstein had taken other bands into his fold and was successfully launching them on the road to fame by way of records and television. With Gerry & the Pacemakers and Billy J. Kramer & the Dakotas also riding high in the hit parade, the public was becoming used to hearing new-sounding groups. If the Stones did not get on the scene soon their arrival wasn't likely to have much impact and they would be in danger of being "just another group." There was also the danger that someone might arrive before them playing the same type of material and the Stones would then appear to be copying them. Although the record was close to release the band still seemed to have made little headway. Everyone had a feeling that it could all begin to happen quite soon, but despite the progress there were still no results and everyone remained in limbo. Everything was now hanging on the success of the record.

About a week before the release date, the boys came back with a promotion copy of the record and put it straight onto the player. As we had with the earlier acetate recording by Glyn Johns, we all stood around eagerly waiting to hear it.

I thought it sounded like crap. It was not what I was expecting to hear at all. The overall effect was totally different and bore no relation to the way the band sounded when they played live. The first thing that struck me about it was that it seemed to be too fast. It sounded as if they had been so keen to record it in the studio that enthusiasm had somehow gotten the better of them. I still did not like the song itself and continued to think it was a bad choice.

They kept playing the record over and over but I still could not find much that I liked about it. They were thrilled that it was going to be released on June 7, knowing that this was the first and maybe the only major chance for the band. They thought that it sounded commercial and poplike but of course this was the opinion of guys who had never even considered doing anything remotely commercial-sounding until about two weeks previously. Maybe the whole project would have been better off given more time for the choice of song and its recording. They might then have even had the opportunity to work on something totally different. Knowing how much this record meant to them, and because they were my friends, when they asked what I thought of it I lied and told them, "It sounds great." Nobody ever mentioned the possibility that the record might not take off.

Life carried on as normal during the remaining few days running up to the release. The band was now playing up to five club gigs each week. This constituted the Stones' first regular income, and although it was still small, there was enough to pay the rent and a few pounds over to finance more regular meals. We started to visit the Ernie less frequently than before and now used it as more of an emergency place. Perhaps it was due to the light evenings, but we wanted to get out of the Grove area when the band was not working. There were two ways from Edith Grove to get into the center of London, the number 11 bus or another bus to nearby Earls Court and from there the underground.

The place we began to visit was a small Earls Court restaurant situated in a cellar called Henrique's, named after its owner. Despite his French-sounding name Henrique was Polish and had only recently opened the place when we discovered it. The restaurant comprised about six small tables covered with white tablecloths and in the center of each stood a Chianti bottle with a candle wedged in the top. With plain plaster walls and dark-colored carpeting, the place had a twilight feel that was enhanced when Henrique lit the candles. Instead of eating the usual fried diet of sausages, eggs, and chips the choice was now orange juice followed by Wiener Schnitzel or kebabs. Henrique used to come and sit at one of the tables and seemed intrigued by the strange-looking band. It made a pleasant change from the Ernies sitting in their overalls and hand-rolling their cigarettes. Apart from its more palatable menu and the better class of customer, the basement had the added advantage of remaining cool during the warm weather. It became our favorite place that summer, to such an extent that we eventually started going there for breakfast.

The only trouble with Henrique's was that we had to catch a bus to get there. The bus route to Earls Court was quite popular and the service was sporadic. There would invariably be a queue of people in front of us waiting to board an already crowded bus. What we needed was a ruse to jump to the front of the queue, so I came up with my mentally-ill Nanker routine.

With our bouffed-up hair and odd mixture of clothes—I still wore my corduroy coat buttoned high to the collar—we continued to look a weird sight. As we hung around waiting in the queue for the bus, I decided to make my way forward to read the timetable mounted on the bus stop.

Using my hands to make a nankering face I stood close to the glass-framed schedule and peered bewilderedly at each line. Shaking my head from side to side to look confused I began to emit the distressed "eek eek eek" noise from the back of my throat. As the Stones stood to one side nudging each other and grinning the remainder of the queue looked on at me with stunned expressions on their faces.

All that is except for a big fat woman who turned her nose up contemptuously and tried to act as though I was not there.

I continued making the "eek eek eek" noises even louder, then stopped. Parting my lips I began to blow big bubbles of saliva that ran down my chin and sprayed over the glass frame. People stepped back away from the bus stop looking horrified at the retard in their midst. The fat woman moved back several feet across the pavement and watched me with her mouth hanging open. Brian, Keith, and Mick stood aside from the queue in hysterics. Seeing the bus approach, I blew more saliva bubbles up over my face and walked toward the people at the front of the queue, who shuffled farther away from the bus stop. When the nearly full bus finally pulled up to take on passengers there was an enormous space at the head of the queue and we immediately stepped into it, jumped on the bus first and scrambled jubilantly up the stairs. The fat lady called out, "You ought to be locked away."

Having found the retard act an excellent ruse to avoid us having to wait in line, I later embellished it. Instead of pulling the nanker face I would just amble up to the timetable with my hands inside my coat pocket, look up at the sky and spit into the air and then let the phlegm land back on my face. I considered that more elegant and it seemed to work just as well. I thought it showed how uncaring the general public was—I could have been genuinely having a fit and in need of help, but no one ever stepped forward to ask if I was all right. Maybe I just wasn't convincing enough as a loony.

People typically held on to their reserve and would stand there avoiding eye contact with each other, trying to make out they had not seen me or were unaffected by my antics. Whatever they thought we always managed to leap on the bus first. I also found a less repulsive method of getting a seat on the crowded underground train. If a full train arrived I simply shouted out, "All change here." Then I would stand and watch the passengers sheepishly look around before getting off the train as commanded. Keith and I would then walk into the empty carriage and sit down as the doors closed and the train pulled away.

14

IT WAS CLEAR from the record reviews that copies of "Come On" must have reached the hands of people who were totally unaware of the Rolling Stones and their type of music. The reviews it received were at best unexciting. Alternatively, perhaps the people who knew nothing of the Stones were the least likely to be biased and would give the most honest opinions. The music journalists seemed to fit into different categories: those who knew nothing of the band or R&B music and those who had heard of the Stones and indeed knew what the music was. Some among the latter group had been to Richmond. We didn't realize at the time that there was also a third section of the press, members of which would sit on the proverbial wall. Their opinions would only emerge later, once something or someone became popular. These "in-between" writers ran with the trends and their main interest was in "hanging out" around the artists to boost their own egos.

The reviews also came in two varieties: those whose authors did not think the record or the band would ever get anywhere and the other writers who felt the record was a letdown but wished the band luck. Most of the reactions seemed reasonable, as no one slated the record or went out on a limb for it.

The Stones themselves were relatively happy with the exposure and faced increasing demand for photo sessions and interviews with various pop magazines. At one such interview they even managed to get thrown out of a hotel lounge because of their appearance—an experience that happened to them many times later.

Oddly enough one of the factors most instrumental in the Stones' early success disappeared just as the record was released. That was the Richmond gig.

The Crawdaddy club had been filled beyond saturation point during the previous few shows, and there were virtually enough people to fill the hall queuing outside before the club had even opened. It was now almost impossible to spend the entire evening inside the club. Body squashed against body, but still people tried to dance. The crowd inside wanted to go out for air, but did not dare leave as they knew their places would be taken thanks to Giorgio's one-in, one-out system at the door. Once outside you might not have made it back in at all. I was fortunate in that I could come and go at will, which understandably upset some of the fans waiting there. The whole situation had become crazy, but it was with some sadness that night when Giorgio announced that we were at the Station Hotel for the last time.

We had all known that the hotel was to be demolished at some future date and that the club would not last forever, but now the owners of the building had become worried that the size of the crowd jammed inside the hall put them in breach of the fire regulations. They had no alternative but to tell Giorgio that the club had to close. Giorgio stood up on stage and made the announcement to a stunned audience, who for the very first time stood quietly and listened. It seemed like a requiem for a lost friend. Then, typical of the man, he ended the announcement by saying that he had been busy. The Crawdaddy would meet again in two weeks at the nearby Richmond Athletic Club.

Following the emotional departure from Richmond, the band picked up another gig a few nights later at the Scene, the place Keith and I frequented to listen to Guy Stevens and his records. The club had now taken to booking live acts, and the Stones were now known as being the most popular band around the London club circuit. The band was now every promoter's first choice to pull a good crowd. It would never replace or compete with Richmond for atmosphere as the place had more of a "contrived" feel inside. Its layout and paint work were not dissimilar to how a trendy beat club might look on a movie set. Nonetheless it had an amiable atmosphere and a knowledgeable crowd, which included some Stones diehards. For some reason I never particularly found the place conducive to live music and preferred just to hear records there. As the place had started out playing records only, perhaps the sound system they used for this was far superior to the average band's PA system. I never realized that "records-only" places would later spring up everywhere and be known as discothèques.

Life was a little busier now with the interviews and photo sessions during the daytime plus the fact that the band was now working five or six nights a week, earning some reasonable money. In between all this we heard the record played on the radio a couple of times and continued our forays in and around London.

A short distance across town from Chelsea, an "in" place to be on a Saturday was Portobello Road. The street was famous as an antique market with many small open-fronted shops displaying their wares. Outside each shop and standing in the edge of the road were market stalls that covered the complete length of the street. Wandering amongst the crowds of shoppers you could choose your purchases from a huge assortment of old-looking goods. Whether any of them were genuinely antique I didn't know. Old grandfather clocks stood in large numbers alongside scrubbed pine tables and dressers. Tin toys that your parents had played with stood alongside jewelry, pictures, ornaments, and fireplace surrounds. I expect some of it was real, including the neckties I bought.

Keith and I wandered down the road out of curiosity, just looking at all the bric-a-brac on display but not really showing too much interest. We had old, broken furniture back at the flat and it never crossed our minds to buy more of it. What we did find at the lower end of the street was a stall that sold secondhand clothes. There was not much on sale that we would have worn; in truth there was nothing at all.

Bundled up on the wooden trestle table was a collection of old and garish ties, which caught my eye. On the side of the stall hung old "demob" suits that the government gave free to soldiers leaving the army after World War II. The ties looked to be from the same era judging by their designs. With their horrible patterns and bad choice of colors they bordered on the edge of looking ridiculous. I bought four of them for a few pence each. When Keith laughed and asked, "What on earth do you want them for?" I replied that they might come in useful sometime. From there we wandered up to the pub on the corner for a beer.

The weather remained warm and sunny and on one of the band's few evenings off we took up a new hobby, which Keith called "Serpin." It was perhaps our subconscious yearning to live on a houseboat that called us to visit London's Hyde Park. Toward the center of the park on the large lake named the Serpentine you could hire rowing boats by the hour. With our various girlfriends in tow we hired two boats, piled into them, and took to the water.

As we drifted out onto the lake, it soon became apparent that none of us had the slightest clue about how to control a boat. Brian was in one boat with Mick and was trying to stand up and use the oar as a pole. The boat rocked menacingly as he probed beneath the water with the oar to see if he could reach the bottom of the lake and push the boat along like a punt. Outside the wooden boat house the owner waved his hands and mouthed words toward us that became lost in the air. The girls in Mick and Brian's boat simply waved back to him.

Keith and I had an oar each and we took a zigzag course out to the middle of the lake but then could not turn around. Eventually we switched the oars around and the boat began to move backward. Brian managed to get close by and used his oar to skim water from the lake's surface into our boat, whereupon a minor battle broke out as we splashed him back. I gave up trying to row and handed my oar to Keith who suddenly seemed able to row the boat quite accurately using both oars. Brian had also found something resembling a rowing technique—I figured that perhaps the two of them could row because an oar was vaguely similar in shape to a guitar.

As our hour approached its end we made it back to the bank and crashed into the wooden landing stage before jumping out of the boats. The guy in the boathouse came out looking for damage to his equipment but said nothing and Brian had the nerve to ask if he had any motorboats for hire. Satisfied with the evening's distraction, we adjourned to a nearby pub.

At the weekend we made the usual Sunday afternoon drive jammed in the back of the van from the Ken Colyer Club down to Richmond. This time the only difference was that we were going to the new venue at the Athletic Club. Almost adjacent to the roundabout before you turned into the town there were two big iron gates that led into the club's grounds. The clubhouse was an almost brand-new single-story building and stood way back from the road. Stu drove the van along the tarmac drive and parked by the entrance. The construction of the building and its surroundings made it seem like you were going back to school. Certainly it lacked any of the character and atmosphere you might expect at a jazz club.

Not knowing what to expect inside, we all gave a hand unloading the van and carrying pieces of equipment through the glass-paneled doors. After being used to the size of the nearby Station Hotel the first thing that struck you was how low the ceiling was, almost to the point of being claustrophobic. Beneath your feet a new mahogany-colored parquet-tiled floor covered the hall. The stage was in the center of the right-hand wall and stood almost five feet high. Racked against the other walls and reaching up to the ceiling were wooden bars built in a frame. We were in what appeared to be a gymnasium.

Giorgio had his man in place collecting the entrance money, and the place seemed to be full even before the band started playing. When they began, it felt odd as you had to look upward at them, making the audience and the band seem isolated from each other. Keith took his usual position to the left-hand side of Mick, who looked as if he would bang his head on the ceiling at any moment. The music came out the same as before and the band did excellent versions of both "Jaguar and the Thunderbird" and "Let It Rock," but the magic feeling of the old club was not there.

Nobody danced at all. Maybe it was too crowded and they couldn't, but no one even seemed to try. Everyone now appeared content to just stand and watch. To get a better view many fans climbed to the top of the wooden bars against the wall and hung there uncomfortably. The curtains were drawn across the big windows to shut out the evening light in a vain attempt to create a clublike dimness. The audience applauded at the end of each song but it was no longer the raving emotion we knew and had become used to. Another section of the new club contained a small bar, but this too lacked ambience, and you felt you were drinking for the sake of it rather than for enjoyment.

During the following week the boys all got some new clothes. Andrew and Eric's management had now landed them a spot on television to promote the month-old single. The format for the image of pop groups—matching suits with ties—still existed from years before, and the tradition continued with the Beatles. Until now the Stones had been concerned with directing their energies toward making a record. Appearing on television had not been part of their game plan and up to a few weeks ago this would have seemed an even more remote possibility than being in a recording studio.

Andrew probably realized more than anyone the implications of appearing on television and what the exposure could do for the band. Playing around the local clubs wearing everyday clothes was one thing, but Andrew felt it would not be an image to present to TV viewers across the nation. Although he had known the Stones for two months and was growing accustomed to their idiosyncrasies and attitudes, he now wanted to make the band look more acceptable. He was moving the Rolling Stones into a different environment, and this necessitated a change in wardrobe.

Persuading the band to wear suits could have been a struggle, but Andrew settled on a happy medium that would look equally smart. He took them to Carnaby Street and fitted them out with black and white houndstooth jackets and black trousers that would also look good in front of the TV cameras.

They came back to the flat carrying the jackets on hangers covered with clear polythene dust bags. The boys dumped an array of plastic shopping bags around the front room and opened them as children would open gifts. The other accessories for the television appearance were black nylon ties and blue shirts with cutaway collars. The bags also contained by far the most fashionable items—blue leather waist-coats, which seemed to be good quality and could be worn for any occasion.

They tried on the jackets one by one. I thought they made them look like a bunch of chefs on their way to a convention. Brian was the only one who looked as if the jacket suited him as it seemed a good contrast to his fair hair. The others all looked as if they had put on someone else's clothes by mistake. It was almost as if they did not know how to wear clothes that had not been regularly dumped on the floor and walked on.

On the day when the show was due for recording, everyone was up early in jubilant spirits for the trip north to Birmingham. We were treated with another display from the Immaculate Dollies but the boys we were soon concentrating more on being ready when Stu arrived with the van. Everyone took turns washing their hair and running my electric shaver around their faces and generally doing the best with their appearance. Keith was putting the final touches to his outfit by sitting on the sofa and using a brush to put polish on his boots.

"Hey, I thought you said it was Ernie to clean your boots, man," I said, recalling his chastisement of me in the kitchen a few months back.

"It ain't fuckin' Ernie to clean your boots if you're going on TV to play your latest record. I don't reckon it's Ernie then," he replied smiling, and carried on polishing.

The television show was *Thank Your Lucky Stars*, the title matched by some equally corny graphics during the opening titles. None of us had watched television since we had been at the flat, but the show had been running for a while and its format and presentation captured the clean image of pop music at the time. The fact that my friends were in it meant I would make an effort to be watching the following week when it was due for broadcast. After Charlie, Bill, and Stu arrived, the whole band set off together across London to make the fateful journey up the M1 motorway.

When they returned later that night spirits were high after the day's experience. We stood in the front room by the radiogram with the naked lightbulb glaring down from above.

"How was it up there?" I asked Brian as they trooped through the door.

"Aw, you should have been with us. We had a great time. Pete Murray's a real laugh."

"Yeah? What'd he have to say?" I wanted to know.

Brian turned to Keith, saying, "Tell him about it, then I'll tell him the other news."

"Murray made a few jokes about our hair at first, but he turned out all right as it went on," said Keith.

"Who else was on the show?" I asked him.

"Helen Shapiro and Johnny Cymbal," said Keith turning his nose up. "Nobody spoke to us, except Mickie Most—he was there too."

I groaned; it seemed the typical bullshit lineup for a pop program.

"There were a few snide remarks about our hair, same old shit," continued Keith. "It was sort of interesting though."

Brian laughed at the memory of it. Then he said, "Guess what?"

"No, go on," I urged.

"Eric's got us lined up to go on tour with the Everly Brothers in September," Brian announced, as if he still could not believe it. It was a *very* big break.

"The Everlys?" I was taken aback, it was all I could say.

"Yeah, we're all real chuffed," said a smiling Keith.

The following Saturday the band departed early from the flat, this time on route to their farthest booking to date. It was way up in

Middlesborough and coincided with the taped television show. I stayed behind and made sure I saw them on television later that day.

The good part about going to visit my aunt in Hammersmith was that she was always generous with food and could muster up a cooked meal quickly. I took up her offer on arrival and sat in a big comfortable armchair in front of the television as I ate my way through the welcome plate of food. The captions rolled for the start of *Thank Your Lucky Stars* and compère Pete Murray began introducing the acts. My aunt sat in a chair on my left, and as aunts and parents always do at crucial moments, she decided to start a conversation.

"Was that food all right? Would you like a bit more?"

"No, that's fine, thanks."

"I can soon do a bit more; it won't take a minute."

"No. I'm OK, thanks."

"Would you like a drop more tea, then?"

"No thanks," I replied, trying to keep the talk to a minimum.

"What do your friends do then?"

"They play guitars and sing," I replied.

"What do they call themselves?"

"The Rolling Stones," I replied, hoping she was not going to talk when they came on the screen.

"Oh, the Rolling Stones." She paused for a few seconds. "They do call themselves funny names nowadays. Why do they call themselves that?"

"They just made it up because they liked it."

Pete Murray introduced another act. "Is this them?" my aunt asked.

"No, I'll tell you when they're on."

I waited as the various acts did their routines then disappeared, my aunt still trying to show an interest and carrying on her talking. It did not particularly bother me—I only wanted to see the Stones anyway. We carried on the small talk and I diverted my attention each time Pete Murray spoke. Then he was saying, "The Rolling Stones." Suddenly they were on the television launching their way into "Come On."

"Is this them?" my aunt asked.

"Yeah."

"Oh my God! Look at them! Are these your friends?" Her reaction was one of shock.

"Yeah."

"Look at them. Look at their hair," she said reproachingly.

I watched the boys and waited for camera shots of all of them. I wanted to see how they all looked.

"Arthur, come and look at this," my aunt called out loudly to her husband. Arthur came in to the room smoking his pipe and stood behind a table watching.

"Look at their hair, Arthur," my aunt said as if Arthur could not see it. Then to me, "Why don't they get their hair cut?"

I made out I was not listening to her and kept watching the television, though I could feel her eyes on me.

"Your hair's long as well, and needs cutting," she said, as if noticing it for the first time.

I gave her a polite "Sshsh."

"Oh, isn't he ugly! Look at his face," she said as a full shot of Mick filled the screen. Arthur grunted in noncommittal mode.

"Look! Look at the faces he pulls," she tutted, and then laughed. "What does he look like? He's got a big mouth!"

"What are those things he's got in his hands?" she carried on.

"Maracas," said Arthur. "They're maracas."

"They all look like they need a good scrub with a bar of soap," my aunt continued as the whole band panned into view.

At first I had been watching them just for the pleasure of seeing how they looked on the television. After a minute or so I realized I needed to try to be objective as they may ask later for an opinion, as they did at gigs. The cameras seemed to pick out Mick more than the others which I supposed was natural as he was the singer, the focal point, but it left me with the feeling that the band did not appear to be one coordinated unit.

Knowing how small Mick's shoulders were, I was half expecting his jacket to slip off as his body gyrated. The jacket looked too big on him I thought; in fact the jackets looked awful on all of them to me, but then again I was not used to seeing them dressed this way. The band certainly did not have the polished look of the other acts and in truth seemed quite amateurish by comparison. None of them appeared very comfortable either—whether it was the outfits or the fact that it wasn't a live performance I could not say. The whole thing was a bit of a charade, a "How Not to Do It" guide to appearing on the box. Toward the end I saw Mick look across to his right where Brian was standing and start to laugh as if to say, "What a load of shit." I quite liked that bit. I felt the performance matched the record—it was not really them.

As the Stones slid from the screen I felt elated for them, even though my aunt continued to pass judgment. I did not appreciate at the time how insular it was to watch television in your own home. It didn't occur to me until later that millions of others in the country had seen them too.

The reaction of my aunt was no surprise to me. In the days to follow I found her response echoed by almost everyone who had seen the band for the first time that night. I spent the rest of the evening watching whatever else the television had to offer and parrying more of my aunt's remarks and questions. By 10:00 P.M. I'd had enough and left to return to the flat. I wondered how long I would be able to sleep before the others arrived back from Middlesborough. It was a gig that was to have some influence on the band.

15

It was about midday and everyone was drowsy. The Stones had arrived back from the northern trip in the early hours of the morning. They were due to play that afternoon at the Ken Colyer Club and later at the new Crawdaddy. The landlord banged on the door for the rent but nobody answered, and he went away.

As we all lay in bed nobody realized that the Rolling Stones were now famous, or infamous, depending how you saw it. The talk between everyone in the band was of Middlesborough the night before. I had not been there but I noticed that the Stones seemed to come back with a realization that they needed more weapons in their musical armory if they were not to be left behind.

The Stones were certainly kings of their immediate territory. They were the best R&B band in London and the surrounding provincial area. They pulled the biggest crowds and had a record out that could be heard on the radio. They had also appeared on television. By comparison bands such as Alexis Korner's and the Cyril Davies All Stars remained unknown outside the jazz club circuit. The Stones had a management and publicity machine to boot. Everything had been looking hunky-dory 24 hours ago, but today there were doubts.

The band was aware of course of the Beatles and other Epstein groups who were breaking new ground in the music business, but had no direct professional contact with them—the Stones were in London doing the rounds while most of their rivals were in Liverpool and the North. Hearing songs the other groups had recorded gave little indication of how good they were live. The Stones' trip up north was a venture into unknown territory, and they were surprised to find more evidence of the healthy northern group scene. On the same bill that night at the Alcove Club in Middlesborough was a band called the Hollies.

Brian had come back to London tremendously impressed by the Hollies, to such a degree that his reaction bordered on panic, which seemed to have rubbed off on the rest of the Stones. He was now convinced that the Stones needed to add vocal harmonies to their repertoire if they were to retain their chance of making it big.

"Phelge, you should see the Hollies," he said. "They're fantastic. They do vocal harmonies on all their songs. All the groups up North do harmonies. We've got to start doing them as well. We've got to be as good as them."

The Monday in Edith Grove started off normally enough. Someone had been out and left the street door wide open and the traffic noise raged into the house. Around midday somebody gave two bangs on the door knocker. Brian stuck his head out of the upstairs window to see who was there. He called out to whoever it was to come on upstairs.

"Who is it?" I asked him.

"It's those grotty schoolkids who are always hanging around across the road," he replied.

The girls made their way up to our first-floor flat and stood in the doorway of the room.

"What do you want?" snapped Brian.

"We saw you on *Thank Your Lucky Stars*," said one girl.

"Oh, that," said Brian indifferently. He seemed to have changed his mind about inviting them to the flat. "What did you think?"

"We thought you were good," answered another of the girls.

"Why were we good, then?" Brian challenged the girl, trying to make the moment as awkward as possible for her. She floundered for an answer. I thought he was being unnecessarily difficult.

"We liked the band and thought the record was great," she said after gathering her wits.

"You're only saying that because we were on TV."

"We'd never seen you before," the girl said.

"You've seen us walking up the street enough times," he answered while continuing to be as difficult as he could. I thought to myself, "Give the girl a break" and wondered if they were going to turn around and leave. Keith came into the room to see who the visitors were.

"I think you only want to talk to us because we were on the telly," said Brian, knowing that this was probably at least partly true. "You didn't bother to say hello to us before that."

The girl looked at Keith. "Which one are you?"

"He plays guitar. I thought you said you saw us on TV?" Brian queried her.

"Who's the one who sings? Is he here?" the girl asked.

"That's Mick," said Brian, at last beginning to lighten up a little. "What do you want to meet him for?"

Whether the mention of Mick by the girl spurred Brian into a charm offensive or not, from then on he became quite amiable. He chatted to them in his best friendly manner, asking questions regarding their lives. He did an impressive job of being a friendly and responsible pop star showing interest in his fans. Mick arrived in the room and he and Keith also spoke briefly to the girls. The boys then gave what were probably the first autographs signed by the Rolling Stones. The girls, as far as I was concerned, became the first real fans of the Stones as pop stars. From that time on they would come back to visit the flat many times and when they did they usually asked for Brian.

Spare time at the flat was spent experimenting with tunes that might lend themselves to vocal harmony. Brian's musical ability allowed him to tell instantly how the harmonies needed pitching and which songs would be most suitable. The other factor he had to consider was Keith's singing voice, the limitations of which he was aware from their ill-fated Everlys duets.

Keith would have been the first to admit he was not the world's best singer and had never shown any aspirations in this field. Brian was going to have to ask Bill to sing on the harmonies to see if he was better than Keith. After sorting through the records at the flat and taking into consideration whether the songs could be used on stage, "Fortune Teller" and "Poison Ivy" were added to the act, these being the only two songs Brian found suitable for harmonies. The need to practice the new arrangements led to them using the Studio 51 club for regular full-scale rehearsals.

A furor had broken out over the band's appearance on the respectable television pop show. The long hair was taken as an insult and a deliberate affront to people's sense of decency. People saw the Stones as symbolizing decadence, their filthy hair ranked alongside illiteracy, degradation, and obscenity as contemporary evils. The Rolling Stones never washed and they were ugly. They were five morons with no apparent talent. They epitomized a misspent youth and a lack of discipline. Even I began to wonder if some of these accusations were true, if only for a moment.

It was not the reaction anyone had expected to an appearance that had only been intended as a plug for the record, and Andrew's publicity machine began to run red-hot in defence of the band. His initial response was to set about proving that the Stones were relatively normal people and not rebellious at all. It would be some six months later, when it was evident that young fans were being drawn to the band because their parents didn't like the Stones, that he saw the rebellious image as one to be promoted. For now, I think he still held hope the boys were going to learn to be more amicable, to temper themselves to an image at least partially acceptable to the establishment. It was going to be a long learning process. The impoverished Stones had nothing to lose anyway. It now seemed everyone didn't like them, and success could end any day with the furor they provoked. Whatever the band did was part of their way of life and beliefs. Eventually I think Andrew came round to seeing "you could get away with murder"—if that's how the public saw it—and began to enjoy the notoriety that attached itself to the band. Right now, Andrew and the Stones were still relative strangers exploring each other, and it would be time that would enable him to see the band's behavior could be turned into a major asset.

The Stones were bemused by all the fuss—hadn't they even dressed up in new clothes for the occasion in order to make a good first impression? No one had given a thought about the hairstyles, especially with the Beatles sporting their mop-top look. For us it was hard to imagine people saying, "Look, they've got long hair so they can't play." Had the Stones appeared on that show with short hair and mohair suits, would the same people have said how great they were? We all thought it was typical of how brainwashed many people were. The reaction summed up the establishment we spent our time deriding.

A blank day came up later that week and Keith and I took one of our trips into the West End again. We wandered through Leicester Square and on toward Piccadilly Circus en route to Eric's office. On the left-hand side we passed a record store where we stopped to glance at some albums on display in the window. Cliff Richard smiled forth at us with his mean rock and roll haircut from a record cover at the center of the display. I made a comment to Keith about his and Cliff's surnames being similar—I don't know if this set him thinking, but later he did drop the *s* from the end of Richards for a while.

We walked on and passed a guy standing around in a raincoat who made a remark. I did not really catch what he said and assumed he was calling out to someone nearby. After we had gone about 10 paces Keith turned to me and spoke.

"Did you hear that?" he asked me.

I looked back at him unsure of what he meant. "No. Hear what?"

"What that turd said back there."

Still mystified, I said I hadn't heard, and was expecting Keith to relate some part of a conversation.

"He called out to us, 'How's trade, boys?' Probably taking the piss out of our hair. C'mon, let's go back and sort him out." Keith turned and I followed him back to the man in the raincoat.

Keith walked up to Raincoat and leaned forward menacingly close into his face. "How would you like a smack in the fuckin' mouth?"

"What's that? What's up?" Raincoat said, looking scared.

"What're you calling out 'How's trade' for?" snarled Keith.

"I didn't mean nothing. It was just a joke, boys." Raincoat moved nervously from one leg to another. I think Keith changed his mind at this point about clocking the guy one.

"Well, it ain't funny to me," said Keith. "You wanna learn to keep your fuckin' mouth shut or someone might put their fist in it."

"I'm sorry, I'm sorry, lads. I made a mistake," bleated Raincoat.

"Because we got long hair, is it then?" Keith asked, still looking enraged.

"No, no," said Raincoat. "I didn't notice. Look there's no harm done, lads. I'm sorry."

Keith swore at him a final time and then, satisfied that honor was restored, we moved on.

We then passed the guy with no face who used to sell newspapers on the corner of Shaftesbury Avenue. He always made you cringe with discomfort when he used to catch you staring at him. His face was disfigured and almost completely flat, with just two holes where his nose once was. The skin looked as if it had melted and spread like warm butter, then been left to dry. I thought it was awful for him and guessed that he had been in a bad accident or possibly disfigured in the war. He caught me looking at him and I vowed that I would walk past next time and pretend he wasn't there. I took a last glance back at him as we crossed the road and shuddered to see he was still watching me.

We went into Eric's office—he was sitting at his desk and Keith spoke with him for a while. There were some girls nearby who handled all the mail for the Stones' newly formed fan club. An assistant busily sorted through a desk piled with letters waiting to be answered. Keith read some and then autographed one of the specially commissioned photos that would be handed out to club members. The office seemed to match Eric's brisk businesslike manner, functional and free of clutter. I felt he would have been quite happy with just a desk and phone. The busy fan club seemed almost like an intrusion. After leaving Eric to his work we wandered out onto the street again in search of something to do.

Like many people I had a built-in sixth sense that on occasions gave me a feeling of instant dislike toward someone. The guy I was looking at now looked a smoothie and was tall and skinny with curly black hair. He also had no clothes on.

Keith and I had spent the evening touring the clubs again and had returned once more to an empty flat. Wandering into the unlit bedroom I could not help noticing the man right away.

He stood framed in the center of the two dollies' window across the way. The light inside their apartment allowed us to see directly through the window, which had no curtains drawn. From what I could see he was totally naked and to add to my annoyance the dark-headed dolly was in the same state. They moved in and out of view and looked to be getting ready to go to bed together. I felt I could be in love with her and did not want her to be with someone else. The guy really pissed me off.

I called out to Keith to come and watch and he came in from the front room.

"Hey look, my dark-haired dolly has some bloke up there with her," I complained.

"We know what they're up to," said Keith.

We stood and watched them moving around, getting ready for bed. Then the light in their room went out and we could see no more. I visualized them in bed together and wondered what could be done to stop them. If only there was a way of suddenly banging on their window. Then I remembered the air gun.

I searched in the dark for the pistol and the lead pellets that accompanied it. I scrambled back over Keith's bed, and he gave me a hand opening our window. We slid it upward just a little until a small gap opened at the bottom. It was enough to point and sight the barrel of the pistol through, but if you looked at the window from across the way in the dark it would still appear closed. I hastily loaded a pellet in the end of the barrel and pointed it through the gap and took aim. I hesitated momentarily as I wondered if the pellet would shatter the glass. That might result in some serious grief coming our way—cops and everything. I thought, "Fuck it," and pulled the trigger.

Whatever they were doing over there must have come to an abrupt end when the pellet hit the glass. There was an almighty crack that echoed loudly around the adjoining buildings and I felt sure the window was now in pieces. The couple inside must have reacted immediately and wondered what the hell had happened. Almost instantly the guy jumped out of bed, ran naked across the room and threw on the light switch.

Keith and I waited with bated breath for something to happen. The guy rushed up to the window and stood there looking out. Keith and I gave ourselves mock cheers of success as we watched him open the window and look around. We were lucky—the glass remained in the frame and there was no obvious sign of damage.

We sat there watching him for a while and eventually he closed the window and stood in front of it for a few more minutes. He then decided it was a mystery he was not going to solve and moved away, turning the light off again. Keith and I lit ourselves cigarettes to mark time before our second assault.

It was Keith's turn to take up the role of hidden marksman. He took careful aim through the opening at the base of the window and once more the noise bounced back around the buildings. The second pellet had landed spot on target and again we waited for the response. The first time the guy had made the elementary mistake of turning on the light, enabling us to see him, but this time he was a little more subtle. It was as if he had concluded that someone was purposely trying to give him a hard time and wanted to find out who it was.

Keith and I sat on the bed watching, but this time no light came on inside the dollies' flat. We waited some more and the reaction finally came. The skinny guy was standing at the window in the dark, surveying the surrounding area. He lit a cigarette as he watched, unwittingly signaling to us that he was there. After a few moments the dolly joined him and they stood there for the next 10 minutes or so, smoking and looking around. I assumed the dolly would, from her experience of the neighborhood, have guessed quite easily who the offending parties were.

Resigned to the fact that what we were doing was only delaying them for a while, Keith and I decided to leave it at that. For me it was some consolation at least that we had put the guy on edge for the night. Satisfied, we put the gun away and made our way out toward the embankment and the pie stall.

Most of the Stones' rehearsals at the Studio 51 club were scheduled to coincide with gigs. If they were playing at the club anyway the rehearsal session would take place beforehand. This meant arriving there about two hours early, but it had the advantage in that the equipment only needed to be carried in and out once.

Working mainly on the two selected songs, the band struggled at first to get the vocal harmonies working. If Keith was mad-keen on this new idea he did not let it show. Brian was the driving force and completely in command of how the harmonies needed to be. He worked out the lines in his head and would sing his own part and then show Keith and Bill what they had to sing in relation to himself. The sessions were of the stop-start variety as Brian patiently kept explaining what was wrong. Either the other two would get their parts mixed up halfway through or the timing was wrong. It all seemed a bit of drag as they went over and over the same thing. Mick looked restless with all the hassle of having to keep singing a song part of the way through before Brian would stop it for the umpteenth time.

Keith looked nervous and self-conscious about having to sing, but he was willing to do anything for the band. Every time they reached the part where the harmonies were due he looked toward Brian for reassurance. Keith knew when he was not getting it right and this seemed to make him hesitant and to sing quieter.

Brian then decided to try Bill on his own to see how that would sound. Bill was not keen on a singing role either, but he did sound better than Keith. Eventually they both did the harmonies and Brian was happy. I did not think either of the songs lent themselves to the

Stones though and could not really see the point of it all. If the Hollies sounded like this, I reasoned that they could not be anything to worry about. In the end, after several sessions and a lot of pain, it all came together reasonably well. Keith gradually grew more confident with each performance, although I would still only have described the harmonies as passable.

Nights off were now getting rare as the band's workload had grown steadily. They had played the first ballroom booking arranged by Eric and there were more in the pipeline. Although the Stones were now masters of the club environment they would have to adapt a new strategy for the bigger venues. Audiences here would be more rock and pop orientated and would not be aware of the hard blues music that was the Stones' forte. The group and the audience would be on learning curves with each other. If the reaction was anything like the one to the band's TV debut they would be more of a visual than a musical attraction.

The image of the band created by the way the Stones dressed had never been given particular thought. Apart from the long hair, it was not a big sensation around Chelsea. Our dress was perhaps a little different but again, unless you visited places like the Ernie, it was no big deal. In other people's eyes we probably just looked scruffy rather than different.

One evening we decided to mooch up the Kings Road for a drink. As the others were getting ready I dug out one of the weird-looking ties I had brought back from the Portobello Market and stood in front of the wardrobe mirror putting it on.

"Look at him," said Keith. "He's only going to wear one of those fuckin' off-looking ties."

Mick turned his nose up from behind the shaver but I continued to tie a nice neat Windsor knot on the tie, which had an ugly red-and-blue pattern. I turned back to Keith when I had finished and asked him what he thought of it.

"It looks really naff," was his frank opinion.

"Ah well," I replied. "If you don't like it I'll fix it." I picked up some scissors, held up the end of the tie and cut it off about two inches below the knot.

"How's it look now, then?" I asked him.

Keith looked at it and laughed. "You're not gonna go out in it like that?"

I looked at it in the mirror. It did look pretty stupid.

"Yeah, why not? Somebody will probably think I don't know it's been cut off." I reasoned to him.

The evening began in the usual aimless fashion. Mick, Brian, Keith, and I, with girlfriends in tow, stopped for a drink at the Man in the Moon pub in the Kings Road. Over the beers we decided to venture back to Hyde Park for another evening of Serpin'. This time our rowing was a bit more coordinated and we ended up wet from sweat rather than from splashing water about. When we ran out of time for the boat we wandered back over the bridge and around the lake. On a summer's evening it was a pretty and tranquil part of the park. If the others viewed it in the same light they never said so—words like *pretty* were not in our everyday vocabulary. We would just have described it as a cool place to come and have fun. With the work for the band increasing, it turned out to be our last Serpin' trip. The other thing we could never have realized was that in six years' time, almost to the day, we would all be back here in rather different circumstances. The Rolling Stones would be playing a historic concert on the exact spot where we were now walking. All except Brian, that is.

On leaving the park it seemed appropriate to go somewhere nearby for another drink and we ambled down Sloane Street until we found a pub. The place was what you would call olde-worlde, with only a few people inside. We walked up to the bar, behind which was an elderly fat guy wearing a waistcoat and tie, his shirtsleeves rolled up to his elbows. Mick ordered some drinks.

"Not in here lads, unless you're wearing a tie." He sounded pleased at being able to exercise his authority.

"A tie? What? To drink?" scoffed Mick, turning to the rest of us to laugh. I thought I might be OK.

"I've got a tie," I informed him. "I'll have a half of lager."

The barman looked at me straight-faced, then fixed his gaze on my tie as if making up his mind.

"A proper tie. A whole one. Not half of one. Are you taking the piss?"

"It is a proper tie," I said as I looked down to where the tie was. I went through the motions of fumbling to pick the tie up from where it should have been hanging to show it to him.

"Hey, Mick! Look! Someone's cut my fucking tie off! It was my best one too!" I tried to sound surprised and hurt. The others began to laugh.

"Where's it gone?" asked Brian, examining the tie.

"Come on, just get out of it. We don't want you in here." The barman was warming to his part now and putting on a show for his regular customers to demonstrate how he dealt with unsavory yobs. He and the people in the pub would now have something to talk about for the rest of the evening. We just left unperturbed and went into another bar a little farther up the street.

In the second pub the barman kept looking at my tie but said nothing. I knew he wanted to comment on it so I decided to make conversation with him.

"Hey, did you know the word *gullible* isn't in the dictionary?" I asked him.

"No," he said. "I didn't know that."

I took my drink over to a table and sat down.

16

THE STEADY UPTURN in fortune for the Rolling Stones had brought with it a good feeling that now surrounded the band. There was an air of relaxed comradeship, with everyone seeming happy with the way things were going. Even the animosity toward Bill seemed to be subsiding. The fact that he had missed a couple of promotional dates when he still held his job as a storeman was virtually forgiven. Bill had played on the record and appeared on television as part of the band. With all the ensuing publicity coming the band's way, the talk of finding a new bass player stopped and Bill began to become accepted. Until now Brian and Keith's attitude toward him had been shaped by their personal beliefs: they held the view that if you were a musician you did not need to have another job, and if you were in the Rolling Stones that was better than a job, albeit that it didn't pay much. A wife and kids were other accessories they felt musicians did not need. If Bill had any reciprocal ill feelings toward the others, he never let them show. He just played bass and seemed to take it all in his stride.

Perhaps the reason the same attitude never applied to Charlie was because they had pursued him to join the band and saw him as someone they had already converted. They also believed from previous experience that good drummers were harder to find than good bass players.

Bill and Charlie, who had worked in an advertising agency, were both soon encouraged to throw in their jobs and risk all with the Stones. Mick no longer attended LSE, although he'd not given any formal indication to the college that I knew of, so everyone became truly full-time and dependent on the band for income.

Brian's role seemed to be that of founder and spokesman. It seemed inevitable that he would be involved in key decisions like the signing of the contracts. He was not a leader who said, "This is my band and you can't do this," but he was able to put himself across to people in a more plausible manner than, say, Keith. He also wrote letters and was good at explaining things, plus he was more musically adept than the others. He was also better at being insincere and telling lies if the need arose. These were all attributes the Stones needed, and Brian supplied them.

How Stu felt in his new role as roadie I never knew—I was too embarrassed to mention it to him. He had always driven the van and in that respect it could not have been much different to him. He continued to play the piano on the club gigs whenever possible and the boys continued to treat him the same as before, but he never said how he really felt about things.

The Offers, who had not spoken to us at all since the toilet door saga, were also more amenable for reasons best known to themselves. Possibly it was because they had seen the Stones on television or they knew the band had a record out and there were potential stars living below. Alternatively it could have been that the band had begun working more and Mick, Keith, and Brian were not at home to make so much noise in the early hours or steal their food during the day. Maybe they were happy because they missed the television slot—the horror of turning on their TV and having the hooligans from downstairs come leaping into their front room could have finally freaked them out. Whatever the reason, Mr. Offer actually said hello whenever he saw anyone.

The Offers' change of mood might also have been helped by the fact that our record player no longer worked. Something mysterious had happened to the radiogram, and it no longer even lit up anymore. Wanting to play some records one day, I turned my attention to Brian's portable record player.

Brian had found that his player no longer worked and believed it had somehow developed a fault. The truth was Keith had done something to it causing electrical damage. In an attempt to keep the peace and avoid Brian throwing a tantrum, Keith never mentioned this to him.

It seemed the deck was immobile, and with Keith looking on I decided to take it to pieces to see if it could be repaired, although I didn't really know what I was doing. I removed the deck from its cabinet to expose its mechanism. The only thing I could think of doing was to disconnect the power wires from the main power transformer, in case that was at fault, and join them directly to the deck itself. We both looked at the turntable to detect any movement but after a few seconds an acrid burning smell wafted up from the deck, followed by a cloud of black smoke and a loud BANG! from the wall socket. I yanked the wires from the socket and looked beneath the record deck, where something had melted and turned black. It was obvious by this stage that it would never work again and we put the deck back into its cabinet and left it. I thought about looking inside the radiogram to see if I could repair that, but then I remembered the blown-apart wall socket. I kicked the remainder of the socket free and the three electricity wires hung protruding from the wall. Feeling a bit guilty about leaving them in such an unsafe condition I took a piece of cardboard, wrote "Arrgh!" in red ink across it and taped it alongside the wires.

The band was now looking for a second single. "Come On" had earned its share of plays on the radio but was now past the point of making any further impact. The song had hung around the tail end of the charts in respectable fashion, reaching a high of number 20, but it was nearing the end of its shelf life.

The two songs the band had rehearsed using vocal harmonies, "Poison Ivy" and "Fortune Teller," were chosen as the follow-up. At the end of July the band went to one of Decca's studios and put both tracks down in a couple of days. Again I was not keen on either of the songs, feeling that they did not really suit the way the Stones played or sounded. With the wealth of material lying around on the floor in the front room, I never understood why they could not find something better or more suitable. They wanted something with a commercial sound, although there were already a number of blues-type songs in the charts. Buddy Holly's version of the tune "Bo Diddley" was there, along with two versions of "Twist and Shout," one of which was on an EP by the Beatles. Ray Charles was also riding high with "Take These Chains from My Heart." Not exactly tunes that the Stones played, but in the same vein. After recording "Poison Ivy" and "Fortune Teller," the band decided neither of the songs were what they were looking for. They asked Decca to put the release on hold while they decided to search round some more.

The band now had a full set of brand-new amplifiers and a PA system. They were the latest Vox models made by Tom Jennings at his factory in Kent. The AC30 model he made was to become legendary. Vox was the market leader in sound equipment and the Beatles also used Vox. On returning to the flat with the new gear Brian told me that the band had bought it all. Later it transpired that Tom Jennings had supplied the equipment to the band as a form of publicity for his product.

Another company called Wall's had been famous for years in England as an ice cream manufacturer, and being a warm summer, sales of their product were probably high. When the Stones went to a gig at the Wooden Bridge Hotel at the beginning of August, Keith also discovered that Wall's made living-room furniture. Arriving back from Guildford at about two in the morning, with the usual noisy entrance, Keith carried in Wall's latest item of home furnishing—it stood four feet high, had a shape like a giant wine glass and was exactly what we needed. He plonked it down in the middle of the room and we all stood around looking at it with admiration. It was a wire mesh basket with a Wall's Ice Cream sign on the side, normally used for people to throw their used ice cream wrappers and cartons into. Keith said he had "found" it and his artistic eye immediately saw our front room lounge as the perfect setting for it. Right then and there I knew he was a genius.

The next night after a trip into the country for a gig in Sussex we demonstrated the ice cream basket to Mr. Ironbar next door. During the day we had filled the basket to the brim with old newspapers, wrappers, and even discarded clothing for disposal. Instead of applying our favorite method of tipping rubbish from the window we now had another option.

Brian and Keith carried the basket plus contents out onto the balcony that also acted as the porch over the front door. Using matches Keith ignited some paper at the bottom of the basket. Very soon flames flared upward into the night sky, followed by billowing clouds of smoke with fragments of burned paper floating in the air.

It was another warm night and most of the neighbors had gone to bed leaving their windows open for ventilation. The amount of smoke increased when the old clothing caught alight, giving off an acrid smell, which filled the air. Mr. Ironbar from next door was the first to slam his window closed, quickly followed by several others in the vicinity. It had started out as an intended distraction for passing motorists but ended up as being another total nuisance for the whole street. Amazingly enough this was another occasion when nobody complained or called the fire brigade as a result of one of our stunts. Mr. Ironbar either thought it was not worth the trouble or did not want to take the risk of having another "delivery" in the middle of the night.

Traditional jazz had become popular in the late '50s and the early '60s, spawning several star bands, some of which had become household names by having hit records. Although "trad" had begun to fade it still had a large following. Apart from hearing the Kid Martyn band briefly with the Stones in the Ken Colyer club I did not really know much about the music. The closest I had been to it was that I knew a guy named Willie who played a banjo and always carried it with him when he rode his bicycle. Willie used to tell the story of how he went out one Sunday and ended up in Belgium. He had told his parents he was going out for a couple of hours and came home six weeks later. When he returned his parents were watching television and without looking up or acknowledging him his mother said simply, "Your dinner's in the oven."

I guessed Willie would probably be at the Richmond Jazz Festival the coming weekend. Although I had never heard of it before, the festival was in its third year and the Stones would be playing in the clubhouse. It sounded like it would be just like another gig at the Crawdaddy.

The organizers seemed to have done a good job with their promotion. The festival was to last the whole weekend with tents erected over the playing fields at the Athletic Club. Some of them sold beer and food, others sold records and other jazz-related items. You could walk around the ground and find two or three jazz bands playing at the same time. The focal point was a huge marquee in the center where the biggest names would play later. It was a nice evening, with several thousand people present, and a carnival atmosphere prevailed over the whole event.

The queue of youngsters waiting to see the Stones stretched back forever. It was obvious that there were going to be hundreds of disappointed fans unable to get in. The clubhouse was full before the band had even arrived, and it looked impossible to even get the equipment inside. Eventually the organizers decided that to accommodate all the Stones fans the band would be allowed to play on the hallowed ground of the main marquee.

To most people this decision made obvious sense, but old prejudices die hard. Some of the musicians who had been antagonistic toward the Stones at the jazz clubs still saw themselves as superior and tried to wield whatever influence they considered they held by objecting to the switch. The electric-guitar-playing layabouts with their awful pop record had no place on stage at a jazz festival. The attempts by the jazzers eventually failed.

The big marquee was so jammed full of people I did not even bother to try to squeeze in to watch the band. The crowd greeted the performance of each song with a tumultuous reception. Looking in through the entrance I could see nothing but well-dressed bodies that looked welded together as one big mass. Occasionally Mick's head would come into view somewhere over in the distance. I wandered around outside with a beer and considered the merits of cutting the guy-ropes that held up the tent. The rest of the grounds now seemed almost empty and I could have captured everyone in a big wriggling parcel.

Whatever the jazz musicians thought of the Stones, the scenes at the festival that night must have been beyond their comprehension. A tidal wave of R&B had swept in and was demanding to be recognized. With the press that was to follow the show it would now be just about impossible for them to persuade a club promoter not to book the Stones and their music. The balance of power had shifted.

After the Richmond Jazz Festival, the Stones diet of club gigs was now becoming supplemented with trips up and down the country to play in ballrooms and village halls. Apart from one day off and the odd canceled booking, the band worked every night in August. The work was now pouring in from all directions. It created a regular income, although despite the extra traveling the boys still found the time to continue their rehearsals.

At one such rehearsal the band was in between numbers on the stage at Studio 51 when in walked Andrew. At first glance it looked as if he had two well-heeled businessmen in dark coats and suits following behind. The pair were in fact John Lennon and Paul McCartney. Andrew had met them by chance in a nearby Soho street and invited them over to the club. The few privileged onlookers watched with surprise as the two Beatles and the Stones greeted each other like old friends. With Paul looking on, John explained that they had a song they'd written for themselves but not yet recorded. They would be happy to let the Stones record it instead as a single if they were interested. Everyone's faces lit up at the prospect. Any tune written by Lennon and McCartney was going to be commercial and virtually guaranteed to be a success. John and Paul said they would run through it and jumped up onto the stage.

Paul took Bill's bass and clowned around in an operatic singing voice to adjust himself to the microphone while John adjusted Keith's guitar. When they were both satisfied that everything was ready for the impromptu session, they burst into "I Wanna Be Your Man." With the famous Beatles' harmony sound on the chorus line, the song sounded like a winner. When they reached the end the Stones were knocked out with what they had just heard. Brian and Keith then held a conference with John to discuss the song's arrangement and ran through the chord sequence with him to make sure they had it correct. Then John and Paul had to be on their way to another engagement and left the club with Andrew. The whole procedure had probably taken around 20 minutes, and the result was that the Stones no longer had a problem regarding their next single.

Now that the band was having to travel further afield for gigs they were arriving back at the flat even later than before. It was not unusual for them to arrive between four and six in the morning.

I was still somehow managing to fit my work at the printers in between all that was going on and used up some of the holiday I was owed. I came home early one afternoon so that I could go to that evening's gig. The three of them were still in bed but awake. Brian had gone into the rear bedroom and was lying in my bed fiddling with the air pistol.

"Hello," he grinned in greeting. Keith was grinning too. It was the same grin as the one they'd adopted when they had thrown the records out of the window. Mick was in his bed smiling. I looked around for a clue to as what was going on and wondered if Brian had been firing the pistol out the window. I went to the window and looked out. Nothing seemed to be amiss, no records or whatever in the garden, all quite normal.

"What are you doing with the gun?" I asked Brian as he fooled with it.

"Just looking at it," he said. "I like these things; they're fun. Wish I had something to shoot at."

Something told me he had already found something and I looked around the room before finding his target. It was the painting of man's survival above Mick's bed. They must have been firing pellets at it for an hour at least. The place where once the surviving man looked out from was now blank. The face was completely gone, replaced by a gaping four-inch hole through which you could now see the wall behind. The remainder of the picture looked fairly well peppered with holes too. I studied the remains of the ruined picture. Brian watched me and laughed gloatingly.

"You've ruined a valuable piece of artwork," I told him in mock anger. "I was gonna take it to Sotheby's."

I moved the picture off the wall and found hundreds of lead pellets from the pistol that had fallen down after penetrating the canvas and come to rest on the back of the picture frame. As I lifted the picture away from the wall, the pellets cascaded over Mick's bed. I held it up and inspected the hole before hanging it back on the wall. The guy in the picture may have survived a holocaust, but not the Rolling Stones.

"We'll have to get one of the girls to darn it up with colored wool," I said.

Later, as the others were making themselves ready for Stu's arrival, Keith was sitting on the bed glancing through the pages of a glossy magazine.

"Hey! Look at this photo!" he said, holding the pages wide open. I came over and looked at the black-and-white picture. It was fashion shot featuring a girl in a garden modeling some clothes. She was a dark-haired girl, a pretty, dark-haired girl.

"It's the dolly from over the back," he pointed out to me. I looked at it again.

"Are you sure?" I asked him—I wasn't.

"Yeah, I reckon it's definitely her. Yeah, it is," he answered conclusively.

"Yeah, it could be. Looks a bit like her," I conceded.

"I reckon they're a pair of models. It's definitely her." It seemed feasible. They did have that look about them.

"I dunno." I hesitated. I was not that good at recognizing people in unexpected circumstances. "You might be right though. We'll have to see if we can chat them up or something." Then Stu arrived with the van, we loaded it up, and then set off for that night's gig.

A lot of time now began to be taken up with photograph and interview sessions. The favored backdrops for the photos were either just down the road by the river or in one of the parks. With the interviews, arrangements were usually made to meet up somewhere like a café, bar, or hotel lounge with the reporters. Sometimes the boys would just go to the offices of the music magazines and go through the question and answer routine there. During one of these trips they picked up a pile of promotional singles and brought them back to the flat. The only record player that was still working was the one that belonged to me in the bedroom. I brought it into the front room, parked it on an upright chair, and plugged it in. The records were a mixed bag and included "Ring of Fire" by Johnny Cash—that was OK, we liked him, although we were not too keen on the Tijuana trumpet sound.

We got down to the last one not really expecting anything much and got a surprise. It was Ronnie Hawkins with his version of "Who Do You Love?" Brian thought the guitar sound was great with all the distortion and sustained feedback. He was so knocked out by the sound he just kept playing the record repeatedly. He had never heard such a wild guitar sound and with the way Hawkins did the vocals the whole thing sounded really mean. The way Brian kept playing it over was as if he was considering doing something similar at a future date. I thought they should have done it as the next single, and as it turned out Brian never did go back to it.

Still excited about being given "I Wanna Be Your Man" by the Beatles, the Stones were now back in the studio. This time it was the Kingsway Studio in Holborn. The studio sessions were slotted in between shows and mostly took place in the afternoons, a time of day when Mick never considered his voice to be at its best. Usually he was not long out of bed and his body had not revved up fully. At the end of August he was lucky—the Stones were to record their second television show one afternoon, but Mick only had to mime.

Back in the late '50s there had been a TV pop show called *Six Five Special*. The program was on every Saturday and the introduction featured film of a steam train, the "Six Five Special," accompanied by the song of the same name sung by Don Lang and his Frantic Five. The clever twist was that the show was broadcast at "Six Five"— five minutes past six in the evening.

I liked the show and watched it whenever I could, as long as my stepfather had not sold the TV that week. Compared with other English TV shows, *Six Five Special* was relatively innovative in its format in that it had a live audience and featured visiting American rock and roll artists. The members of the audience were mostly teenagers dressed up in the latest fashions and would dance or sit around swooning over stars like Bill Hayley or Britain's own Tommy Steele. The show that Mick and the rest of the Stones were going to appear on was called *Ready, Steady, Go!* The theme was similar to *Six Five Special*, although there was a larger studio audience and the presentation was far slicker. By chance many of the studio audience were dedicated Stones fans, some of whom we knew quite well. Members of the *Ready, Steady, Go!* team had originally come to the Crawdaddy looking for dancers to appear on the show, and this led to them discovering and subsequently booking the Stones.

The compères were similar in age and dress to the audience, most of whom were fashion-conscious mods. Little time was wasted on chitchat between the artists, each of whom mimed the words to their latest single. Most people in the audience were good dancers and would cheer loudly for their favorites when they came on stage. When you watched the show it gave the impression that a lot of people had casually turned up to have a ball and that anyone could be doing it. The brief rehearsals before the show went out on air were also fairly informal—just a matter of timing the acts and organizing the running order. From the studio floor to the backstage areas it felt as if a big party was taking place. Up a stairway above the studio was the Green Room, where complimentary drinks intended for the artists and their associates poured freely. I spent most of my time there drinking vodka while the Stones performed below.

This second television show led to further condemnation and letters of protest, but it also won the Stones many new fans up and down the country.

With all the traveling they were doing, the boys were beginning to spend less time at the flat. It was not unusual for them to be away for two or three days journeying from one gig to the next. In the days following *Ready, Steady, Go!* they went to Manchester for yet another television show and then traveled directly to Wales. They also fitted in another recording for *Thank Your Lucky Stars*. This time the show was a little more up-to-date, featuring the Searchers and the Tremeloes. The acts also included teenage ballad singer Craig Douglas of "Only Sixteen" fame. The main highlight of the show as far as the Stones were concerned came at the end during a photograph session. Keith told me the story.

"We all got together to have a picture taken at the end of the show. They wanted Craig Douglas to sit on a chair in the front and he refused because of his trousers. He had this brand-new mohair suit on and didn't want to sit down in it.

"He told Pete Murray he wouldn't sit down in his new trousers in case they got creased. So Pete Murray said, 'Well, I'm not too big to sit down and crease my trousers; I'll sit on the chair.' As he sat down he crossed his legs and wiped the bottom of his shoe all the way down the side of Craig Douglas's trousers. He went berserk."

When they did get back to the flat they would spend the time either asleep or rushing out to Eric's office or a rehearsal. To me it seemed as if they had now moved out of the flat and were living in the van. Edith Grove was just another stop-off point. Although my relationship with the band remained the same, I did not go everywhere with them at this time. I still needed an income so I had carried on working at the printers. The other factor was that television and recording studios were unknown territory. Turning up at a club with the band was OK, but to begin with we weren't sure if this would be acceptable at the studios.

One afternoon around 4:30 I was in the kitchen making coffee when I heard the street door open and the three of them come up the stairs. They came into the kitchen.

"We've got a copy of the record," said Brian, looking pleased with himself.

"Show it to him," said Keith.

"Yeah, take a look at it," said Brian and handed it to me. I could not imagine why they wanted me to look at it, other than to prove it existed. I took it from Brian and looked at it. I read the title on the A side first. It was laid out normally like any other record—the name of the song, "I Wanna Be Your Man," was at the top and underneath that it said: The Rolling Stones. I turned it over to see what was on the B side. It was something called "Stoned," not a song I'd ever heard.

"'Stoned'? What's that?" I asked, looking at each of them in turn.

"He's missed it," said Mick.

"Read it again," Brian told me. I did so, and it still said "Stoned," as before.

"Stoned, by The Rolling Stones," I read out to them as they all looked at me as if I were half-asleep.

"Look underneath where it says 'Stoned,'" said Brian patiently. I looked underneath the title and in brackets where the writer's name would be credited it read "Nanker-Phelge."

"Hey, it says 'Nanker-Phelge,'" I exclaimed in complete surprise. I took my eyes from the record and saw the three of them standing there watching me intently, their faces lit with broad smiles. At that moment I felt proud they had taken the trouble to think of me and associate me with their accomplishments.

"I hope you don't mind us using your name?" Brian asked. "We wanted to put it on the record."

"No, that's great," I said and read the label one more time. "What is 'Stoned' anyway?"

"Just something we made up in the studio," said Keith. "An instrumental."

"Yeah, we had some time left over and decided to make something up for the B side. Everyone does it," said Brian.

"I never really noticed," I replied. I never usually bothered to read who wrote the songs.

"Well," said Mick, explaining, "You get the same royalties as the song on the A side. If the A side sells a million copies, that means the song on the B side has sold the same amount."

The thought hadn't really occurred to me before, although it obviously made sense.

"Andrew's organizing us our own publishing company called Nanker-Phelge," said Brian.

"Anyway, what does it all sound like? When is it coming out?" I asked.

"We don't know yet," said Brian. "Maybe they'll release it to coincide with the Everlys' tour."

17

WITH THE INCREASE in the band's work since Eric Easton and Andrew Oldham took over, the boys had enjoyed a boost in income. Apart from the luxury of not having to count pennies before deciding whether they could afford to eat, they could now buy clothes. New shirts and fashionable jackets and trousers were now being worn by all, in keeping with their growing status. Mick had bought himself a corduroy coat that was very similar in style to my own, except his was brown. He was wearing it as he stood alongside Keith in the front room.

"We've decided to leave the flat," he said. "Andrew's found us something over in Kilburn."

The news had come out of the blue—I had not really thought about leaving Edith Grove.

Brian was crawling over his bed behind me, probably looking for either his inhaler or the bottleneck.

"OK, when are you going?" I asked him.

"Probably Friday," replied Mick. "We're gonna move in over the weekend sometime."

"There's only room for two, but come over next week," said Keith. "It's in Kilburn—33 Mapesbury Road."

"OK, I will probably go to my relatives in Hammersmith for a while," I replied. I knew there was a spare room I could use temporarily. I asked Brian what he was doing.

"I don't know. I think I'll stay down at Linda's for a few days. I feel like a rest," he replied. Brian had missed playing on some gigs a week or so back because he felt unwell, a decision that had not pleased the others too much. He had stayed at Linda's then, so it was no surprise that he had decided to go there now. The irony was that Brian had originally considered playing bass instead of Bill and thereby trimming the band to a four-piece. Now the band had played several gigs in this formation, except it was Brian who had been the one missing.

It seemed strange that Brian had suddenly taken to being ill, as during the long hard winter, when there was little money or food, he had never missed a gig.

Leaving the flat certainly seemed like a natural progression. They had followed their TV appearances by playing a big pop concert at the Albert Hall just a few days previously. Opening that show, which had the Beatles headlining, the Stones had received a crazed reception, which must have made them a hard act to follow for some of the other support artists. With the extra money coming in and their growth in status, it didn't seem worth suffering 102 Edith Grove just for the sake of it. Also the Everly Brothers tour was now imminent— they would be away four to five weeks—and after that who knew?

Brian moved out to Linda's parents on the Thursday as the gig the Stones were due to play that night was in Watford, not too far from where she lived. The rest of us left about midday the following day, September 20. There was no sentimentality about it at all; we just packed our things and went.

The broken radiogram, which was Brian's as far as I knew, we left behind. We sorted briefly through the records and Keith gave me most of the singles we had played in the bedroom late at night. He also gave me the promo records he had picked up at the interview a few weeks before. I was going to ask him if he wanted the Perry Como album in return but did not bother. Some items of old clothing and other unwanted personal effects were also left behind. We walked out more or less as we had arrived. All I carried was some carrier bags and a record player. Nobody even bothered to tell Morgan-Morgan we were leaving and I imagined him coming over to look at the flat for the next couple of weeks and assuming we were still there.

On the Sunday after our departure from Edith Grove I met up with them at the Studio 51 club. From there we made the cramped journey in the back of the van down to Richmond. This was now the final week before the major tour with the Everlys. All the regular club gigs that had featured in the band's development were now coming to an end, they were playing at each for the very last time as a resident group. I felt Richmond had never been the same since the demise of the Station Hotel; certainly I never had the same affection for the Athletic Club site. The Ken Colyer club had been fun in its own way but the nights I would miss most would be those spent at Eel Pie Island. The bouncing dance floor, the minstrel gallery, the humping of the gear over the footbridge — these things provided irreplaceable memories.

We sat with our various girlfriends about 20 rows back from the center of the almost-empty auditorium. It was the latter part of the afternoon and rehearsals were taking place at the New Victoria Theatre in London. We had come around from the backstage area to sit and watch the man who was now playing guitar in front of us. Bo Diddley was patiently playing the same piece of music over and over while a drummer tried to put the accents of the Diddley riff in the right place. As Bo kept stopping and starting, people with cables and tools strolled backward and forward behind him shouting instructions to each other. The stark lighting highlighted the bareness of the wooden boards that made up the stage. The stage did not look in any way as glamorous as I expected, it just looked big—big enough, I imagined, to have housed the whole basement floor of the Ken Colyer club with room to spare. After several attempts Bo called across to the drummer, "That's it, man; you got it. See, it's not hard." You could tell Bo had been through this routine at least a thousand times before with drummers unfamiliar with his music. Eventually satisfied that the drummer had indeed "got it," and probably hoping he still "had it" later, Bo finished rehearsing almost without playing anything. Then the Everly Brothers walked onstage, looked around for a minute or so, and walked off. That was twice I had seen them and they hadn't sung on either occasion. Reaching the conclusion that nothing interesting was going to happen, we left the theater while the Stones went off to Eric's office in Regent Street; I bid them farewell and headed home.

Over the next few weeks I spent most of my time either working or drinking in the rear of the Bulls Head in Barnes, which hosted a modern jazz club. I had found myself a single-roomed apartment in St. Anne's Road about one minute's walk from the club. I knew most of the musicians who worked there and had received drumming lessons from one of them.

Going back to the Bulls Head after living with the Stones and experiencing their gigs was like visiting a rest home. The guy in the leather jacket and horn-rimmed glasses was still sitting there with a half pint of beer, still expertly making it last all evening as he clicked his fingers in time with the music. Black polo neck sweaters were also still the best clothing for listening to modern jazz so it seemed. I still liked to listen to the music, although the highlight of the evening was watching the guys sneak out to the toilet to smoke a joint when they announced, "We're just gonna take five." That was jazz cool talk for a five-minute break that usually lasted four times as long.

The resident setup for the club involved a house trio who would usually support the main act. During my earlier visits I had become friendly with a guy named Terry Smith who played guitar but went to the club to enjoy the jazz. Terry was still there but he was now head-lining as a guest player and we renewed our friendship. I still liked the music, although I found that most jazzers were still terrible snobs when it came to other types of music.

The Beatles had somehow mastered the knack of making hit records that went straight to number one in the charts every time. They only had to announce the recording of a new single and it sold enough advance copies to be number one before its release. Even if they'd only said, "We are thinking of making a new single," that probably would have been enough to ensure a number one.

Right now the Beatles were again topping the hit parade with "She Loves You," a well-written song with a good melody line. Standing at the bar in the Bulls Head early one evening, before the session began, the musicians were discussing the tune. It was difficult to tell whether their attitude toward it was borne out of financial jealousy or artistic superiority. Maybe it was a combination of both. The supposedly technically superior jazz men were working for about £3 a night and resented the fact that a group like the Beatles, whom they considered knew nothing about music, were making a fortune. From their perspective "She Loves You" couldn't possibly be a good song—it had too few chords in its structure.

I ordered another beer and let them get on with their discussion, but felt like saying that it stood up as a good tune regardless of how many chords it used. Why did a tune need to have loads of chords before it could be considered good? There were probably many worse tunes that used vast numbers of chords. As the put-down of the Beatles continued, my respect for the jazz musicians diminished rapidly. I saw their criteria for good or bad pieces of music as classic examples of the arrogance that existed. I made a point of not mentioning the Rolling Stones to them.

Back on the Everly Brothers tour, rock and roll legend Little Richard was added to the bill at the end of the first week. Although the tour was attracting good crowds on the day of each show, the promoters preferred the financial security of advance ticket sales, and hoped Little Richard's fans would boost advance sales to the desired level.

The tour was giving the Stones good exposure across a large area of the country that included Brian's hometown of Cheltenham and the Beatles' heartland in Liverpool. Having started in the southern half of England, the tour looped through Wales and the Midlands. It then went on to take in the northern towns plus a one-night excursion into Scotland before descending gradually to the finish in London.

A couple of days before the tour came to its end the second single, "I Wanna Be Your Man," was released by Decca. As it was a few weeks since I had first heard the song, it took me a little while to recognize it when I first heard it on the radio. It also jogged my memory about the fact that the band was coming back to London any day.

The final night with the Everly Brothers was at the Hammersmith Odeon. The Odeon was essentially a cinema, but with the screen removed it provided a very large stage. It was also a fine-looking building with a white-tiled art-deco fascia, although its splendor had been largely lost behind the Hammersmith Flyover, an elevated section of the Great West Road that had been erected immediately in front of it. Only the cinema's neon sign remained barely visible.

I had forgotten that the tour was ending that Sunday and did not remember until late in the evening, when I decided I would go and pay them a visit. I walked under the flyover and over the Odeon's concourse then around to the stage door at the rear. The poor lighting made the illuminated stage door sign stand out like a beacon and a group of about 10 girls stood around it like moths. I went up to the window alongside the door and waved my hand to attract the attention of the attendant inside. He looked at me disdainfully from beneath his peaked hat and made his way over to the door.

The girls were standing around flapping autograph books around in their hands and seemed desperate for someone to write in them. I smiled at one of the girls who immediately demanded, "Who are you?" I smiled at her again and said, "Nobody. I've come to mend the toilets. Who are you waiting for?"

The girl looked at me suspiciously, then said, "The Rolling Stones. Who *are* you?"

"I've never heard of them," I teased as the attendant opened the door. He looked at me and I said the first thing that came into my head, "Rolling Stones management."

He looked me over slowly from head to toe. I could see him thinking and then deciding that I looked weird enough for it to be possible. Finally he said, "Up the stairs on the right."

The girls immediately started trying to push their way through the door, protesting that the doorman should let them in as well. I left him to argue with them and made my way up the stairway.

Despite the amount of people milling around, the naked lights and painted concrete walls still made the room seem stark. People were mostly standing around talking and drinking. The final show must have finished about 15 minutes beforehand and a party was just underway. I had missed the Everlys yet again. Keith stood across the other side of the room in conversation with someone. I wandered over and just interrupted.

"Hey, what's happening?" I said from behind Keith without him seeing me. He turned around smiling.

"Hey, man," he said, letting his breath out in surprise. "Get a beer."

I got a beer from a table.

"Well, how'd it go?" I asked with good-natured impatience.

"Aw. It was great, man. The fans were going mad for us everywhere," he answered.

"Great, so how were the Everlys?" I asked, meaning that it must have been exciting working with artists we both admired.

"They were fantastic, but they kept getting booed off wherever we went."

"No!" I said in disbelief. "What happened?" I could not believe they had been so bad that nobody liked them.

"People were throwing paper cups and stuff at them," said Keith. "Whenever they went on stage, the kids were still screaming out for us."

"You're kidding, throwing stuff at them?"

"Yeah, they weren't too happy."

"That's a shame," I said. "Great for you guys though to get the best reception."

"Yeah, but it's a pity it was the Everlys. They were good and they're nice guys, but that's how it goes . . ."

We stood there mulling over the situation. We were both fans of the Everlys and felt a little sad at the way they had become a sacrificial lamb to the growing popularity of the Stones. Despite our feelings toward them though it was an immensely happy occasion for the Stones and boded well for the future. Although we did not realize it right then it was another sign of how things were changing both musically and socially. Then I noticed Keith was not wearing his showbiz jacket.

"What happened to the jackets?" I asked him.

"Gave them up ages ago," he replied. "We kept forgetting them and getting them mixed up. Charlie lost his and then someone else would forget. In the end we just gave up with 'em; it was pointless."

Brian also sounded thrilled at the reception they had received throughout the whole tour and seemed in equally high spirits. For him and the others the tour had been a brief step inside the world of pop stardom and they wanted more.

Reality came back with the appearance of Stu. There was only so much hanging around and talking that you could do; people were starting to leave and Stu was ready to join them. The theater would be closing soon, and the gear was still on stage. Stu wanted a hand getting it packed and out to the van.

The whole theater was empty now and lit with normal lighting. We wandered out on to the stage where others were packing equipment. The bare wooden floor gave you the feeling of being on the deck of a wooden ship. Looking like the ship's captain was a policeman in uniform who had come onto the stage and wanted some autographs.

I had always wanted to try one of the helmets worn by British "bobbies" and as the boys were about to do the autographs it looked like a good opportunity to find the cop in a receptive mood. I simply asked, "Hey, can I try your helmet on?" He duly obliged and handed it to me.

It seemed to perch on top of my head OK, and the others looked on amused as I did some nankering faces while I wore it. I began to prance around the stage in it, much to Brian's delight. The cop thought it was funny too to begin with, but then he asked for it back.

"No, no, no," I said. "I gotta keep it now." As the cop moved toward me I moved away nankering and making noises. The cop started to run after me so I began to run too. I led him around the stage and down the steps to the auditorium and ran between the front aisles. The cop chased after me looking panicked as the others stood on the stage laughing at the scene. I led him around the aisles and eventually back up to the stage. I guessed by now he was not going to let me keep it. Knowing I would only be able to go so far with this gag I stopped and let him catch up with me. Taking the helmet off I said to him: "I dunno, I think I've gone off it now."

The cop took the helmet and immediately put it on and relaxed again. Apparently, so he explained, he would be in trouble if he lost it and would have to pay for a replacement. I never knew that, just as he probably never realized that he could have been famous as the first cop to lose his helmet at a Stones gig.

The next day the boys were back on the road again. Eric had them booked into various clubs up and down the country including a return trip to Liverpool. This time it was not a theater but an excursion right inside the Beatles' den, the Cavern Club. The Stones received a fantastic reception there from the Liverpool fans—ironically the Beatles were in London on the same night.

While the Stones seemed to inspire hatred among anyone over 30, the tidy-looking Beatles received a kind of treatment more suited to a new puppy. Whereas the Stones represented everything degenerate and rude, the Beatles were four loveable young men with a zany sense of humor. So accepted had the Beatles become, they were chosen to appear on the prestigious Royal Variety Show attended by members of the Royal family. The show was supposedly meant to consist of acts the Queen had commanded to see, but I was sceptical about whether it actually worked like that. The Beatles further endeared themselves to the establishment figures present when John told the audience that those in the front rows could just rattle their jewelry instead of bothering to applaud. As I watched on television I tried to think what Mick might have said to them.

Before the Stones returned to London a couple of weeks later the newspapers were filled with another story apart from tales of the Beatles and Stones. In America President John F. Kennedy had been gunned down by an assassin in Dallas, Texas. For those of us who were young it was a very sad time. In Britain we saw Kennedy as someone we could have done with for our own country. We regarded our politicians as a group of old farts. They were mostly ex-Eton schoolboys who ran the country as if it were their own private club. They did not want the boat rocked by controversy or a thinking public. Kennedy was closer to our generation, almost like an elder brother figure who was fighting his own battle against the established order. Whereas our politicians appeared to kowtow to foreign powers and made appeasing noises, Kennedy simply told the Russians to "fuck off!" which they did. His spirit in some way seemed to relate to ours. Musicians at the jazz club were however quick with their sick humor and a few days later they were asking everyone, "What's Jackie Kennedy giving her kids for Christmas?" The answer was "A jack-in-the-box." Life went on.

Under the reins of the Easton/Oldham management partnership the band had now notched up more than 150 appearances across the country over the past six months—a staggering total. Fans were packing every venue to capacity, although many of them still knew very little about the band or the music they played.

The Stones had progressed from the club scene to theaters and ballrooms, but they had not made any real concessions to changing their repertoire of hard-core R&B songs. As they were reaching a wider audience it would have been reasonable to expect they would now play a few recognizable pop or rock and roll songs to make the band more acceptable. They never strayed for a moment away from their beloved pure blues songs. Even "Come On," one of the few songs recognizable from its TV airing and record sales, was discarded as the band decided they no longer liked it. The first new song the boys added was the second single that was now in the lower part of the charts. "I Wanna Be Your Man" was receiving more air play than "Come On," possibly because it also gave the disc jockeys yet another chance to mention the Beatles. I thought much of the Stones' national popularity was due to their television appearances and the strong reactions that these provoked. At the concerts you could somehow sense two sets of emotions: the girls loved the wild man look of the band and would call out the boys' names and scream; the male section remained quiet and often seemed to stare with hostility, as if waiting for an opportunity to beat the boys up. Whatever their reasons, though, the fans continued to pack the theaters.

With the second single out it was obvious the Stones were going to need another song in a few weeks' time for their third release. Andrew cajoled Mick and Keith into putting their heads together with a view to writing some original songs for the band. The other motivating factor was the potentially lucrative royalties earned from writing and publishing successful songs.

The fact that this task fell to Mick and Keith could be put down to opportunity created by the sudden evacuation of Edith Grove. Brian was more preoccupied with his domestic situation and seemed to have no spare time. Bill also lived at home in Penge with his family, as did Charlie with his parents in Wembley—arguably drum kits did not lend themselves to writing songs anyway. Mick and Keith now shared a flat, making it easier for the two of them to work together. If things had worked out differently after leaving Edith Grove, or if even they had stayed there, the arrangement might have been different. Keith and Brian would have perhaps been the most logical partnership as they both played guitars and had deep musical interests. Or maybe all three of them would have collaborated. Whatever the possibilities, in reality it was Mick and Keith who were writing the songs.

The Stones' outlook remained that they saw themselves as likely to be just another group who would be popular for two or three years before becoming unfashionable. That was the lesson of most pop music history. The ambition was to have some success and make some money for later in life—the more the better. Keith and Mick in particular could not imagine themselves being on stage as pop stars when they were 35. In 1963 it was only old "has-beens" who stayed around that long, deceiving themselves they were still as popular as ever. The

Stones couldn't identify with this—as they saw it, the band would have a three-year life span at most.

Somehow, between all the gigs, rehearsals, press interviews, recordings, and being driven around the country at all hours, they managed to come up with a handful of songs within the next couple of months. To add to the growing workload Andrew had them booked into a studio to record demos of these songs. The place he had chosen was a small studio in Denmark Street called Regent Sound.

Denmark Street was perhaps more famously known as Tin Pan Alley, the backbone of the British music industry for decades. This small ramshackle side street lay off Charing Cross Road close to the sleazy Soho club land. Music publishers had offices here and the "old boy" network unashamedly flourished. This was the place where behind-the-scenes deals took place and favors were repaid. Being at the center of the music publishing industry meant nearly all songs passed through Denmark Street one way or another.

Most of the music was crap but the sheer volume meant there would also be a percentage of good material as well. The people in control of Tin Pan Alley could secure publishing deals for the corniest songs purely on the strength of who they knew. The street had now attracted ancillary businesses such as independent recording studios and musical instrument shops. Around the corner was a members-only club named the Artiste and Repertoire, the "A&R," to which many of the music "fixers" and their friends belonged. The Stones were now recording inside the very walls that had blocked them out previously. One of Mick and Keith's songs from these sessions, "That Girl Belongs to Yesterday," was later used as a single release for Gene Pitney.

As the Stones continued to tour the country hitting the youngsters hard with R&B they slowly began to learn the craft of presentation. The singer was naturally looked on as being the leader of any band and Mick began to look for ways to manipulate audiences. Originally he would often just be plain rude about the fans' ignorance regarding music. When he announced a song as having been written by Chuck Berry or whoever, the people would look back at him blankly.

One of the first efforts I saw the band make to get the audience more involved came at St. Marys Hall, Putney, about six miles up the Thames from Richmond. During one of the songs Mick introduced a counting and clapping routine designed to involve the audience. When they got to the chorus section of one particular tune he would get the audience to clap and count to 10 along with him in time to the music. I thought it was a shitty idea but it seemed to work and everyone joined in. That was their first concession to showmanship and they kept the routine for a short period. The Putney gig was also notable for the presence of another band on the bill that day—the Detours, who would later evolve into the Who.

Two of the last gigs the band played in 1963 were back in London. One was in my old North London stamping ground at the Club Noreik on the junction of Seven Sisters Road and Tottenham High Road. The club had formerly been a small cinema before the seats were pulled out to create a dance floor. The place opened late and the acts would come on well after midnight. Fortunately the stage was set quite high as many of the crowd would be a little the worse for wear after a Saturday night's drinking. High stages were welcome under conditions like this as they would act as a deterrent to stop anyone who was drunk and antagonistic from reaching the band.

The Noreik was also only a couple of miles away from the Manor House pub where they had played the midweek gigs organized by Giorgio back in March. These now seemed ages ago.

The other gig was back in the crowded Studio 51 club. This was again treated more as a live rehearsal for new numbers than an actual gig. Something about it being over the Christmas holidays and the presence of many of the band's original followers made it seem almost like old times.

18

I STILL TRAVELED to work at the lithographic printers in Fulham, although the trip from my small bedsit flat to work each day was a real hassle. It was necessary to get a bus to Hammersmith then catch a train to Parsons Green via Earls Court. The bus service out of Barnes was often erratic and inevitably my bus became snarled up in the morning rush hour at Hammersmith Bridge, which was a major bottleneck. I eventually gave up any real pretence of attempting to get there on time and relied more on fate.

Most of the people I came into contact at with at work knew I was friendly with the Rolling Stones. At first they just used to make jibes at the band—these were easily ignored as I'd heard most of them before. The band was now being seen regularly on television and in the papers, and the comments began to subside and be replaced with questions. Most of the questions were either mundane or stupid. Workmates would still ask if the Stones ever washed or had any decent clothes. The other assumption was that they took drugs and were homosexual—the latter seemed to be a label some people tagged to anyone for a while when they first became famous. As for drugs, I laughed at the suggestions. No one realized that most of the time we did not have money for food, let alone drugs, even if we had wanted them.

Despite the jibes and innuendo it seemed people were accepting the Stones gradually, if only as knocking horses. They would look in the papers each day for any latest scandal. Quite often they would say, "I see your mates are in trouble again."

Other attitudes were gradually changing too. Following the success of the Stones around the London club circuit it seemed the owners wanted more. The departure of the Stones from these venues had obviously left a void. It was now evident the traditional jazz bands were never going to bring those crowds back. The doors were now open for virtually anyone calling themselves a blues band. There were some good ones like the Downliners Sect and Jimmy Powell and the Fifth Dimension. Even Manfred Mann switched from modern jazz, importing blues singer Paul Jones on the way. Blues was now the magic word.

With the Stones and the Beatles claiming most of the headlines the kids on the street inevitably began to copy their hairstyles. The Stones had started out with long hair more as a symptom of poverty than as a fashion statement, but now they took pride in it and there was no way they would have had it cut because of pressure from anyone else.

The Beatles had taken the chart honors over the New Year period with "I Want to Hold Your Hand" at number one. The Stones' "I Wanna Be Your Man" lurked outside the Top 10 and never rose any higher. The Stones were recording during the daytime throughout the first part of January then fulfilling bookings in and around London in the evenings. Invariably if the gig did not involve too much traveling we would end up visiting the Ad Lib club by Leicester Square until the small hours of the morning. Brian used to revel in telling me the latest episodes of their travels over a few drinks. Highlights included a recording session, which featured Phil Spector, Gene Pitney, and two of the Hollies. The session had turned into an impromptu party with everyone getting drunk and a little carried away. The two Hollies had ended up playing a bottle on one of the tracks.

Brian also told me about a gig in Scotland where he described the audience as animals. He made it sound as if the club was providing acts for the crowd to demolish. The band played on a stage protected by a metal grille as the audience hurled empty bottles and whatever else they could throw at them. The bottles crashed up against the grilles and the Stones had taken to antagonizing the audience even more by pulling faces and hurling insults. "They're all mad up there," said Brian. "It's like throwing Christians to the lions. I'm sure they would have killed us if they could. Apparently they treat all the acts like that. It's their way of having a good time. The guy pays out money for a band so they can all get drunk and wreck the place. A sort of live Aunt Sally."

The Stones' success was now beginning to be reflected in the lifestyle of the whole band. More work meant more money and most of the engagements paid a reasonable sum. Clothes were now a priority item and everyone's wardrobe now contained a wide choice of outfits. Nobody was restricted to wearing the one and only set of clothing they owned, as they had at the outset.

Mick and Brian had acquired themselves a car each and the band's equipment was much better quality. Management fees accounted for a slice of the band's takings, as did the cost of food and accommodation during road trips, but even with all the overheads taken into account it did leave each member a decent weekly wage, though not a fortune.

Andrew Oldham's profile had increased—he was the manager of a popular and successful group. He now had prestigious offices at 138 Ivor Court, Gloucester Place, near Baker Street. Ivor Court boasted a uniformed doorman who checked everyone entering, after which a short ride in a polished wood and carpeted elevator took you up to Andrew's office. It contained four or five main rooms, all newly furnished, and overlooked the edge of Regents Park. Andrew later told me it was really an apartment that he should not be using as an office at all. The band he was managing was already soaring in popularity despite the limited success of the two singles and an EP that made up their catalog to date. What would an elusive hit record do for the Stones?

Mick was driving us back to London from a gig a few days after the "Not Fade Away" release. Keith knew that the record was due to be played on a late-night show on Radio Luxembourg, the station based on the European continent, which was the only place you could hear pop music in the evenings in Britain. He leaned from the backseat of the car and started fiddling with the radio. Radio Luxembourg's reception was intermittent at best, but he finally managed to get a decent signal. We sat back waiting and listening as the DJ went through the latest records. Finally, a few minutes before midnight, the opening chords of the song started up. Except for the radio the car was silent until the record finished.

"That's the one," said Keith. "What'd you think?"

"Yeah, it's good. I like that. It's the best one so far," I said. "It seems a bit short though."

"It's meant to be, one minute 53 seconds," he replied.

"It sounds OK, just seems a bit short that's all."

Keith explained, "You may as well make them that length—they fade the records out before the end anyway. This way we get the whole record played because it's not too long."

This made sense as most singles played for an average of two minutes 30 seconds but were usually faded out before the end, as Keith had said. I looked out of the car window and saw we were somewhere in South London.

"We've got time to make the Ad Lib," said Mick.

"Where are we now?" I asked. South London was not too familiar to me.

"Yeah, Clapham Common right now," he announced across the smoke-filled car as we sped into London.

The Ad Lib club was situated in a penthouse on top of a building in a side street off Leicester Square. The glass front doors at the entrance made it look like an office building. This image was enhanced by the marble-floored foyer and the fact that there was no visible sign for the club—word of mouth was the only method of knowing it existed. A plush elevator at the rear of the foyer carried you up to the club. When you reached the entrance the club's owner would invariably be standing by his wooden desk vetting those who wanted to enter. The clientele consisted mainly of the rich and famous and their friends, although celebrity status was no guarantee of admission. Smoked-glass mirrors lined the walls and recessed lighting shone down dimly from the ceiling. Beneath the mirrors were expensively upholstered benches, with knee-high coffee tables in front of them. The dance floor usually contained a selection of attractive young women, but if you grew tired of watching them there were more private tables at the rear.

An unspoken pecking order determined who sat where. The first three or four tables on the right as you entered had become the natural preserve of the Beatles or the Stones. Whenever we arrived and the Beatles were in town they were always there before us, seated at the first table. We mostly had the second table right next to it.

The members of the two bands most likely to be found at the Ad Lib were Mick, Keith, Brian, Ringo, and George. Other pop stars mooched around mingling with film stars, politicians, and titled people. As you sat chatting, a mixed selection of tasteful music featuring artists such as Tony Bennett played seductively in the background. If you wanted to learn the words to "Green Dolphin Street," this was the place.

On one occasion Mick and John Lennon were having their usual discussion-cum-argument regarding blues music and its popularity. Sitting at the adjoining table I broke off from my conversation with Paul and interjected some remark. John stopped talking and threw his arms up in mock anger and surprise.

"Who's this? Oh it's Phelge!" he exclaimed, turning back to Mick. "I thought we were having a conversation between the two of us. If you're gonna bring all your friends in to take sides I'm gonna get my uncle. I may as well get me granny and 'er mates as well."

I saw the familiar look on Mick's face that showed he was paying full attention and wanted to be sharp.

Lennon carried on, "My mum and dad could back me up too."

"Yeah, well," said Mick, pausing. "They'd all be wrong as well!"

Brian's car was a plush gray Humber saloon. On one occasion I was riding with him on the long drive north for a gig at the City Hall,

Sheffield. As Brian drove along the motorway in the dark the head-light beams picked out glimpses of the barren countryside and the occasional road sign. Mainly there was nothing to look at except the writing on the side of trucks that we kept overtaking. After a while a light flicked on and glowed from the dash but Brian did not see it. I sat looking at it and after a couple of minutes asked him what the red light meant. He looked down at it and said, "How long as it been on?"

"About a minute or so now. What does it do?"

"I don't know. It probably means something though." As he said that the light magically went out. "Ah, it's gone out now. Just one of those things I suppose."

We drove on unperturbed, until a few miles later when the red light came back on again for a few seconds, then went off again. Then it happened once more.

"That light keeps coming on and off," I told Brian again. "Does anything feel wrong with the car?"

"No, the car seems to be OK. It's probably a loose wire or something."

The light was now staying on longer than it was off. I leaned across to inspect it. "I'll see if I can take the bulb out to shut it up," I suggested.

"I don't know what it is; it doesn't seem to be doing anything. Chuck it out the window if it comes out. I can't stop or we'll be late," Brian said. He remained in the fast lane—we were touching 90 miles per hour.

I began to run my hand around under the wooden dash panel, trying to feel if it was possible to reach the offending bulb and remove it. The light was now on permanently as if challenging us. Then there was sound like a bump and the car shook for a second or two.

"Shit, shit, shit," said Brian. "The steering's gone! Everything's gone, the engine's cut out. I'll have to try and get over."

We were still in the fast lane but slowing down rapidly. Brian tried to steer toward the hard shoulder of the motorway. He managed to glide into the center lane as the car slowed some more, then crossed the last lane, and brought the car to a stop about 50 yards from a roadside phone. We sat there thinking about what to do; then Brian tried starting it again. There was some sort of noise, but nothing from the engine. Brian cursed, then decided to climb out and walk back to the phone. About 20 minutes later a tow truck arrived.

"I don't think you're going to see it for about a week," the tow truck driver announced to Brian cheerfully. "My guess is you've run out of oil and the engine's seized up."

Brian grunted. "What do you mean, seized up?"

"Well, if there was no oil in it and you kept driving, the engine will probably be all welded together by now," the man said. "There's a service station a few miles up; I'll drop you there and you can decide where you want to go."

The driver waited at the garage while Brian asked the manager if he would call a cab to take us the last 14 miles into Sheffield. Satisfied that he did not have to go any farther out of his way, the tow truck driver asked for an autograph, then towed the Humber off into the night. When the car was finally returned to Brian the bill came to a massive £350 and the diagnosis was that we had indeed run out of oil.

One of the people who surprised us backstage when we finally arrived in Sheffield was none other than Judy—the girl who had lived at Edith Grove and had been one of our recording stars in the toilet sessions. This time we were a little better behaved and bought her a drink.

Andrew's office had now become a hive of activity as he added new personnel to the Stones' backup team. This now included a receptionist who handled all of Andrew's appointments, a guy named Tony Calder, and the publicist Andy Wickham.

Andy was a big fan of an American group who were as yet unknown in Britain and played something he referred to as "surfing" music. He would invariably color his conversations with words that he would explain were surfing terms. Anything he considered that was fantastic or great became referred to as a "wipe-out" and he became known as Andy "Wipe-out" Wickham. The band he would spend so much time extolling the virtues of was apparently called the Beach Boys, although the name meant absolutely nothing to me. His dream at that moment was for the Beach Boys to come to England and he assured everyone that "surf" music was going to become big very soon. Andy always seemed to be on the phone to California talking about his pet unknown band. I never knew the exact role of Tony Calder but he came across as the most stable person there, and I assumed from this that he ran the business end.

Andrew was also dealing with another company from Manchester called Kennedy Street Enterprises and began to have publicity material for other artists flowing through his office. During a visit to the office with Keith, Andrew asked me if I could print some publicity material for him and I said I could. Most of the work comprised an enlarged photograph of the artist with publicity blurb printed on the back. The first thing I produced for him was a press handout regarding Herman's Hermits. From then on, Andrew passed all of these things my way. Keith later showed me a magazine article on the band featuring a column devoted to me. All nicely presented with a black border, the article began, "Not all of the Stones' friends are rich. One of their best friends is Jimmy Phelge the printer . . ." They had obviously arranged that and thought it quite funny.

"Not Fade Away" was faring well in the charts but it was the B side that sounded more like the real Rolling Stones from the blues clubs. Andrew had a copy of the record lying around in the office, which I picked up and put on his player.

As "Little by Little" played, I said to Andrew that I thought Mick and Keith had written a very good song. It sounded almost like a track that could have been taken from one of the records back at the flat.

"Well, it's not bad; it's OK for a B side," said Andrew who seemed almost pleased with it. "They're gradually getting better at writing, but they're not there yet. They need to think a bit more commercially.

It takes time." Andrew had a different slant on listening to songs than anybody else and although he did not write he knew exactly what he was looking for.

Apart from hit records Andrew was also looking for more people he could turn into stars. It was as if somehow the successful promotion and arrival of the Stones had given him a new self-belief. He had turned possibly the five most-hated people in the country into a marketing and money-making success. The Stones, with their misunderstood unruly behavior and unconventional appearance, had become role models to the young while continuing as hate figures to the older generation. Andrew seemed to believe that having accomplished this he could turn anyone into anything and then sell them. He was the master of the moment.

One person I was surprised to see hanging around the office was the dapper George Bean. George was one of the hard-core Stones fans and a former drinking partner of mine back in the early days at the Ealing club. How Andrew had come across him I had no idea, but here he was sitting behind a desk. George said he "sort of worked here," though I never saw him actually do anything but sit at the empty desk day after day.

For some reason Andrew had decided to record one of Keith and Mick's songs with George as the vocalist. I had stood drinking and chatting with George many times but remained completely unaware of any musical ability. As far as I knew he never played an instrument or sang and his main talent seemed to be wearing smart fashionable clothes. He always looked well turned-out, complementing his polite and friendly disposition toward everyone. Maybe he was another dark horse like Eric Clapton, or Andrew just liked the image he projected.

Another of Andrew's ventures at this time was a female singer named Adrienne Posta. She was a small dark-haired girl, and although I knew nothing of her history, she could certainly sing and Andrew arranged for her to record another of Mick and Keith's songs.

The last nine months had been virtually nonstop. The band had been continually on the road and seemed only to stop to do more work.

In between the gigs they slotted recording sessions, press interviews, rehearsals, TV appearances, and radio shows. In March, after the band finished touring with the Swinging Blue Jeans and with "Not Fade Away" sitting pretty in the charts, they had seven days off for a well-earned break.

As the Stones' single climbed to number 4 in the *New Musical Express* charts, another London-based blues- and jazz-oriented band had a single on the way down. Manfred Mann, the jazz pianist I had seen at the club in Barnes, had charted with his new band. The record "5-4-3-2-1," a catchy if somewhat corny song, had reached number 7. The rest of the Top 20 consisted of 11 new groups and three new solo acts, one of which was Gene Pitney with the Mick and Keith song called "That Girl Belongs to Yesterday." By comparison the Beatles at this time had records that held the top three places in the American charts, where Andy Wickham's favored Beach Boys stood at number 5 and another Beatles record was at number 10.

The first real sign I saw of Brian's falling status within the Stones came at the first gig after the band's short holiday. Meeting up again at Andrew's office, the boys discovered that Charlie had not yet returned from his holiday abroad with Shirley. With a gig to do, a last-minute search took place to find a competent stand-in. After several names were mentioned they finally agreed that the experienced Mickey Waller would be an apt replacement if he was available. Another option was Carlo Little. Both had played with several well-known bands, including Cyril Davies, whose recent tragic death had shocked those who knew him. Either of the two would have been an adequate deputy as they both had a familiarity with R&B. Mickey was currently backing rock star Marty Wilde but he was free that evening so he got the job.

The demand for the Stones to play at local clubs was huge and resulted in many strange bookings. Many of the clubs were little more than village halls and not designed with built-in facilities for stars. Often there would be no separate stage or dressing room entrance and the makeshift stage was badly placed and too easily accessible by crazed fans, although in a way these factors contributed to the frenzied atmosphere. We pulled up at just such a venue shortly after arriving in Chatham, Kent.

The exterior of the building gave no indication as to the chaotic arrangements inside. We drove past an orderly queue at the entrance and around to the darkened rear. The back door and the dressing rooms were on opposite sides of the stage, which meant crossing behind the act that was currently playing. The fans started screaming and pushing as they saw the boys making their entry. The dressing room was dim and very small and doubled as the hall's storage area, with an array of boxes and broken chairs.

The main hall gave the illusion of looking big if not spacious. The ceiling was lower than at most clubs and with the vast amount of people packed inside the only thing your eyes focused on was a sea of faces. As you looked toward the far end, the faces and ceiling seemed to merge like a horizon. Around the sides people seemed to be squatting on the walls like flies. Girls waited, pressed up against the front of the stage and easily within reach of Mick's legs if he went too close to the edge. It seemed impossible for anyone to move. You could almost see the moisture in the air from the sweating clammy bodies pushed against one another.

A slightly tense atmosphere seemed evident between Brian and the other members of the band as they were getting ready. Bill was much his normal self, looking as if he was making mental notes of his surroundings. When Keith looked at Brian it was as if he was pissed off at him and he would only speak to him if absolutely necessary. Mick never looked Brian's way at all and made no attempt to speak to him. To me it was very noticeable that Mick purposely avoided any contact with Brian. For his part, Brian seemed subdued around the others and kept himself occupied with anything that did not involve conversation. I wasn't aware of any specific problem and put it down to the fact they were tense at the prospect of facing such a large crowd without their regular drummer. Apart from Bill the only one who seemed his normal self was Stu as he went about his business of sorting out the equipment.

The backstage areas were now always busy and it would usually be just the promoter plus a privileged few who were allowed in to meet the band. Some just looked at them and others spoke awkwardly or just asked for autographs. With all the distractions I was not really listening to any one conversation in particular.

Mickey Waller wore dark-rimmed glasses, but these apart he could almost have passed for the real Charlie with his jacket and tie. The only drummer I could think of who never wore a tie was Ginger Baker and no one could have passed for him. I had no knowledge of any arrangement the band had made with Mickey regarding his fee, and when Mickey brought the subject up it sounded as if he did not know either.

"What's the split on the money?" he asked Brian straight out.

Not wanting to commit himself, Brian looked vague and replied, "I'm not actually sure. I don't know how much we're getting. See Mick."

Mickey then asked Mick, "Is it a five-way split tonight?" I guessed Mick was going to nod his head in approval, and that would be that.

Mick looked him squarely in the eye. "No, it's union rates." He was referring to the agreed conditions of the Musicians Union. "It works out about 17 quid."

Mickey was unhappy at this—he was expecting an equal share of the £350 fee the band was being paid.

"Surely it should be one fifth?" he persisted. "I should get the same as the rest of you." It sounded a reasonable argument to me.

"You know it's union rates under the circumstances," replied Mick. "That's the normal deal."

"I should get 70 quid—that's a fifth," replied Mickey.

"It doesn't work like that," replied Mick. "There are expenses and commissions to be paid as well. It's 17 pounds for the night." His argument sounded equally reasonable.

The argument continued along those lines, with Mick sticking to his guns. Brian kept a low profile across the other side of the room, not wanting to be involved. I could not imagine him backing Mick's tough stance. At one point it seemed Mickey might refuse to play at all. The whole episode made the atmosphere in the dressing room even more strained. I felt sorry for Mickey Waller but on the other hand admired Mick's tough businesslike approach. £17 was more than the whole band had earned at some of their early gigs. It was hard to decide who was right. Mickey Waller had not helped the Stones achieve anything, so maybe it was fair.

Mickey eventually went on stage with the Stones and played the set in front of an almost-hysterical audience. I stood at the side of the stage with Stu and watched, barely being able to hear the band above the screaming fans. Girls were throwing things and trying to scramble on the stage. Mick teased them by almost letting them reach him. The staff around the stage area kept themselves busy preventing girls from climbing on the stage, but they'd have been little use if anything serious had happened. The Stones played for about half an hour but it was the audience that ended up being worn out. Girls were fainting from the heat and everyone's clothes looked soaking wet. It was a great show, and Mickey Waller had done a good job.

We all hung around in the dressing room afterward, waiting for the crowds to disperse before attempting to leave. Eventually I left with Brian in his car, and he drove Mickey and me back to London. The discussion continued over the gig money, Mickey saying he thought Brian was the leader of the band and Brian confirming that in fact he was. Then Mickey said how unfair it all was and Brian told him, "Everyone was feeling a bit off tonight. Don't worry; I'll sort it out. I'll see you all right."

Away from the others Brian was still his old self, but the balance of power within the band changed forever that night. Brian had opted out of any leadership role in dealing with Mickey Waller. It was reminiscent of him not wanting to tell Giorgio to his face about Andrew being the new manager. His "I'll see you all right" promise to Mickey also made me remember his words to Stu.

Any criticism toward Brian for being indecisive could equally have been levied at me a few days later, although I would have claimed it was a question of priorities. At a gig the band had played in Rochester, Kent, I met a girl who came from the nearby town of Gillingham and was the local beauty queen. I duly spent the evening chatting her up and invited her up to London for a date. The arrangement was that I would meet her at Waterloo Station beneath the famous suspended clock, the rendezvous for countless couples in the past. However on the way to the station to meet her at midday I changed my mind and decided I would get rid of her and go to the Stones' gig at East Grinstead later that night. What had seemed a good idea at the time did not appeal much to me now. I thought about the hassle of taking her back all the way across London if she was planning to go home that night. Taking her to the Stones' gig was not going to be all that practical either. Car and van space for a lift back would be short, and there was no public transport out of East Grinstead in the early hours. The other alternative was hanging around in London entertaining her. Weighing it all up I decided I'd prefer to hang with Keith and the guys instead. Understanding the girl had made a considerable journey to London to meet me I decided it would be courteous not to leave her standing around, so when I reached the station and spotted her waiting, I found a porter and paid him a tip to deliver a message to her. My instructions to him were to tell the girl in the blue coat beneath the clock that he had received a phone call saying I was unable to be there owing to illness.

I stood near one of the exits to make sure the porter delivered the message to the right person and when I saw him talking to her I went into a nearby toilet. Satisfied I had escaped from that situation and thinking the girl would be on the other side of the station by now, I left the toilet and took a roundabout route to leave the station. Walking out into the street I bumped straight into her.

"Oh, there you are!" she said. "I just got a message from a porter who said you were ill. Was that a joke?"

I lied and told her it was. Having walked into her there was now no alternative but to take her to Portobello Road as promised. When we arrived there I took her around the market and we ended up in a pub where we met a few people I knew. I was still scheming of how I might get rid of her and meet up with the band before they left London that evening. At an opportune moment I said I was going to the toilet, which was conveniently out of sight and near an exit. Excusing myself, I headed toward the toilet and kept going until I was out into the street, after which I made off as fast as I could. I figured it was a bit mean, but at least I had been nice enough to leave her with someone who would be able to give her directions on how to get home. I was able to make the Stones' gig after all.

10

BACK IN RICHMOND, Giorgio had found the ideal band to replace the Stones at the Crawdaddy. Rumor had it that he also had his new band tied to a management contract. This no doubt was in some way due to his experience in dealing with Brian. Giorgio obviously knew he now held a strong bargaining point for any up-and-coming band—his club was now known as the famous venue that had launched the Stones on their way to stardom.

With the success of the Beatles and the Stones, record companies seemed ready to sign almost anything with at least eight legs. Just as *blues* was now the magic word to obtain a club gig, so the word *group* became the key for a fast trip to the recording studio. No one wanted to be another Dick Rowe and turn down the next Beatles, because it was unlikely they would have his luck in finding the Stones straight afterward. The Crawdaddy would be a magnet for the talent seekers, just as the Cavern Club had become *the* place to be seen in Liverpool. Any band that played at either place would be off to a good start, just like Giorgio's new group, the Yardbirds.

Unfortunately my views were biased from the start. To me the Yardbirds were the first band to copy the Stones. It looked as if Giorgio had set about creating clones of his former charges. Whether they were actually any good or not seemed secondary as far as I was concerned.

It was not so much that they played the same songs as the Stones, but that they dressed the same and had long hair. Obviously I was not bigoted about long hair, but I felt that with the Stones there had been a reason for it—it was part of an attitude. With the Yardbirds it seemed as if someone had told them they'd have more chance with long hair, but perhaps it had just grown more fashionable than I thought. The Crawdaddy gig was physically the same as when the Stones had left it, but felt different. People seemed to think that if everyone stood around long enough trying to re-create the past, it would eventually come back, along with the Stones.

An unlikely addition to the Stones' circle was songwriter Lionel Bart who had written a hit musical called *Oliver* based on the Charles Dickens book *Oliver Twist*. Lionel had a musician's sense of humor and I recalled seeing him on television a few years before wearing clothes similar to those now favored by the Beatles, especially a jacket with pointed shoulders that stuck out sideways.

Andrew turned up with him at the Noreik, but this time Lionel dressed more conventionally in a dark overcoat. He also had a very conventional and expensive car parked outside, about which he was enthusing. I decided to offer him the world's most badly written song, which I had just made up while listening to his car story.

"Andrew said I should let you listen to this song I've just written," I told him.

"A song! A song! I'm always interested in a new song," said Lionel. "Tell you what . . ." He fumbled through his pockets and produced his business card. "Ring my office tomorrow; hang on . . ." He went back to his pockets and produced a silver pen. Writing on the back of the card he said, "This is my personal number. Call me there tomorrow."

I took the card and read it. "It's called the "Doo Wot" song. You wanna hear it?"

"No, call me tomorrow."

"I'm sorta busy and the Beatles are a bit interested," I lied to him.

"Er, well, let's hear a bit; go ahead; let's hear it," said Lionel, all attentive.

"Well, it goes like this." I said. Then all on one note I sang, "Doo wot doo wot doo wot doo wot Shepherds Bush. Doo wot doo wot doo wot doo wot Notting Hill. Doo wot . . . "

I continued on the same theme, substituting the names of different railway stations between the "doo wots." Lionel looked at me as if I was mad.

"The good thing about this song, Lionel, is that you can make it as long or short as you like. You just add or subtract as many railway stations as you want. What do you think?" I asked him with a straight face.

Lionel was thinking of being somewhere else. "'Er, well, is that it?" he said meekly.

"Yeah, the "Doo Wot" song. That's it." I said. Everyone was looking at Lionel for his response. Finally he recovered then asked if I still had his card.

"Yeah, sure," I replied.

"Let me see," said Lionel. I placed the card in his outstretched hand.

Lionel took the card, tore it in half, and threw it on the floor. "Don't worry," he said. "We'll call you."

Just as there had been a routine a year ago in the Edith Grove flat, there was now another, albeit on a different level. The odd visits to the Ernie and the sparse collection of low-paid gigs, interspersed with periods of hunger, had been replaced if not forgotten. The prejudices of the jazz clubs and record companies now remained only as distant memories. The current lifestyle was now a diet of theaters, recording studios, radio shows, and television programs. If this was not contrast enough there were the additional bonuses of adoring fans and public recognition or in another word, fame. The only place that served as a reminder of the past was Mick and Keith's new flat at Mapesbury Road.

In earlier times the living space inside the huge house must have been vast when occupied by a single family. Nowadays the house was divided into several self-contained flats and the two Stones occupied the one on the first floor at the front. The flat contained two rooms of which the smaller was Mick's bedroom. Keith had the larger room, which could have been used as a lounge but was furnished mainly as a bedroom. Entrance to the flat came by climbing a winding staircase overlooking an expansive hallway. Decorated throughout in a deep Regency-red color, the hallway and landing gave a sense of opulence that made you feel you ought to keep quiet. Close at hand lay a communal bathroom and a coin-operated telephone attached to the wall in the hallway.

Once inside Mick and Keith's flat any feel of Regency opulence disappeared immediately.

Keith's room had a huge dark oak wardrobe in the far left-hand corner in which hung a couple of jackets and some trousers. The rest of his clothes were generally strewn all around the room, mostly on the floor. His bed was on the opposite side of the room, permanently unmade. Being a divan, the bed was low to the floor and he had placed a record player close by on the carpet at arm's length. This enabled him to operate the machine and change records without going through the unpleasant hassle of getting out of bed. Also placed close to hand was an ashtray overflowing with cigarette butts.

Keith was fooling around with his shirtsleeves, deciding if he was going to wear cuff links or not as Mick's electric shaver buzzed in the background. I wandered around the room picking up records to see what was new. Keith went over to the player and placed the singles already loaded back to the replay position. The Everly Brothers' "Hello Amy" filled the room as I looked at a Joe Brown album featuring a Johnny Cash song. I went over to where the records played and saw a pile of books. All nicely stacked one on top of the other in a neat pile they stood wedged underneath one corner of the bed to replace a missing leg.

"Who is this guy?" I asked Keith, waving an album in his direction.

"He's guv'nor," he replied, glancing my way.

"What's he like? I see you got two of them."

"Sort of folky, modern stuff, good words; put one on and have a listen."

"Bob Dylan, never heard of him," I replied preferring to listen to "Love Hurts," which was now playing. Mick came in half-dressed.

"You wanna make some coffee before Stu comes?" he asked and then disappeared again.

They had put a huge blown-up photograph on the wall in the kitchen—it had been taken during a recording session. Mick looked down at me waving his maracas as I opened the fridge door to look for some milk. The usual bottle of green stuff was standing there to greet me. It was almost like being home. Over in one corner, dumped on the floor, was an ancient film projector and I wondered if it still worked. A box with spools of film hanging out was next to it and some of the film had come unwound and hung over the edge. Waiting for the kettle to boil, I pulled it up and looked at the still frames but they were too small to make any sense of. I then washed out some half-filled cups that had been piled high with cigarette ends.

I took a coffee for Mick into his room where he was getting dressed. Apart from its size, the only difference to the other room was that it did not have a record player. What clothes Mick owned that were not on the floor were hanging on the outside of a wardrobe or on the picture rail that ran around the room. Mick had either risen in a hurry or decided that the bedclothes also looked better on the floor. With nowhere to walk I went back into the other room.

Loose gravel rattled against glass in the window as I restudied the Dylan albums.

"What's that?" I asked Keith, not immediately sure of the sound.

"There's a group of kids of hanging about down there. Tell 'em we're not here." He was trying a jacket on and viewing himself in the full-length mirror.

"You get many round?" I asked.

"There's always some ringing the bell and stuff. Found the phone number too—we had to change it."

There were about eight girls standing around the driveway clutching various items they wanted autographed. They all appeared to be around 14 years old and were looking up toward the flat trying to obtain a glimpse of someone. I opened the window and told them there was no one around except me. Then it was the usual cries, "You're lying; tell them to come down." I gave up and closed the window on what was going to be a pointless conversation. The girls looked up with menacing faces so I waved to them and went back to reading the Dylan album cover. Keith took the Everlys off the player and put the Dylan album on. A jangling guitar followed by a harmonica filled the room. Finally a whining voice droned over the top of the instruments. I felt glad it was just Bob Dylan and not the Dylan Brothers. I decided to put the Joe Brown album on at the first opportunity.

The Empire Pool at Wembley was buzzing with activity when we arrived shortly before midday. The reserved stage-door car park was full of TV outside broadcast trucks. They all spewed out an endless supply of thick black cables that crept everywhere like some form of self-multiplying spaghetti. The gate attendant gave a look as if to say, "So you do look just as bad in real life as on TV," and waved us in, but not before exercising his authority by telling Stu where to park. Stu said, "Bollocks," and parked in a completely different spot, almost as a matter of principle.

In daylight the interior of the building seemed nothing more than an aircraft hangar with rows of banked seating along either side of the covered ice rink. The far end had a row of windows about 30 feet above the ground and reminded one of the projectionist gallery in a cinema. The control rooms for the building's spotlights and sound system were housed up there next to the security office. A makeshift partition erected completely across the end where we came in had created an area behind the stage like a huge separate hall. This part was very sparse with plain bricks and a tangle of iron pipes being the only thing to look at. A row of trestle tables stood end-to-end to form a simple counter, behind which several women dispensed drinks and snacks. Other tables and tubular steel chairs lay scattered throughout the area. The whole place resembled a wartime canteen. The stage was the other side of the partition and you could hear the events taking place there but not see them. There were no television monitor screens backstage for anyone to watch.

The show was the *Ready, Steady, Go!* Mod Ball. Virtually the entire British pop elite, new and old, were performing except the Beatles. The show was possibly the biggest pop concert ever held at the time, perhaps the first to be shown live on television. It would later prove to be a landmark in other ways.

The Stones were pounced on by photographers and press as they walked around the concert area discussing the show's format with the producers. Someone had come up with the novel idea of using a moving stage. It was a large wooden plinth on wheels that would be appear to float across the floor, under which was the covered ice rink. The only problem was there would be approximately two thousand fans dancing at the same time, and the plinth was not very high. Mick was very apprehensive.

"You mean, er, tow us through the audience on it?" he asked one of the producers.

"It will be quite safe. We'll have security people out here at the same time," replied the producer.

Mick cringed toward the others and said, "We'll get bloody killed being pulled around on that."

I thought the guy was mad—it was obvious he had not been to a Stones concert recently and witnessed the scenes. Back in the television studio he might have his audiences under control, but this was the real world. The likely result of going ahead with the idea seemed obvious, but after some more discussion and further reassurances the Stones agreed to go along with the producers' wishes.

Underneath the banked seating ran concrete corridors, which gave access to a number of small rooms. Pop stars wandered around freely from one room to the other using them as dressing rooms and many new friendships started that day. The easy part of being recognizable meant that the stars could talk to anyone they recognized without either party having to introduce themselves. They all knew each other at a glance. The place had the air of an underground town.

As the afternoon rehearsal progressed the canteen became the social center for a gathering of the stars. At one point lined up together along the wooden trestle tables were the Merseybeats, the Stones, the Searchers, and Freddie and the Dreamers. They all stood taking their relevant turns to buy a cup of tea along with a cold meat pie, egg sandwich, or packet of crisps. They may all have been stars, but there were no stars here.

Eventually the Mod Ball sprang to life and the acts got under way. The aircraft hangar underwent a complete change with the dimmed lights and audience of thousands. It was now the world's biggest party for youngsters and everyone was in the spirit. I went up into the stands where *Ready, Steady, Go!* presenter Cathy McGowan stood positioned and spent the time chatting with her. Occasionally from there she would interview a nearby audience member and introduce the next act. I watched them all, patiently waiting to see what would happen when the Stones appeared.

Depending upon what you were expecting the whole performance was a disaster or a coup. I had made my way down to a seat close to the front just as the Stones were announced—the signal for the fans to go crazy. People descended upon the mobile stage before the Stones had even reached it. The record to which they were meant to be miming played away on its own as the boys fought to climb aboard the rostrum. They were completely stranded in the crowd and had still to make the stage. Somehow they got there and managed to struggle on board, except for Charlie. Keith and Mick saw him and reached down and took hold of his arms and upper body, then tugged against the fans who had hold of Charlie's legs.

With Charlie finally on board, they tried to mime to the latter part of the record as the fans tried to climb on the stage as well. Mick kept being tugged toward the front and was fighting to maintain his balance. After being pulled, Keith disappeared but somehow managed to claw his way back. At this point all pretence of carrying on with the act went completely out the window. It became a good-natured tug-of-war set to music.

I knew the questions they were going to ask afterward, and quickly left my seat to make my way to one of the control rooms. The room had a television and I went in to watch. The security guard was watching the screen showing events down below. From here you could see both the television broadcast and the live action through the window. The TV pictures showed close-ups of the now disheveled Stones laughing at their predicament. The music continued, unaccompanied by the band. Mick's sweater looked twice its normal size after having been pulled around. From the window I could see that the stage only moved when the fans surged—the official handlers had no control over it. One minute it was stuck against the barriers, then it slowly twisted around in circles to the center of the floor.

I went back downstairs to the seats as the last few songs of the set were played. The girls were screaming out the name of their favorites and still trying to grab or just simply touch one of them. At one point Mick had to hold on to Brian in an attempt to prevent him going overboard. The last number ended, but the stage continued its haphazard journey through the crowd.

I went back to the security room to see if the episode was still being broadcast. The black-and-white television still showed the pictures of the chaos, but now without any music to accompany it. The show was completely disrupted from its scheduled format. Eventually, the airtime ran out and the program credits rolled over pictures of the out-of-control situation.

It must have been 40 minutes that the Stones spent being wheeled around by the fans before rescue came. A determined effort by all the security personnel eventually got them back to the main stage. I went down to the dressing room below.

The boys were laughing almost uncontrollably at the turn of

events. Brian was almost shrieking with laughter.

"Did you see that? How did we look?" Brian asked immediately.

"It was fantastic. The whole thing looked great. You really stole the whole show," I told him.

"I wonder what it was like on television. I'd love to have seen that," he said.

"I saw it," I said, smiling.

"Ah, no, how was it?"

"It came across totally ridiculous. Showed lots of close-ups of you guys being mobbed," I said. "No one's ever seen anything like that on TV before. It'll be in all the papers tomorrow."

The whole band was overjoyed with their reception, which by far exceeded any reaction given to the other acts on the bill. The complete episode had turned into a major publicity success for the band to boot. The producer also had a memorable show, which many saw as great television. Miraculously, given the mêlée, none of the fans suffered even slight injury. Though it hadn't come off as planned, the evening had been a major success for everyone involved.

The timing of the Mod Ball and the ensuing furor could not have been more fortunate if it had been planned. The television publicity coincided nicely with the release of the group's first album a couple of days later. Titled simply *The Rolling Stones* it was mainly a collection of songs that the band had performed during their stage act around the country. Although the album did not include any of the records issued as singles, it did feature "Little by Little" and two other Stones compositions. A week later the band would be in the somewhat unique position of having a number-one-selling album plus an EP that had also reached the top of the charts. To achieve these feats it was usually necessary to have a number-one-selling single, but the Stones were used to doing things unconventionally.

Another event that practically coincided with the release of the album was the opening up of the airwaves to commercial radio.

Enterprising Irishman Ronan O'Rahilly, who had an interest in the Scene club, became involved with the launch of this new phenomenon in Britain. Teenagers had long been aware through films that America was a mecca for radio stations that played pop music. In England there was only one station called the "Light Programme" broadcast by the BBC. The Light Programme was a mixture of comedy, panel game shows, and drama as well as music programs featuring big bands with resident singers. Pop records were broadcast for just a few daytime hours each week. The longest program was *Saturday Club*, which was a mixture of records and live music that lasted a whole two hours. To hear pop music regularly it was necessary to tune to the distant Radio Luxembourg that played pop from 7:30 P.M. until midnight.

The new commercial station, named Radio Caroline, was declared illegal by the British government. The station's location was aboard a ship anchored in the North Sea. These were international waters, but the ship's radio signal could be heard on shore. Caroline began broadcasting pop records 24 hours a day and within a few weeks most of Britain's youngsters had tuned in to it. Later on other stations such as Radio 390 and Radio London anchored offshore and further increased the flow of pop music. Whereas in the past the BBC could ban a record or classify it as "not suitable" for its playlist, the new stations had no such restrictions. With the stations being based on ships and the government's "illegal" tag, they became known as pirate radio stations.

The new radio freedom brought more exposure for bands like the Stones. The pirates also brought with them a new generation of disc jockeys. The programs at the BBC were nearly all presented by old men, some of who were ex-comedians. The pirate presenters were all young and knowledgeable about current trends. The government would spend the next three years issuing restrictions and laws against the pirate stations. These included making it illegal to advertise on them and to sell supplies to the ships. Eventually the ships were forced off the air but not before they paved the way for legal commercial radio onshore.

Brian had tired of his spell living with the Lawrences on the outskirts of Windsor and moved back to London. Somehow he had found himself a flat at 13 Chester Street in the upmarket Belgravia area. It was difficult to determine exactly whether it was a flat or just a room and if he indeed paid any money for it. The properties in Chester Street were big old Victorian houses, which would originally have been occupied by members of the gentry whose servants lived in either the attic rooms or the basement.

It was mainly the basement that was occupied and this seemed to be where any activity ever took place. A guy named Andrew lived in the basement and had a bedroom at the front. Brian's bedroom was in between Andrew's and the lounge at the back. French windows opened from the lounge into a small yard with a tree growing in the center. On the first of the six floors was a very modern-looking furnished flat, which Brian referred to as his. The only room he ever used however was the smart new kitchen and that was mainly for washing his hair in the sink. The floors above that were all unoccupied although expensively kitted out with period and antique-style furniture.

We were in the lounge, and across the room on a table stood a record player and a handful of albums. For something to do I went over and looked through them. The only one that appealed to our taste was one by Johnny Tillotson featuring some of his country-style hits. I took the record and placed it on the player, and after a few seconds Johnny started singing "Take Good Care of Her." Andrew was unfamiliar with the Stones' taste in music and must have assumed they only listened to blues. He immediately leapt up in the air and said testily, "Take that rubbish off. We don't want to hear that."

"Rubbish?" said Brian. "We like that stuff. It's guv'nor gear. Leave it on."

Brian came over and looked through the small pile of records, casting each one aside dismissively. "There's nothing else here anyway—it's a right load of shit."

Andrew, suitably chastised, said nothing more. After that it was not unusual for him to give the Tillotson record a play whenever Brian was around.

Brian made a couple of phone calls before both of us went

upstairs—it was time for his hair-washing routine. Scattered around the sink he had an assortment of different shampoos, which he would try out to see which gave the best result. As he washed his hair every day, it always had that just-washed, fluffy texture anyway. I could not see that the various brands were any different—they were all just soap—but he seemed convinced otherwise.

Brian's idiosyncratic approach to washing his hair also meant he couldn't just stick his head under the tap like anyone else, but always wanted someone at hand to pour water over him from a jug. Whenever he asked me to do this I always made sure some went down the neck of his shirt. The next part of the routine was for him to sit there in front of a small mirror and blow-dry it. If he didn't like the end result he would start over and wash his hair again. He was fiddling with his hair in the mirror when I brought up the subject of songwriting.

"I didn't realize that Mick and Keith had written "Little by Little" when I first heard it. It sounds pretty good." I ventured. Brian's face immediately dropped a little and I knew straight away I'd raised an awkward subject.

"Hmm . . . it's all right," was his sullen response.

Trying to appease him, I continued, "What about you? Have you written anything?"

"It wouldn't matter if I did; they wouldn't do it. You have more chance of getting a song recorded than me."

"Oh," I said, sensing Brian's irritation but now finding no way out of the subject. "Have you written anything though?"

"Yeah, some stuff, but they won't even listen to anything of mine," he complained. "They're not interested in anybody else's songs. Everything has to be done by them. If it's not theirs, it's no good."

The emotion in Brian's voice toward Mick and Keith was almost venomous. He clearly felt hurt and this saddened me as I'd never known him to feel like this before. I wondered if there had been a falling-out between him and the others—it was difficult to imagine them still not being close friends.

If Brian's relationship with Mick and Keith was becoming

strained, then his private life away from the band was in equal turmoil. His girlfriend Linda Lawrence was now almost six months pregnant. Much of the time they now spent together was very tense and would often result in an argument if not a fight.

Since his move back to London, Brian had begun enjoying the high life and all the perks that came with it. He loved the novelty of being easily recognized and his new life of socializing at night clubs with fellow celebrities. Linda, because she needed care during her pregnancy, was seeing less of him as she remained at home in Windsor with her parents. For her the situation must have been one of undue stress.

Brian's concept of responsibility had not changed. Often he would tell Linda he was coming to see her and then at the last minute decide to do something else. Other times he would promise to phone and then just simply forget because he was out on the town. The series of broken promises must have made Linda feel she was being deserted now that she had a child on the way. Eventually she would take to arriving unannounced at Chester Street in a highly emotional state just to grab an hour or two with Brian. This in turn would put Brian in a bad mood and they would lock themselves in his bedroom, arguing ferociously. It would invariably end with Linda sobbing and Brian making more promises he was unlikely to honor. In the midst of all these events Brian was seeing another girl who lived in nearby Chesham Place named Dawn Molloy. It was a secret he kept well hidden—no one else knew about her at the time.

As if further evidence of his talent for creating stars was necessary, Andrew decided he would start work on another total unknown. This time it was a nervous-looking female singer named Marianne Faithfull.

I was at the office handling more publicity flyers and reading through the Stones' itinerary for forthcoming gigs. Andrew was smiling and joking with a small group of people, who looked like a group of relatives who had come to London for the day to visit him. The young girl with blond hair had pale skin that enhanced her frail appearance. I looked at her, trying to decide if she was an albino or had bathed that morning in some new miracle soap powder. Possibly it was the white dress she wore that made her look so ethereal. By contrast the people with her were two middle-aged ladies, both dressed from head to foot in black. What really caught the eye was the style of their clothes, which were like those from another age, covered with fussy little edges and lace. With the long hair and clothing sported by Andrew and myself, anyone entering from the outside could have been forgiven for thinking they had stepped into a time warp. Andrew's horn-rimmed sunglasses with the specially fitted pale green lenses seemed the final touch of absurdity.

Marianne was Andrew's latest protégée, picked out from the crowd at a record promotion party for Adrienne Posta. The two other women, her mother and aunt, were acting as her chaperones, a job for which they could not have been more aptly dressed. Later I would find out that Marianne's mother was an Austrian countess, and then the origins of the clothing fell into place.

Andrew was at his most affable, working hard to gain himself credibility with Marianne's protectors. I presumed the two ladies had heard of the Rolling Stones and their reputation, but perhaps they were blissfully ignorant. The talk centered on the possibility of the young Miss Faithfull making a record. The women seemed wary and suspicious of the flamboyant Andrew's real intentions, but his polished publicist patter eventually won the day and the strange trio became part of the widening Stones circle.

The Stones had just completed their first trip abroad to Switzerland for a unique edition of *Ready, Steady, Go!* filmed at the Montreux International Television Festival. The trip had lasted three days and was a glamorous break from slogging around Britain in the van. Arriving back home it was straight back on the road again for a few days before another trip to the Empire Pool, Wembley, the scene of the eventful Mod Ball. I met up again with Keith and Mick at their Mapesbury Road flat on the morning of the show. As it had been raining there were no fans waiting outside by the gateway on this occasion.

The flat hadn't changed. Mick was on the phone and Keith was replying to some fan mail. I put the Joe Brown record on and selected the part I wanted to hear before Keith decided to play Bob Dylan again.

"Brian was saying you won't record any of his songs," I said to Keith.

"Do what?" said Keith, looking annoyed and a little startled.

I repeated myself.

Keith turned his head and called over his shoulder to Mick, "Here, do you fuckin' hear this?"

"What?" answered Mick, who was now in the kitchen.

"Fuckin' Jonesey's been moaning to Phelge that we won't record his songs. Fuckin' typical." Then Keith turned to me. "Have you ever fuckin' heard any of them?"

"No, what are they like?"

"Fuckin' crap," came Mick's laughing voice from the kitchen.

"If you'd heard any you'd know why we don't record them," said Keith. That sounded reasonable. "You want to ask him to play them to you sometime. Everything he writes ends up sounding like a fuckin' hymn."

I smiled. "Does it?"

"Fuckin' right it does," said Keith. "They're all dirges of doom. You'd need a fuckin' Welsh choir to record 'em."

I laughed. Whenever Keith argued he always showed his talent for getting right to the core of the subject.

The guy operating the gate of the artists' car park at Wembley waved us straight in—he didn't bother to give parking instructions this time. He waited until Stu had parked then came over, looked at the van, and then said authoritatively: "It's OK there," to which Stu replied, "Yeah I know, mate."

The event this week was hosted by the weekly music paper *New Musical Express*, or *NME* for short. Every year the paper had a vote among its readers and put on the *NME* Poll Winners' Concert. This was the Stones' first appearance at an awards show. Inside the setup was exactly the same as for the Mod Ball, although this time the Stones commandeered a large bright corner room, which had plenty of space. The Beatles were a few doors away and looked in to say hello.

The show was generally a mixture of the new groups who had emerged over the last 12 months and more established artists. Among those flying the flag for the new wave, along with the Beatles and Stones, were the Applejacks, the Dave Clark Five, the Searchers, Manfred Mann, the Merseybeats, and Brian Poole & the Tremeloes. Previous generations of pop were represented by the Joe Loss Orchestra, Cliff Richard & the Shadows, Eden Kane, and Joe Brown with his group the Bruvvers.

The dressing room quickly filled up with throngs of people coming and going, either to congratulate the band for their album success or just to hang out. I slipped out and made my way through the underground corridors and up into the seats to watch some of the acts. The dividing line between the two eras of pop was starkly evident.

A classic example of the old school was Eden Kane. In his shimmering white suit he prowled around in the spotlight like a tiger waiting to pounce. With everything seemingly under control, from his deft body movements to the skillful tricks with the mike and its stand, he looked very polished, the epitome of a '50s pop star. For sheer looks and presentation he should have stolen the show. It was hard to believe that his latest record "Boys Cry" was his first chart entry for two years—it would also prove to be his last. I also saw the Shadows in their mohair suits swinging their choreographed legs and guitars from side to side in time with the music. Those two acts represented the established image of professional showbiz stars.

The Stones—of course—were the complete opposite. Their stage clothes were back to being whatever they had fancied wearing that day. If they decided to move around at all it would only be to the feel of the music rather than in a coordinated routine like a bunch of puppets. The other new groups went both ways—some, such as Brian Poole & the Tremeloes, dressed uniformly but in a casual style. Much to Keith's amusement their Wembley outfits included blue leather waistcoats identical to those the Stones had once worn. The other acts dressed in suits but wore their hair long—this gave the impression they wanted to be rebels, but weren't really sure about it.

Out in the concrete canteen, disc jockey Jimmy Saville held court at one of the tables while his smooth counterpart David Jacobs introduced the acts on stage. Saville was smoking one of his huge cigars and between puffs he demonstrated his famous trick of holding about nine conversations at once. Stu and I sat close by drinking tea and listening, but it all proved too confusing to follow. Stu was complaining about the problem of removing lipstick marks from the van's paintwork. As fast as he cleaned it off, the fans would scrawl the name of their favorite Stone back again. To him it was a wanton act of vandalism and to everyone else's amusement he took it personally.

The Beatles and the Stones both performed in front of an ecstatic sea of fans who erupted during both acts. Up until the two groups appeared, the audience had given a reserved reception to the other acts in the lineup. The Dave Clark Five, who still featured in the charts with their hit "Bits and Pieces," finished to an almost embarrassing round of polite applause. This gave the impression that people would have paid the entrance fee and then been prepared to sit there all day watching nothing until the Beatles or Stones appeared. At the end of the day it was impossible to decide which of the two bands provoked the louder response—honors were truly even.

From Wembley we drove back to Soho for another meal at the late-night restaurant where we had been over a year ago. This time there were no Scottish soccer fans indulging in baby talk and collecting loose change. Instead we had to make do with talking to Brian Poole & the Tremeloes, who had also found their way there.

If the situation regarding the lack of radio stations was bad, then television was no better. For years there had only been the one BBC station showing general entertainment. A second commercial channel had later been added, with advertising breaks during the programs. The BBC now had a second channel that broadcast during the evenings only, its programming dedicated to the arts and documentaries. All three stations of course broadcasted black-and-white pictures. Stereo radio did not yet exist, although the BBC was experimenting. During such experiments you had to turn on both your radio and television. With the television tuned to BBC 2 you could receive the right-hand sound channel. You then tuned the radio to a BBC station and that would play the sound for the left side. If your radio and television happened to be situated in the wrong place, the stereo channels would be reversed. I assumed only purists would move their furniture to accommodate the BBC. Most people thought that having stereo was just a matter of having two speakers.

The evening after the *NME* Poll Winners' Concert the Stones were back again at the Royal Albert Hall, this time not carrying the Beatles' guitars for them or even opening the show, but appearing for a live TV broadcast on BBC 2. As the show was also being broadcast on the BBC Radio's Light Programme, I assumed it was going to be one of the stereo experiments. As it turned out the two programs were broadcast at different times and the opportunity for the Stones in stereo was missed. After the evening at one of the country's most hallowed venues, the subsequent trip to a village hall in Wallington, Surrey, could not have provided a more varied contrast.

If the Stones were running the Beatles close in the popularity stakes when it came to live performances, on the record front they were nowhere in sight. Although they had taken the top spot in the album charts away from the Beatles, their singles sales lagged way behind.

The Beatles had also surged ahead in cracking the American market and had already scored a number of Top 20 hits. After several changes of mind, the Stones finally opted for "Not Fade Away" as their U.S. debut release. The single soon charted, but remained lost somewhere in the lower half of the U.S. Top 100. With talk around the Stones camp of a possible American tour, the band decided to release their successful U.K. album. One track was replaced by "Not Fade Away," and the album was retitled "England's Newest Hitmakers" before being released across the Atlantic in readiness for the proposed tour. Before that adventure was to take place the band had to switch their attention back to another road trip around the U.K.

Following a few days back at Regent Sound in Denmark Street, the band headed north again. I was in Andrew's office toward the end of the week collecting some artwork proofs and mentioned that Brian had suggested I meet up with the band in Manchester.

"Are you going up there?" Andrew asked me.

"I dunno, I might do. I have a friend who is going to Liverpool who could drop me off," I said—I hadn't made up my mind yet.

"I think that's a great idea. Look, can you go up there and keep an eye on them?" Andrew asked in all seriousness.

"Keep an eye on them?"

"Yeah, you know what I mean. Make sure they don't get into any trouble or anything like that. Tell them I sent you. See that they behave themselves a bit."

I looked at him blankly and wondered if he had gone mad. The last person you would have asked to keep them out of trouble would have been me. On top of that there was no way Mick, Keith, or Brian were going to take any notice of anything I said. I imagined telling them not to do something and them retaliating by deliberately making the situation three times worse. I wondered what Andrew was thinking of. Maybe he had in mind the recent press reports concerning Mick's arrest for driving without insurance. I was bemused, but I simply said, "OK!" to Andrew and left the office.

When I arrived at the Queen's Hotel in Manchester I checked in and booked myself a room. The first person I ran into in the foyer was Brian.

"Phelge!" he exclaimed in greeting. Then his face dropped a little. "What are you doing here?"

"You said to come up here, so I have."

"Yeah, I know but . . . " He hesitated. "The thing is, I know I said come up here, but you can't come with me. I don't have any room in the car."

"Oh, is it full?" I felt like an idiot for asking.

"Well, sort of, I've got someone with me and I can't take anyone else," he confessed.

I looked at him thinking, "Why are you such an asshole, Brian?" I was annoyed with him, but just said, "That's OK."

He realized I was pissed off and said, "Look, Stu's got room in the van. I can't take you. Go with him." I walked off and left him there.

The truth of the matter was of course that there was plenty of room in the car, but that Brian had a girl with him and didn't want any other passengers. I could not see what the big deal was, but maybe he was pissed off about something else. I was used to Brian's moods although I still found them exasperating.

The rest of the guys were downstairs in the bar waiting to take part in a photo session. The place was quite full when I walked in but it did not stop Keith from greeting me.

"Hi, Phelge," he said, genuinely pleased. "Where did you come from?"

I grinned and told them about my mission from Andrew.

Keith turned to the others saying, "Hey, get a load of this. Andrew's only sent Phelge up here to make sure we don't get into any trouble." The others burst out laughing as I knew they would.

"Bloody hell," said Stu. "It's gotta be bleedin' desperate if he sends you up here. I've got enough trouble with this lot." He probably wasn't kidding.

"Any room in the van?" I asked him.

"I can't get anyone else in; it's crammed full now that we have Spike in there as well," Stu told me. Spike was his new assistant, who helped with the equipment now that the others were prevented from carrying it by screaming fans.

"I guessed it was," I told him. "Brian told me I could go with him if I came here but now he says he's got no room."

Keith turned to Mick and said angrily, "Fuckin' Brian's only invited Phelge here and then told him he can't go in the car. What's the matter with him? Fuckin' wanker."

Mick frowned and looked at Keith. "I don't know. Let him get on with it. I'm pissed off with it all."

Keith shook his head. "Fuckin' big star bit." Then he turned to Stu and said, "Phelge will have to come with us. We'll have to squeeze up a bit more so we can fit him in."

"Yeah, s'pose so," replied Stu. "We can probably get one more in there."

Brian came into the lounge a few minutes later along with the girl, went to the bar, and bought himself a drink. No one bothered to talk to him and he remained at the opposite end of the bar, keeping his distance. Again there was evidence of the strained relationship between him and the others. It crossed my mind that anyone who was friendly with Brian would probably be less popular with the others. If you were in his company and the others were ignoring him it was reasonable to assume they would shun you too. It felt like a time to take sides, but as I was not talking to him at the time it wasn't an immediate problem. I decided to let it ride and see what happened. Maybe it was because of the girl.

Brian made his own way to the photo shoot, following behind the others who were traveling in an old vintage car. The vehicle was enormous with an open top and resembled something a German officer might have used during World War II. The driver must have felt exhilarated at having some of the Stones on board for when the car reached some open motorway he put his foot down hard. The old car had probably never traveled so fast before. As the car raced along everything must have been vibrating. I was in another car close behind but after a few miles we had to drop farther back. Huge chunks of dried mud that were at least the size of tennis balls began to fly through the air. The chunks of flying earth had probably been stuck to the underside of the vintage car's chassis and wheel arches for years. Now it was all being shaken free, hitting the tires then being thrown into the air in the face of following traffic. The car looked as if it was either going to take off or collapse in trying.

Other motorists were gawking in amazement at the sight of the speeding car with the long-haired Stones on board laughing. As other traffic began to overtake them Keith began to acknowledge the passing motorists, forming a Hitler moustache with the fingers of his left hand and giving a Nazi salute with his right.

The rest of that weekend was relatively uneventful and after the final show in Manchester we began the long drive back down to London in the van. As we traveled down the motorway in the early hours, a police car pulled alongside and ordered Stu to stop the van. The problem was that one of the taillights was broken and shining white instead of red. Apparently someone had broken or stolen the red plastic cover over the bulb and it was an offence to drive without two red lights at the rear. The cops told Stu to get off the motorway and wait until it was light. It seemed like they were just being awkward, so after a short delay Stu found some red paper from somewhere, covered the offending bulb, and we continued.

I lay sprawled on the floor in the back of the van. We had started out talking but eventually everyone ran out of things to say and then gradually we all dozed off. I was in a huddled position against the side of the van feeling relaxed, warm, and sleepy when suddenly there was an almighty yell.

"Stu, for fuck's sake! Look out!" Keith was yelling at the top of his voice. I woke up with a jolt and saw Keith looking panic-stricken out of the front window. We were going headfirst toward an embankment at the edge of the motorway. Stu's body was slumped over the steering wheel—he had drifted off to sleep momentarily. He woke with a start just in time to slow the van and veer back onto the road.

"For fuck's sake, Stu, try and stay awake, man. We'll be fucking killed," Keith shouted at him again

"Yeah, all right!" snapped Stu irritably—he was as tired as anybody else. Everyone had woken for a minute or so and except for Keith and me, they drifted back to sleep. The two of us had a smoke before Keith fell asleep with the others. He just passed out in a position that would have normally been impossible for sleeping. I stayed awake, watching Stu to see if he was going to drop off again and after a few more miles he did just that. I called out as his head went down, and he immediately sat up and this time opened the window to let some fresh air in. The others remained asleep, oblivious to it all. After that I couldn't sleep anymore—it was too cold and I just sat there. The nonstop journey to London seemed to last forever. Any novelty I had enjoyed regarding being in the van with the band on a long road trip had long since worn off. When we arrived back, dawn was breaking. It was a year to the day since the Stones had done their first full professional gig in Battersea Park.

The following weekend we spent most of Saturday at a television studio just around the corner from Hammersmith Odeon. Hanging around television studios was not a particularly exciting pastime. You did see the various artists rehearse their routines once or twice but most of the time was spent standing around. Even if the band was only scheduled to perform one song you could be there five or six hours doing nothing but waiting. Radio shows such as *Saturday Club* usually worked out better. The BBC recorded that show in an old theater and usually the Stones would just go in, play their songs to an empty theater, and then leave. Sometimes there was only Stu or I in the audience, and it always seemed deathly quiet between the numbers after the hysteria of live gigs.

When the recording finished, the band should have gone to Catford in South London for a show later that evening. But first of all we headed in the opposite direction to North London and the Finsbury Park Astoria. The Astoria was another former cinema that was now a venue for live shows, and this Saturday the entertainment featured Chuck Berry and Carl Perkins. It served to show how quick and shrewd the promoters were to latch onto a trend. Just a year ago R&B would not have been a commercial proposition. Now, due to the surge of the Stones and the groups following in their wake, both Bo Diddley and Chuck Berry had already been brought over the Atlantic to play live shows.

We gained admission through the stage door entrance without any problem and made our way backstage. As we reached the wings, Chuck Berry pushed past on the way back to his dressing room. He did not look particularly approachable at the time. Another guy dressed in a cowboy suit and boots was on stage, playing guitar and bouncing around to cheers from the audience. I asked Keith who he was and he said, Carl Perkins. He did not look as I expected, and we both thought his flashy western suit looked a bit outrageous for a rock and roll show.

When Perkins came to the end of his act, the others went off in search of Chuck Berry, hoping to meet him. It turned out that he had locked himself inside his dressing room and that the visiting Stones were not at all welcome. One rumor doing the rounds that night concerned Chuck Berry's terms of payment. The story went that after having been cheated so many times in the past by unscrupulous promoters, he now did not trust anyone and insisted on payment before he walked out on stage. The figure mentioned on this occasion was £1,000, in cash. The detour trip to see Chuck Berry had been disappointing—not only had we missed missing seeing him play but he had shown no interest in meeting the Stones. Quite possibly he had never heard of the Stones and had no idea that they played his very own music.

As the month progressed the proposed tour of America became a reality. One of the last things the band would do before leaving was a small seven-day tour featuring singing duo Peter and Gordon. They had come to prominence through a connection with the Beatles. Paul McCartney was dating actress Jane Asher and arranged for her brother, Peter Asher, and his friend Gordon Waller to record a Lennon and McCartney song. Their version of "A World Without Love" was a hit, reaching number one in England and later matching the feat in America during the Stones' tour.

After a couple of shows in Coventry I traveled back down to London with Brian the next day, when the band was again recording *Saturday Club*. This time it was just him and me in the car—the incident in Manchester had passed without any further reference. Brian had taken some time getting ready and was running late. On the M1 motorway he pushed his Humber to its limits. The car was probably not meant to do more than 100 mph. As he pushed the speed up to 110, it sounded as if the engine was at its absolute threshold. Brian just had to push that bit extra though and kept his foot down until the gauge reached the 120 mph mark. The steering column was visibly vibrating and making the most awful metallic noises while the rest of the car shuddered in unison. I had visions of something breaking and the car going out of control, leaving us splattered on the roadway somewhere. Despite my suggesting he slow down a bit, Brian kept his foot down and the car careered onward at the crazy speed. I tried to put him off driving so fast by mentioning the incident regarding the oil running out and the resultant expense. Brian was in one of his devilish, couldn't-care-less moods, laughing and saying, "I want to see what happens." He was lucky that nothing did happen, except that we arrived early at the BBC having completed the journey in exactly one hour.

Following a show in East London we went back up north to Birmingham and stayed at the Grand Hotel. A couple of weeks earlier the Stones had stayed at the Grand Hotel in Bristol and made the newspapers after being refused lunch in the hotel restaurant because they were not wearing ties. The whole thing seemed petty and stupid and some of the reporting depicted the event as a victory for the establishment. The restaurant manager had made some inane comment about treating a king exactly the same. It probably never occurred to him that there was little chance of a king staying at his hotel if he was going to be treated like the Rolling Stones. This time in Birmingham they chose to wear some ridiculous-looking ties, which made a mockery of the house rule.

The Grand was one of the traditional hotels where you still left your shoes outside your room for cleaning overnight. Having read escapades in comics about someone swapping all the shoes around during the night, I had always wanted to do it. Rather than just swap one pair of shoes with another a few rooms down I had to make it more confusing. After midnight I began taking the shoes from my floor and changing them over with the ones on the floor above. On one of the trips back down I rounded a corner and came face-to-face with the night porter. With a pair of someone else's shoes in my hand I promptly asked him, "Excuse me, where can I take these shoes to be cleaned for the morning?" The porter replied politely, "Just leave them outside your room, sir; I'll make sure they're done. We come round and do them during the night."

The next morning I was with Stu when we checked out at reception. Behind the desk was a big pile of muddled shoes, while a busy clerk in the background spoke into the phone asking, "Can you describe them to me?"

The compère for the tour was a comedian named Tony Marsh who had also toured with the Beatles. I had met him a few nights earlier in one of the dressing rooms although not in the friendliest circumstances. The Stones were tuning their guitars and Tony was sitting on a table talking to someone. He had a resonant, booming voice so that it seemed impossible not to overhear the topic of conversation. He was relating some funny story and I chipped in with a humorous remark of my own. Tony took exception to the interruption and leapt up from the table.

"Who are you, you flash bastard? What are you doing here? Fuck off out of it," and with that punched me straight in the head. While I was still off balance he came at me again throwing more punches and shouting, "Who let you in?" Keith had turned and seen what was happening and without even removing his guitar he jumped to my aid. "You bastard," said Keith. "You fuckin' leave him alone." Keith punched Tony in the face and then Brian joined in, aiming more blows at him.

"He's with us. He's our mate so mind your own fuckin' business," said Keith.

"He doesn't have to ask you to come in here; he's with us," Brian reiterated angrily, joining up with Keith. "Fucking lay off him."

Mick turned around asking, "What's going on?"

"It's this fuckin' asshole having a go at Phelge," replied Keith, still with his face a few inches from Tony's.

"You fuckin' bastard," Keith continued. "You touch him again I'll stick this guitar in your fuckin' head."

"All right, all right. I'm sorry, fellas," Tony said. "I thought it was some flash bastard who'd found his way in here. I didn't know he was with you."

"You pick on him and you pick on us," said Brian.

I was touched by the boys' response in coming to my aid. Later Keith told me Tony was forever pissed and losing his temper. It was true Tony liked a good drink and unfortunately it was always Scotch and he would end up getting aggressive. The next night when he saw me in the dressing room he came over and apologized.

"Look, man, sorry about last night, but I'd had too much of the old jolly. I didn't know who you were. Why don't you come round to my place for a drink when we get back to London?" I accepted his offer and after that we became good friends.

The short tour finished a week later at the Adelphi Cinema, Slough, just west of London. The final night of a tour always led to an end-of-term party atmosphere with members of the bands' entourages often playing practical jokes on each other during the acts.

This tour was no exception, except that one of the stunts went disastrously wrong.

Poor Tony. The misfortune that befell him that night was pure accident. The Stones had been on stage and Tony decided to try to put them off their act by "mooning" at them from the wings. He dropped his trousers, bent over, and pointed his back side toward the stage. Unfortunately he was a foot or two too far out of the wings and was seen by some of the audience. These people turned out to be parents who then lodged an official complaint. Tony had to appear in court later and was duly fined for his misdemeanor. The whole episode became one of his favorite stories and I heard him recount it many times afterward.

The day after the "Marsh Moon," the Stones were yet again back at Wembley. This time the occasion was the Pop Hit Parade, which was very similar to the previous show with its mixture of old and new acts. This time the slick professional with the polished presentation was Adam Faith, who had a brand-new backing group called the Roulettes. I had seen him several times before and made a point of going to the seats to watch him again. The material he used that night was arguably not his best, but he certainly worked hard at being dynamic. Wearing a gray mohair suit he made full use of the stage and, as would become popular with other singers later, took his jacket off with a flourish and hurled it to one side. Even this was carefully orchestrated though—I noted that he threw it to the side rather than into the audience; otherwise, he would probably never have seen it again.

"The Rolling Stones went down an absolute bomb in San Bernardino on Friday night." So spoke Tony Calder on the message on Andrew's answering machine. Peter Meadon laughed, saying, "I wonder if he realizes what he's said." The phrase "absolute bomb" signified a terrific show in England, but in America the meaning was the complete opposite. I guessed it depended on the nationality of the person calling and was sure Tony used it in the English sense.

Peter Meadon was a freelance publicist, the same occupation as Andrew before he took on the Stones. A frequent visitor at Ivor Court, Peter was a natural comedian who always had a quip or two ready and got on well with everyone. Even his clothes made you laugh and looked as if they had been handpicked to match his personality. He favored light-brown suits covered in large check patterns, which made him resemble a bookmaker or an off-duty clown. Anyone who he considered to be hip or cool he referred to as a "face." Other people he would categorize as "a bit of a pleb."

While the Stones toured America, I stayed at Keith and Mick's flat in Kilburn and spent my evenings as usual visiting the clubs and socializing. One evening I met up with Peter at a bar in Shaftesbury Avenue. From there we went on to a party at a small mews house near Kings Cross that lasted about three days. It started out as a one-night affair, but people had such a good time they just hung around afterward. The highlight was when somehow American blues artist John Lee Hooker got to hear about it and arrived at the door with his guitar and suitcase. He was accompanied by a girl and a very large guy who looked every inch a bouncer or bodyguard, so nobody was going to try and stop them coming in. John Lee also brought his personal supply of booze, the sign of a man who has been to a few parties where stocks had been running short at the end of the night. Wisely he kept his liquor in his pocket. He eventually got around to taking out his guitar and entertaining everyone for about an hour, finishing off with "Boom Boom." With the entertainment over, the three of them commandeered one of the bedrooms overnight and left early the next morning. The whole occurrence left one with the classic image of a traveling bluesman with guitar in one hand and luggage in the other.

One of the "faces" on the scene was a midget. Always dapperly dressed in a smart suit and tie, he was often seen on the club circuit in the company of Peter Meadon. The two of them could have easily been mistaken for a vaudeville act. Peter was known for his charm and wit, but also for being unusually squeamish at the hint of any trouble or physical violence, no matter how slight. People who knew this often pretended to be annoyed and would threaten to hit Peter just to watch him squirm and try to talk his way out. To everyone's amusement Peter would perform the same routine of mock bullying on the midget whenever they were together.

The midget's first name was Mickey, but Meadon had dubbed him "Mickey the Monkey," and everyone referred to him as that behind his back. On the second day of the marathon party Mickey the Monkey, badly in need of some sleep, had flaked out in his suit in one of the bedrooms. Peter discovered him spread-eagled across the bed in a deep sleep, oblivious to anything going on around him. Tiptoeing stealthily around the room, Peter gradually bound Mickey the Monkey by his wrists and feet to the bed using telephone cable and some pull-cord from the curtains. Satisfied with his handiwork, Peter closed the bedroom door, expecting to hear his victim wake up and start yelling for help at some point. A couple of hours later we were discussing what to do next and everyone made a spontaneous decision to leave the flat and go on to a gig, forgetting all about the hapless victim. It was nearly two days before the girls who lived in the flat returned to set Mickey the Monkey free.

A week later I became Peter's latest victim outside the *Ready, Steady, Go!* studios in London. Fans seemed to develop the powers of detectives when it came to finding out every little detail about their heroes, from ex-directory telephone numbers to the identities of all their friends. Some of them had come to recognize my name and identify me after I'd been seen in the company of the Stones. A large group of more ardent fans would always wait outside the studios hoping to obtain a glimpse or autograph.

That Friday, as I left with Peter intending to go for a drink, the usual gathering of girls was clustered around the door. Normally it was no problem for me unless I was with Brian or one of the others. As we walked out, the girls pushed forward expectantly before noticing the lack of Stones and asking disappointedly who we were. Peter turned around pointing at me, said, "This is Phelge," then jumped into the waiting taxi. Suddenly about 30 girls screaming my name jumped on me and subsequently bundled me onto the pavement like a sack of potatoes. Hands were pulling at all parts of my body and clothing as I rolled about beneath them with visions of being crushed or suffocated. The whole experience was becoming quite frightening, but after one of those moments that seem like an eternity a nearby police officer came over and somehow dug me out. Needless to say, as I got up Peter's laughing face greeted me from the taxi window as it pulled away. Eventually I got another cab and asked the driver to drop me off at the pub. I walked in looking like a tramp with my shirt torn and body covered from head to foot with dust from the pavement. I was cursing Peter and felt a complete fool as everyone stared at me, sniggering behind their drinks. Peter of course did not show up.

The incident reminded me of one of the Stones' gigs I had been to where the venue was a ballroom or theater on the end of a pier at a seaside resort. Having parked the cars on a hill nearby we had to run the whole length of the pier immediately after the show ended. The surface of the pier consisted of wooden planks with gaps in between and the Cuban-heeled boots we were wearing seemed just the right size to slip between the planks. The Stones set off at speed but I just loped along casually a few yards behind with my hands in my pockets, not taking it too seriously and mainly concerned with keeping my boots out of the gaps. Keith turned around and called back, "For fuck's sake run!" When I looked over my shoulder the pursuing fans seemed to have reached the speed of Olympic sprinters. In the end I was running flat out as they closed in fast. It was only a security guard slamming closed an iron gate behind us that ensured our safe escape from their clutches. Having experienced what happened when the fans did catch up with you, I realized why the Stones always ran like mad.

While the American tour continued I decided to renew my acquaintance with the obstreperous Tony Marsh. He lived close to the Whiteleys store in Bayswater where I had bought the Miles Davis record during the shopping trip with Charlie. Tony's premises belonged to a bookmaker and a sign on the street door indicated that his flat was on the first floor. When you rang the bell he would open the window and throw a bunch of keys down and shout, "First floor."

Everyone was welcome at Tony's, day or night, and if you brought something to drink so much the better, although it was not a condition. The guy just loved to party at all hours of the day. There might be no one else there when you arrived, but by the end of the evening there would be a roomfull of people. Tony knew every pop star and an equal number of film stars, some of whom occasionally dropped by unannounced. Tony would stand in the middle of the room, drink in hand, entertaining everyone with his stories and the caustic wit that spared no one, not even himself.

The cricket season had started and an international "Test" match was being shown on television starting at 11 o'clock one morning. Tony and I decided to get a few beers in and relax in front of the TV. Like so many cricket matches this was a long and drawn-out affair featuring long periods of inactivity that made us feel even more lethargic. We sat there drinking beers, only talking occasionally and gazing at the TV. Trying to liven things up, Tony broke the silence.

"What did you do last night?" he enquired uninterestedly. I sat there watching some rare movement on the screen and a few moments passed until I answered.

"Went to some party." More silence followed.

"Who was there?" asked Tony. The question hung in the air for a while.

"The Dutch Swing College Band," I told him. "They played a few tunes."

Tony grunted. "Any chicks around?"

"Yeah, some. I ended up with some bird from Sweden."

"Malmo?" asked Tony. I thought for a while.

"Dunno, I can't remember. Malmo? No, I think her name was Ingrid or something."

We sat there silently as a few more seconds ticked past.

"You stupid bastard," growled Tony, not taking his eyes off the television.

"Do you know her then?" I asked him. Tony turned his head and looked at me in disgust.

"You stupid bastard," he repeated. "Malmo's a fucking city not a bird. Was she from Malmo?"

I laughed. "I didn't know that."

"A fucking bird named Malmo!" He scowled, shaking his head. He must have decided the cricket made more sense and stopped asking me about the Swedish girl, whatever her name was.

One night after leaving Tony's place a little the worse for drink I decided to pull a stunt on him. At the corner of the street stood a phone box and I stepped inside. Dialing the emergency number I waited for a reply and asked for the police. A voice came on saying, "Scotland Yard."

"Can you come quick?" I blurted out, trying to sound panicky. "A guy named Tony Marsh has been shot. There's blood everywhere." I gave them the address and got out of the area as quick as I could.

Back at Keith and Mick's flat I wondered how Tony had got on with the cops and after about an hour the hallway phone rang. I went out and answered it.

"You bastard!" I recognized his voice.

"What's up?"

"What's up? You bastard. I'll tell you what's up," said Tony.

"What?" I asked, laughing to myself.

"The cops. I must have had every fucking police car in London here," said Tony.

"What happened?"

"They came rushing up the stairs, dogs an' all," he said. "I was in the lounge and heard all this pounding on the door. I thought someone was breaking in. When I open it, there's a load of cops standing there."

"Really?" I said.

"One of them asked me who I was and when I told him he said, 'You're supposed to be dead!' I told him I only die on stage. Then they all came in and looked around. Took my details. They were really pissed off. There were about 12 squad cars outside. It was a great gag, fucking great gag, Phelge."

I laughed. "What did they say?"

"I've got nothing to worry about, man. No problems. I'm only ringing you because I had to give them your name and address and they'll be there soon. You bastard!" With that he hung up.

I looked out the window at the half lit deserted street. Was he kidding or not? I hung around for a while smoking and half-expecting to see flashing blue lights as a police car came screaming down the road. Eventually I decided on a policy of not answering the door or the phone and went to bed. Nothing happened that I knew of. Tony had just been getting his revenge by spoofing me.

Not much news was getting back to the office regarding the Stones' progress on the tour. I rang Keith and spoke to him at one of the hotels where they were staying. He was generally "knocked out" with America, saying they had been to the Chess studios and that the tour was going great. We only spoke briefly as he was busy with a press conference and I was running out of change for the pay phone, so I didn't find out much more. I had to wait until they arrived back in England, when we met up again at the office for a full debriefing.

The boys had spent a small fortune on clothes while they were away and were determined to show them off back home. Most of the clothing was lightweight American summer wear and Charlie looked particularly cool in a finely striped blue-and-white jacket. Andy Wickham described it as "Surf Wear." Some of it certainly looked as if it belonged on a beach.

I asked Keith about the television show when the band had met Dean Martin. He turned up his nose, describing Martin as "a right fuckin' offer." Apparently he had given the band a hard time, making them the butt of sarcastic jokes at every opportunity. Mick had tried to be sarcastic in return by saying it was "so nice to have Mr. Martin on our show," but that sounded somewhat tame, if not childish. The band had been both disappointed and annoyed at being treated that way.

If the Martin show had been the low point, it soon became overshadowed by the trip to Chicago and Chess records. Brian was still incredulous at the fact that he'd discovered one of his musical heroes at the studio painting the ceiling. Muddy Waters was up a ladder when they arrived and had climbed down to welcome the Stones and help carry their guitars into the building. Keith revealed that some of the "live" recordings issued by Chess were not recorded that way at all. In the Chess archives were reels of tapes with nothing but audience noise recorded upon them. Chess used these to dub the "live" effect onto whatever tracks they chose. When I asked Keith what the likelihood was of getting the same taped audience on two different records he replied, "Not much chance, they've got fuckin' miles of it."

Andrew's staff continued to grow and the latest member was Reg, who for the want of a better description was Andrew's personal aide. Depending on who you spoke with, Reg's function was described as assistant, driver, or bodyguard but was probably a combination of all three. Reg was well-spoken and articulate and dressed in dark blazers or suits, always with a tie. Most of the time he was friendly and easy-going but he could suddenly switch and take on a menacing air. Sometimes it was difficult to tell if he was just acting or was really annoyed.

The Stones were standing around Andrew's desk as I stood out in the hallway looking up at a poster-sized photograph. The neatly framed portrait showed Andrew, looking dominantly down from behind his green-tinted sunglasses. Reg suddenly came running out of the office over to where I was standing and grabbed me by the throat. In his other hand he held a gun that he placed at my head.

"Right, Phelge, it's all over. We're going outside." With one hand still at my throat Reg used the hand holding the gun to open the door and dragged me out into the hallway, then pressed the elevator button.

"Stop fucking about!" I said as he bundled me into the lift.

"Shut up! We're going up to the roof. I've had enough of you," roared Reg. "You open your mouth again, I'll shoot you right here."

The lift reached the top floor and Reg pushed me out in front of him and through the fire exit door onto the roof. I guessed he was kidding, but did not have much option other than to go along with him. From the roof you could see over London, and it looked a long way down. Not being one for heights and with a gun behind me I did not feel too secure.

"Right, Phelge, good-bye." Reg pulled the trigger.

An enormous bang went off from somewhere behind me and Reg started laughing. I turned around and saw he had been pointing the gun in the air. "That had you worried, didn't it?" he said.

"No, I guessed you were kidding," I said.

"What? What? So, you think I was kidding, do you?" said Reg. He grabbed me again and pointed the gun back at my head. Then he shouted, "Bang!" and started laughing once more. Then he fired the gun toward the sky again.

"What if that lands on someone's head? Will it stick in them?" I asked, imagining the bullet hurtling back to earth.

"No," said Reg letting his breath out with a sigh. "It will just float back to earth. There won't be any impetus left. You want to try it?"

He held the gun out and I looked at it. "No, thanks," I replied. "Where did it come from?"

"It's Keith's. He brought it back from the States with him. Come on, let's go down," ordered Reg, now happy with his little joke. Once back in the office he informed Keith that his gun seemed to be working OK.

One of Reg's tasks was being in charge of Andrew's new car, a brand-new metallic-blue Chevrolet Impala convertible. The soft top opened or closed automatically at the push of a button. Andrew loved demonstrating how it worked particularly when lots of people were around to watch. On one occasion when Brian and I were passengers, Andrew parked outside a cinema in Leicester Square. Leaning forward he pushed the magic button and the roof lifted high up into the air and gradually folded itself away at the back of the car, just above the rear seat. People on the pavement paused to watch the smart American car. With a look of satisfaction on his face Andrew decided to close the top a minute or two later, in case anyone had missed seeing it the first time. Pushing the magic button again the roof began to unfold and rise in the air until suddenly it became stuck halfway. Pressing the switch again moved the roof backward and forward but would not close it. The motor driving the mechanism whined under the strain and the roof waved about above us like a gigantic flapping umbrella. Andrew had now attracted quite a crowd of amused onlookers. Finally, thinking it was some sort of stunt, a policeman came over and told him to stop mucking about and clear off. We drove off with the roof still in the air.

On Friday June 26, just after the Stones arrived home, their next single came on release. "It's All Over Now," newly recorded at the Chess studios during the American tour, had been rushed back across the Atlantic for release. At lunchtime Brian and I went to a small pub off Shaftesbury Avenue called De Hems, which was a known hangout for members of the music press. With the sun streaming down outside Brian had chosen to wear a thin black-and-white hooped sweater to stay cool.

Once inside the pub we sat by the open door to catch any breeze. Brian decided he was not going to buy any drinks but would instead take advantage of the eager-to-be-friends journalists. He answered a few questions and when offered a drink kept choosing something that was two or three times more expensive than the average beer. He had all sorts of "long" drinks, but mainly Pimm's. I sat back as the pressmen pontificated about R&B and fawned all over him. I recalled Keith describing them previously, "A bunch of posers in their 30-quid suits that they saved up for all month."

After finishing the liquid lunch off with a couple of Scotch and Cokes we finally made our way over to the *Ready, Steady, Go!* studios. Brian met up with the others to get ready for the broadcast while I went to the Green Room. Sitting on the far side, like a queen observing a troupe of court jesters, was one of Marianne's ladies-in-waiting. Andrew was talking with Marianne and seemed to be trying to prize her away from the watching eyes. I concluded that Andrew had brought them there as an introduction to the glamour of show business.

It was now well known that Mick's girlfriend was Chrissie Shrimpton, but a stupid rumor had begun circulating that linked him romantically with the show's presenter, Cathy McGowan. Someone had probably imagined the two of them as a fantasy couple and it had built from there. After the Stones performed the new single, Mick did an interview with Cathy and poured cold water on the stories of their impending marriage.

Later that night we ended up at a special party-cum-concert at Alexandra Palace. As befitted its name the venue was indeed palatial and had been built at vast expense in 1873 on top of a hill overlooking North London. The Palace had burned down almost immediately after opening but was rebuilt in 1875. In the 1930s the BBC used parts of the Palace, and it eventually became famous when the first black-and-white television pictures were broadcast from there. With a huge transmitter on the roof that stretched up toward the sky it was now a well-known landmark.

The party was to welcome the Stones back from their U.S. tour and they duly obliged by playing a couple of short sets. The celebrities strolled about and mixed freely with the other guests, who included a few familiar faces. One of the first people I spotted was the irrepressible Peter Meadon who greeted me by saying, "I see you're still alive, then?" We had a few drinks and a good laugh together over the "mobbing" incident outside the television studio. With Peter as ever was Mickey the Monkey, who looked none-the-worse for his two days in captivity, although he seemed even smaller than before—perhaps he'd shrunk through dehydration. To complete the memories of the legendary party, professional lodger John Lee Hooker was there and performed again on the stage. Then someone tapped me on the shoulder saying, "Hello baby, you on the run?" I turned round and looked into the laughing eyes of Tony Marsh.

If the Stones had made some progress toward becoming acceptable to the general public, their attempts came unstuck during another TV show the following week. The occasion was their performance or perceived lack of it on *Juke Box Jury,* which I suspected was going to be eventful even before I saw it.

The show had been popular for a few years and had a simple format. A panel of four celebrities would listen to a section of a record then vote by pressing a buzzer and triggering the illuminated scoreboard, which would indicate if the record was a "Hit" or a "Miss." In between the listening and the voting each panelist would give his or her comment on the record. Another panel made up from the studio audience would vote afterward to show if they agreed with the "jury." BBC stalwart David Jacobs hosted the show, although I thought he had little talent beyond his dinner jacket and posh voice. Jacobs was from the old school of BBC disc jockeys, most of whom seemed out of touch with modern music trends. I always got the impression that Jacobs was snobbish and would not normally listen to pop music other than when he was being paid to do so. Putting him with the Rolling Stones was like trying to mix oil with water.

I'd given up watching the show after a program in which the panel had agreed that the Pat Boone record "I'll See You in My Dreams" was the best of the evening, then promptly voted it a "Miss." However, as the Stones were due on I had to watch it and settled down in front of the television at Brian's place in Chester Street. I wasn't expecting the boys to partake in the usual showbiz platitudes that were favored by most guests. It was not going to be the usual, "Ha well, Johnny's a friend of mine; he'll be disappointed I'm voting it a 'Miss.' He'll probably keep my lawn mower now." The Stones were going to say it was either "crap" or "great." As it transpired they were almost polite and seemed to be bending over backward so as not to offend anyone. The records that came up on the playlist were really uninspiring, the sort of stuff that the Stones would have immediately turned off. But rather than sit there slating everything or making inane remarks, they clammed up and said very little, perhaps for fear of being misconstrued. They also seemed to be waiting to hear a record they could talk positively about.

Immediately I heard the first few bars of the next song I knew they were going to like it. That was the Everly Brothers' "Ferris Wheel" and although not the Everlys greatest it was by musicians they respected and was arguably the best record on the program. After enthusing about the Everlys, they caused outrage by describing the next number, one of Elvis's mundane film songs, as "dated." This incensed rockers up and down the country who saw this as an insult to their King. The Stones, with cigarettes in their mouths and little to say for themselves, had somehow done it again.

There was another flood of criticism the following week from people who saw the band as boring, rude, illiterate, and arrogant. I just thought it reaffirmed what we knew all along—that the whole Stones thing was a question of attitude or how you perceived things. Some people still did not understand what they were all about.

I was in the West End on a shopping trip when I took a short cut down a side street. Engaged in thought, I was not taking too much notice of what else was going on around me. A black cab pulled alongside and expecting the door to open I moved away from the edge of the pavement. I kept walking and the cab began to crawl along beside me with its passenger door now wide open. Still not taking any real notice I just kept moving and the cab followed. I thought I might be in the way and looked round to check. Propped up in the doorway of the moving cab, with one arm on the roof and the other over the open door, stood Keith. He asked curtly what I was doing in a manner that suggested I was jerking him around by making the cab follow me. I got in and we ended up in Act One, Scene One, a coffee bar the band sometimes used as a meeting point before gigs.

Following a trip to a shirtmakers in Soho we spent the afternoon wasting time before eventually making our way to meet Brian who had been making a solo television appearance as a panelist. From there we traveled around with Brian in his car, flitting aimlessly from club to club and still unsure about what we wanted to do. Somehow we ended up driving around the Earls Court area and decided to make an impromptu return trip to Edith Grove.

We pulled up outside the front door as we had done many times before and I noted the iron bar was still missing. The street door was wide open, as if it had been like that since we left, so without even considering if we would be welcome we marched straight inside. There were still no lightbulbs it seemed, and we climbed the stairs up to our old kitchen.

A young guy in a suit was holding a candle and looked out to see who it was. He turned to some friends behind him and said excitedly, "It's the Stones." There were three of them in the kitchen, all looking like office workers of some kind. Keith and Brian chatted with them and I looked around the room as much as was possible in the gloom. "Jenkins" and "Humphrey," the evidence of my gobbing on the walls, were still there but I did not point them out to the newcomers. The place looked as slimy and repulsive as it always had and I wondered why they wanted to live there. Maybe it was because the Stones had. They were nice friendly young guys and one of them offered us coffee. We declined—everything was so dirty and it was not our dirt anymore. Maybe it actually was still our filth, but it didn't seem the same. The guys asked where we were going next but we side-stepped this by saying we were just passing. When we left we had an invitation to "come back anytime."

Leaving the flat we decided to go back to the West End and maybe visit the Ad Lib club. As we reached the center of London Brian asked, "Aren't the Beatles having a reception or something, somewhere?"

"Yeah, at the Dorchester, I think," said Keith.

"We could call in there. Shall we?" Brian sounded pleased as if his idea showed great genius.

"Yeah, why not?" said Keith. "Let's go!"

After parking the car the three of us strutted boldly through the main doors and over the plush carpet like intruders entering a castle. Pillars of ornamental marble footed by green plants surrounded us as we made our way across the lobby and up a few stairs with gold handrails either side. We looked for an indication of where the Beatles might be; then a stout man in a gold-braided uniform and top hat strode out and barred our way. Looking down at us he said, "Yes, gentlemen?" It was a polite way of asking what the fuck we thought we were doing.

"We're the Rolling Stones, and we've come to see the Beatles," Brian announced.

"I see, sir. They are in a private reception," said the man. That meant, "Fuck off. You're not invited."

"Can you tell them we're here?" Brian asked, meaning, "Go and fucking find them."

The man had by now realized it was the Rolling Stones. "Could you write your names down, sir?" he asked. Brian wrote something on the pad and the guy took it saying, "Wait here please, gentlemen." This was Dorchester-speak for "Don't touch anything or burgle the rooms."

The uniformed man returned shortly and gestured with his arm. "This way, gentlemen."

"Thank you, my man," said Keith, showing uncharacteristic restraint. The pair exchanged hostile glances, but nothing was said and the we were led through the hotel and into another world.

ALL ACTIVITY IN the room ceased, as if the world had stopped turning for a second. A man in a dinner suit, who was bald except for traces of white hair above his ears, turned and squinted through his monocle at us. A glass of red wine in his hand that was en route to his mouth stopped in midair, and he stood motionless behind a cloud of cigar smoke. An elderly woman in a tiara nearby also looked in our direction, her face frozen and her mouth hanging open. Even the pearls around her neck, which looked like accessories to match her teeth, momentarily stopped moving. The remaining occupants of the room, including the string quartet, stood hushed and motionless. Eventually a few people began whispering, this grew to a buzz, and soon sound levels in the room returned to normal.

All the men were elderly and wore black dinner suits. It felt as if we were in an expensive club for ex-colonels and their ladies. Velvet sofas, ball gowns, and jewelry made up the backdrop along with aspidistras and palms. From somewhere amid the aristocrats, also wearing dinner suits and bow ties, John Lennon and then Paul McCartney emerged to welcome us. Paul obviously felt self-conscious about meeting the Stones in such formal circumstances. He seemed sheepish at first, like a schoolboy who had been discovered doing something naughty.

"We're only dressed up like this for the bigwigs," said Paul, indicating his suit. "They're all here tonight."

"Don't worry," Brian replied. "We were just looning around and thought we'd drop in."

"We're glad you came," said John in a hushed voice. "It's really boring, but it's one of these things we have to do."

"These are all the money and EMI people," Paul explained, looking round.

A waiter appeared with glasses of champagne and wine on a silver platter and held it before us. As we took our drinks some photographers who I hadn't previously noticed appeared from nowhere and cameras began to flash.

"I think the new record's great," said John. "It should get to number one."

"Thanks," said Brian, going on to explain how the band had recorded it in America at Chess. Paul puffed on a big cigar as he listened.

"I think it's gonna go straight to the top; it's a winner," Paul said after Brian finished. Brian Epstein then called John away to meet someone more important.

The sight of the two Stones talking on friendly terms with their counterparts won us the seal of approval from the gathered hierarchy. Some came and stood close by to listen to the conversation before being introduced, while others were waiting for the chance to be photographed alongside one of the stars. An elegant woman with a crusty voice asked me which one I was. I told her my name was Henry and that I'd come to fix the drains. Thinking I was being loveable, she smiled and said it was nice to meet me. Judging by the way people were reacting it was obvious no one in the room watched *Juke Box Jury*.

Walking in unannounced had been a real novelty at the otherwise staid and formal occasion. It was ironic that a section of society that would have looked down on the Stones with disgust a short while ago had been happy to stand there drinking champagne with them because they were famous.

The next morning Keith and I arrived at the office in Ivor Court and a cheerful Andrew met us waving a newspaper in his hand. He wanted to know what had been going on the night before. The casual spur-of-the-moment visit to the Dorchester had ended up splashed across the front of every daily newspaper, most of which also had a photograph featuring Brian and Keith. The accompanying articles said that Brian Jones, Keith Richards, and Bill Wyman had gate-crashed a reception for the Beatles at the Dorchester Hotel the night before. With the furor from *Juke Box Jury* still raging, the Dorchester incident was cited as another example of bad behavior by the ignorant louts.

Andrew thought it was brilliant. It was rare to achieve such huge publicity completely by accident. His second reaction was one of surprise at Bill being involved and he had a good laugh when Keith told him it had been me instead. A short time later Bill arrived at the office. He had seen the papers too and had been even more surprised to find out he had been out enjoying himself instead of being in the process of moving house. Smiling, he asked Keith, "What was that all about last night?"

"It was me, Brian, and Phelge," Keith told him, laughing. "We stopped off to see the Beatles out of the blue. The press thought Phelge was you. After all this time they still don't know which one of us is which!"

There were two more new faces in Andrew's office, John Paul Jones and Doug Gibbons, and Andrew wanted publicity handouts produced for the newcomers. John Paul traveled in from South London on a motor scooter that was standard transport for the mod fraternity. He was a relaxed and pleasant person to talk to, and had taken George Bean's empty desk. He described himself simply as an arranger. Where George had disappeared to I had no idea. I knew that Andrew had gone to the lengths of issuing a record by him, but no one spoke of it. Doug, who occupied the desk when Jones was not there, had been another one of my drinking friends at the Ealing club. The *Ready, Steady, Go!* show had been running a lighthearted competition where members of the audience mimed to a record. Doug managed to get himself picked from the audience and did an impersonation of Mick while a Stones record played in the background. He had come to Andrew's attention, not so much because of his impersonation skills but because Andrew thought he resembled Mick in some manner. I could not see any likeness whatsoever, and as with George Bean I was unaware of any musical talent Doug may have possessed. Someone told me Andrew thought Doug had a "smouldering" look about him, whatever that meant.

I continued to spend quite a lot of time at Chester Street, and Brian and I took to drinking at a small pub just a few yards away. The Queens Head lay hidden away in a cobbled mews street and with the weather continuing mostly warm we liked to sit at one of the wooden tables outside. Among the visitors now coming to Chester Street regularly was Gordon Waller of Peter and Gordon, who would often join us for a drink. Brian had struck up a friendship with him when the duo played on the pre-America short tour. One afternoon as we sat drinking in the sun, Gordon asked Brian a friendly question.

"Who is the leader of the Rolling Stones, you or Mick?" Gordon, like many others, was not sure.

Brian looked across at him and said, "I am, although Mick likes to think it's him on occasions." I sat there, thinking it seemed more of a cooperative nowadays.

"I wasn't sure, but I thought you were," said Gordon.

"It's my band," replied Brian. "I signed all the management contracts and I make the decisions."

"I see," said Gordon. "Is it split five ways?"

"Well," replied Brian. "It is, but I get an extra five pounds a week more than the others. Turning to me he said, "By the way, don't mention this to any of them at all. Give me your word."

"OK!" I said. I had no intention of mentioning it, mainly because I thought he was talking a load of crap. I could not see the point of him of saying he was receiving £5 more. Given the amount of money they were now earning each week it just sounded stupid for him to say that. An extra fiver did not seem worth bothering with. I guessed he was just trying to impress Gordon in some way and I didn't think anything more of it. Only later did I find out that it was actually true, at which stage

Nankering with the Rolling Stones

I was suddenly clearer about the background to the on-off niggles and occasional irritation that existed between him and the others.

While the band had a few nights off, the round of socializing continued. Chester Street was becoming a meeting place. Long John Baldry, Peter Meadon, and Mickey the Monkey dropped by regularly to party along with the Pretty Things, another R&B band now doing the rounds. I saw the Pretty Things as another Yardbirds-type band in that they seemed to copy the Stones. Again it was the long hair and the same songs; they even had their own Stone—guitarist Dick Taylor, who had played with the Stones in the very early days. The Stones' road to success was now one that other bands wanted to follow.

Brian and I left Chester Street one night to visit Tony Marsh. I suggested that I should drive Brian's car as I knew the way and Brian agreed. Although I had neither formal driving tuition nor the legally required insurance I did not do a bad job—until we had to execute a right-hand turn into the street where Tony lived. The Humber was a heavy car that lacked power steering and the turning of the wheel became like a wrestling match. Having begun to turn right I put my foot down but did not turn the steering wheel enough. It felt as if I was trying to maneuver an enormous truck. The car careered onto the pavement and I could not get it back on the road. Brian was panicking. "Turn the wheel! Turn the wheel!" he was shouting. I told him I was trying. The car continued along the pavement heading straight toward a pedestrian and a lamppost.

"Look out, look out! We're going to kill him!" yelled Brian. "Mind the post." He started yanking the steering wheel and one side of the car went over the curb and back on the road. The pedestrian was a big black guy who suddenly turned and leapt for his life as I managed to stop the car just short of the post.

The guy came to Brian's open window. "Hey, man! What do you think you doin'?" he shouted. But then he recognized Brian and said, "Oh, it's you guys."

Brian grinned. "Yeah, you nearly were swinging on a star then!"

"Man, I'll walk in the road next time. You cats are crazy!" said Big Dee Irwin, who was also on his way to Tony's. Big Dee was in England on tour following the success of his single "Swinging on a Star," the title which Brian had referred to as a possible literal occurrence if we hadn't stopped in time.

Our near accident was not the last mishap of the day involving Brian's car. After partying with Tony for a few hours Brian decided to stop at Earls Court for something to eat. After his experience of me nearly killing Big Dee, Brian decided he would drive. Approaching a stop sign the brakes failed and the car rolled on at about 30 miles per hour. Brian was shouting again.

"We can't stop, the brakes have gone!" he screamed. We approached a side turning with a parked car beyond it.

"Drive into the back of the parked car," I shouted back.

"No, we can't," said Brian and heaved the steering wheel so that the car swerved left into the side street. Finally he ran it into the edge of the curb, which dragged the car to a stop. As he sat there, trying to pump the brake pedal, somebody knocked on the window.

"Are you a lunatic? You will kill someone," said the policeman. I laughed.

"I couldn't stop the car," Brian snapped at him.

"I'm not surprised, coming round a corner at that speed," said the cop.

"No, you don't understand. The brakes have gone," Brian told him.

"Well then, you should have slowed down to come round the corner."

"I've got no fucking brakes," Brian screamed at him. "I couldn't slow down."

"Well, it's an offence to drive a vehicle without brakes," the policeman informed him.

"I know," said Brian. "You don't understand; they just failed at the corner. I'll have to leave the car here."

The policeman looked at him for a few seconds then said, "You can't leave the car here, sir."

"It's got no brakes," said Brian. "What shall I do? I'll have to come back for it."

"Well make sure it's before eight o'clock in the morning," the officer told him.

Leaving the car there we hailed a cab, went for the meal, and then headed back to Chester Street. We spent most of the next morning sleeping and it was past noon before we got back to the car. Miraculously it was still there—it hadn't been towed and didn't even have a parking ticket. Brian's plan was to drive the car slowly to a garage using the hand brake to stop. Having started the engine he put the car in gear and drove away. At the first corner the brakes worked perfectly and presented no problems from then on. The whole sequence was to remain one of life's mysteries.

Most of the publicity during the last week concerning *Juke Box Jury* and the Beatles incident had been unfavorable. Whether that made any significant difference to the band's commercial success could not be gauged, but certainly it didn't stop "It's All Over Now" going to number one in the charts. The Stones now had that elusive major hit record.

Although the hit was welcome, it was not something they had been openly worrying about. The importance of the record was that it meant the band finally had the chart success that befitted their status as one of the most popular live acts in Britain. Touring the country, the Stones had played to packed houses and received crazed receptions as lively as any for the Beatles—this had seemed bizarre without a big hit. The relative success of rock and pop bands was measured mainly by their record sales, and at last the Rolling Stones really had arrived. Coincidentally their number one coincided with the first American chart-topper for Andy "Wipe-out" Wickham's Beach Boys, with "I Get Around."

With Linda still pregnant and living with her parents—the baby was almost due now—the artful Brian brought his new girlfriend out into the open. Dawn lived with her parents, who Brian claimed were live-in staff at a big house just around the corner from Chester Street. I was with him a couple of times when he gave her a lift home and it soon became obvious that Dawn was pregnant as well.

I found it difficult to comprehend how Brian could possibly get himself into the same predicament with two different women almost simultaneously. I had no idea how he was going to deal with both situations and never bothered to ask him. It seemed that if he was going to stick with anyone it would be Linda, but their relationship had been pretty combustible recently. Knowing Brian was unlikely to make a decision that would be unpopular with either of them, I waited for him to come up with some easy way out of it all. I also wondered if the rest of the band knew about his predicament.

One afternoon after returning Dawn to her home in Chesham Place, Brian and I were driving along the Cromwell Road between Knightsbridge and Kensington. We began to crawl through the traffic and came alongside a large expensive-looking black car. Thinking it was just another chauffeur-driven Rolls-Royce I did not pay much attention, but Brian saw who was in the car straightaway and began to wave. Without bothering to look round I asked him who it was.

"It's David Jacobs and his wife," said Brian.

I looked round at the car that was now slightly behind us. There was David Jacobs driving in his dinner suit. Probably thinking I was Keith or Bill, he smiled back at me superficially and waved. Maybe he wanted to make sure we noticed that he had a better car than us. I waved back to him and could see he was explaining to his wife the weirdos in the gray car were the Rolling Stones.

"It's a wonder he even acknowledges you," I said to Brian. "After all the shit about his poxy show."

"He's all right," replied Brian. "All friends with us now he's getting publicity as the good guy."

The waving nonsense continued for a mile or so until he turned left into Earls Court. We then became stuck across an intersection and peered ahead to see what was causing the holdup. Another car, equally black and expensive, appeared to have broken down and was being pushed along very slowly. As if meeting a required condition for owning one of these posh cars, the man straining away to keep the car moving was also wearing a dinner suit. We gradually began to make our way past it and I looked at the man sweating as he pushed the car along. A petite woman who looked like a doll sat behind the steering wheel looking straight ahead as she guided the car. I felt sorry for the guy pushing behind.

"Hey, you know who that is?" said Brian, laughing.

I tried to think. They did look vaguely familiar but I could not quite place them. "It's, er, whatsisname . . . "

"Princess Margaret and Lord Snowdon," Brian answered correctly. I turned to look at them again as we began to move quicker, leaving them behind. The people who said Princess Margaret looked like a doll in real life were right.

"I'm surprised there are no police or security with them," I remarked. "Maybe we should go back and give them a hand."

Brian looked in his rearview mirror as he thought about it. There was a huge amount of traffic behind us and finally he said, "They're too far back now and there's probably nowhere to turn."

He was right. We were in a one-way system and it was not possible to get back to the beleaguered Royals without an extensive detour, by which time help would probably have arrived anyway. It was a pity, but there was nothing we could do except watch a golden opportunity for some of the ad-lib publicity that Andrew loved slip away. I sat there musing over possible headlines—something like "Rolling Stone Rescues Royals" would have been suitably ironic and further shocked the establishment.

Stones concerts were gaining a reputation for the fans getting out of control. Some of the problems stemmed from simple overcrowding of the venues. Promoters put shows on to make money and obviously the more paying fans they could squeeze in, the greater the profit. Many promoters also grossly underestimated the number of people who would turn up. These conditions were the prime cause of girls fainting from the heat and ending up in ambulances. With little room to move at the average gig, security staff found it more and more difficult to keep the fans from the stage. It was now almost commonplace that at some point during a show one or two fans would rush the boys on stage. At the end of the shows it seemed they all tried to scramble up there and retrieve whatever they could as a memento. Often one of the boys would end up with torn clothes if the band did not escape quickly enough. Sometimes they appeared on stage wearing new jackets or shirts only to have them ripped up half an hour later. For the most part the band took this in their stride and treated it as an amusing game, but there was nothing funny about what was to take place at the Empress Ballroom in Blackpool.

Down at the front of the stage a group of guys gathered whose main interests lay in baiting the band rather than seeing them play. An attitude still remained among the rocker element that long hair was "soft" and the Stones were the perfect example of the trendy "softies." Usually these guys just jeered, but on this occasion it got way out of hand. The small group set about antagonizing the band by swearing at them and eventually spitting on the stage, particularly at Brian.

Keith had a thing about people encroaching on what he saw as his work area. At previous concerts I had seen him once or twice throw his foot out as a warning in the direction of someone who was pissing him off. At Blackpool he purposely made sure that it connected with the ringleader's head. As he said afterward, "I 'accidentally' stuck my boot in his head." This resulted in the injured party and his cronies being joined by others who wanted a taste of the Stones' blood. The band ended up being chased from the stage and only just managed to escape. Unable to kill the Stones, the mob vented its anger on the band's equipment and the theater. They managed to heave a grand piano from the stage and smash it to pieces along with all the band's equipment. The rioters even managed to bring some of the building's chandeliers crashing to the ground, and virtually every policeman in Lancashire was called in to deal with the situation.

There had been mini riots before in the good old days of rock and roll, when Teddy Boys had ripped out cinema seats during Bill Hayley films, but this was on a larger scale. Naturally because the Stones were involved they were portrayed as the masterminds in a national plot to undermine law and order. Television and newspapers covered the incident extensively over the weekend, giving the Stones a fresh burst of publicity just in case their bad-boy image was slipping. Comedian Bruce Forsyth, appearing in a televised show from Blackpool a couple of nights later, was playing the maracas and held up one that was not making much sound. "This one's not too well; it must have been here Friday," he quipped.

Back in London, when I asked Brian what happened at Blackpool he put his hand in his pocket and pulled out a small piece of wood about the size of a matchbox. "It was crazy. Look, that's all that was left of my amplifier. Eric had to collect new ones from Vox the next day and bring them up to us," he said. "Oh, and by the way, Linda had a baby boy on Thursday."

Brian spent the next couple of weeks running backward and forward. He would travel down to Reading to stay with Linda and the new baby for a couple of days and then come back to Chester Street to meet up with Dawn. The band's commitments gave him the perfect excuse for not staying in either place too long, meaning he could just about keep the two girls reasonably satisfied. Just to add to his troubles, I sometimes arranged dates for him with another woman.

There were several female journalists working on the various pop magazines at the time, and one of them had a bit of a crush on Brian. She was a nice person but not that attractive, at least not to Brian who had absolutely no designs on her at all. Finding I could imitate Brian's soft-spoken voice over the telephone, I used to call the girl up saying I was Brian and invite her over to Chester Street for an intimate liaison. She would arrive saying, "Brian asked me to come over," and I would simply let her walk in. Brian would be inwardly going nuts at her turning up again, but she was a journalist so he had to act polite and amicable. With the pregnant Dawn a few feet away, hidden in the bedroom, Brian would be squirming at the journalist's heavy flirtation and trying desperately to get rid of her without being rude. The last thing he wanted was the spurned woman to write a story about his pregnant girlfriend, which would then appear in the papers. The journalist remained convinced Brian had invited her and consequently she was not in any hurry to go, ignoring all his hints, which almost became pleas, that she should leave. One particular day the only way to get rid of her was by saying he had an appointment in town and offering to give her a lift back to the West End. Not wanting to be alone with her, he asked me to accompany him to Eric's office for the fictional appointment.

After dropping the woman off, Brian headed for the Scene club in Ham Yard. Pulling up outside we saw the club door open and ventured inside to see if anyone we knew was there. Inside we found Lionel Blake, who ran the club, talking with the boss of Radio Caroline, Ronan O'Rahilly. Brian chatted with Ronan for 20 minutes or so about how the radio station was able to evade the law and keep broadcasting. Eventually it was Ronan's turn to excuse himself and we remained there with Lionel. The conversation then somehow turned to the art of self-defense. Lionel said he practiced some obscure far-eastern martial art and to demonstrate how it worked he told Brian to attack him as if he had a knife.

Lionel was the complete opposite of Brian, powerfully built and much bigger, so it seemed inevitable what would happen, but Brian was undeterred. He took his jacket off and attacked. After sliding down the wall and picking himself up following Lionel's counter, he decided he liked the pain and wanted to try it again. Brian gave no thought to the fact that he might have ended up with some arm or hand injury that would render him unable to play with the band and stupidly he continued to roll around the floor. By the time he had cut his lip and hurt his wrist the penny finally dropped that he was not going to be able to inflict any harm on Lionel with his imaginary knife. Covered from head to toe in dust and hurting, Brian was in no condition to go anywhere else after this cultural exchange, so we made our way back to Chester Street. Brian decided he was fed up with London for the day, so he changed his clothes and drove off to Linda's.

Later that evening Gordon Waller came calling and we headed for the Queens Head. The mews pub was undergoing decoration prior to featuring in a period film early the next morning. Gordon and I sat outside at a wooden table watching how set designers could transform a building in a couple of hours with lights, flowers, and other skilled touches. Looking for some extra socializing when the pub closed, we caught a taxi and made our way to the Ad Lib.

Gordon was quite a refined person, always very tidy and wearing a suit. With his polite and respectable disposition anyone who approached him would assume they were dealing with a responsible young man. That would have included the lost-looking tourist who followed us into the club entrance. As we stood in the chintzy lift the man called out as the doors were closing and Gordon pressed the button to hold them open.

"Excuse me," he said. "Is this the way into the Ad Lib club?"

I leaned against the mirror at the back of the elevator waiting for Gordon to step aside and let the man board. I had not quite placed his accent, but thought maybe he was American or Irish. Dressed in a pinstripe suit, I thought he looked like a lawyer or businessman. His face looked familiar and I wondered if I had met him somewhere or seen him on television. I tried to decide if he was a program announcer or newsreader. Gordon stood firm, blocking the lift doors.

"Yes, it's in this building," replied Gordon.

"Do you know where the entrance is?" asked the man. I kept looking at him, sure I had seen him somewhere else. Maybe he was in films. Maybe he was a gangster.

"Yes," replied Gordon. "It's on the top floor."

"Is this the way up?"

"Yes," said Gordon. "If you were going in. It's members only, I'm afraid." I wondered why Gordon was giving the guy such a hard time—the owner would do that once we arrived at the club entrance. I stood back and let Gordon carry on.

"Oh, I see," said the man. I still couldn't quite recognize him but felt sure I should have.

"I could take you up to the entrance," Gordon told him. "But I'll have to search you first." I figured the guy was a London gangster and Gordon was pushing him to see how badly he wanted in.

"That's perfectly OK, I understand," said the man, who didn't seem bothered.

"You'll have to raise your arms," Gordon told him. The man lifted his arms and Gordon began frisking him and patting his body for concealed weapons. He bent down and ran his hands over the inside and outside of the man's legs, like a cop in a movie. Standing up, he said, "You seem OK; I'll take you up, but don't speak in the lift."

Brian Morrison, the club's owner, was waiting outside as usual. After greeting him Gordon nodded toward our new acquaintance, saying, "I found him lurking about downstairs wanting to come in." Gordon and I strolled off , looking for a waiter to show us to a table. I still couldn't place the man in my mind.

"Hey, he was wearing a bullet-proof vest," said Gordon. "I felt it when I searched him."

"Was he?" I asked in surprise. "I know he's a fucking gangster but I can't remember his name."

"Don't you recognize him?" asked Gordon, smiling. "He just looks like a gangster, that's all."

"No, who is he?"

"That's Robert Kennedy," answered Gordon.

I knew I recognized him.

Charlie and his girlfriend Shirley had moved into a spacious flat at Ivor Court, one floor down from Andrew's office. The inside was somewhat sparse and had bare wooden boards on the floor, but with the few furnishings they had, the place acquired a certain artistic style. Previously they had lived at their respective homes and Charlie occasionally stayed with Shirley at her parents' place in Fulham. One morning Stu had driven the van over to Fulham to pick Charlie up before going on to a television rehearsal. Charlie would normally have been ready to jump straight on board when we arrived. This morning he came out looking a little sheepish and saying he was running late. He explained that while he and Shirley had been in bed during the night the ceiling had fallen down and landed on his head. When they had eventually gone back to bed they had lain there looking at a big hole above them and worrying about more falling debris. The new flat was unlikely to have any such problems, unless Andrew continued to move more people into his office above.

The Stones' second EP was now out, along with Marianne Faithfull's first release, "As Tears Go By." The song had been written by Mick and Keith and was also released by Decca, but I did not like its folky overtones and thought Marianne's vocals sounded weak. The Stones' EP release *Five by Five* featured tracks they had recorded in Chicago on their American tour. One of the tunes, "2120 South Michigan Avenue," had been named after the address of their beloved Chess Records.

The demand to see the Rolling Stones was now international. Their calendar was now jam-packed with bookings following the success of "It's All Over Now." Among the events on the horizon, following an excursion to the Channel Islands of Jersey and Guernsey, were another British tour and a second trip to America. Looking down the list I could tell I was going to see very little of them over the coming months. The work had started in earnest after they topped the bill at the fourth Richmond Jazz Festival, now renamed the National Jazz and Blues Festival. This time there had been no hassle about whether they would be using the main marquee or not—the Stones headlined at an evening session dedicated to R&B.

Before going to Richmond we had been at a party celebrating the first birthday of *Ready, Steady, Go!* On the way to the studio there had been nine of us in Andrew's open-top Chevy, with Reg driving as usual. I was in front fiddling with a new record player fitted in the dashboard. It worked OK until you went over a bump or the car braked suddenly, making the needle skip. Reg was swerving the car in and out of the London traffic and those packed in the back were cheering each time he forced another driver to give way. Someone complained to the police who later turned up looking for Andrew, assuming he had been driving. During questioning by the officers, Reg and the others denied seeing anything untoward and the matter did not go any further. The police viewed it as an everyday traffic incident and seemed to agree that there had only been a complaint because the Stones were involved.

We left the studio by the same entrance door where I'd been bundled by the fans, and this time they had some real Stones to mob. The frenzied fans set on the hired car that was waiting to take them to Richmond and totally ripped off one of its doors. Brian was the last in line and had to retreat back to the building while the car left without him and made its way across London with a large hole where the door should have been. Brian escaped later through a service exit, and I used the same route for fear of being attacked again.

It was becoming more and more difficult to determine exactly who was living at Chester Street. Brian was away seeing Linda whenever he could—the bedroom was still his although he rarely slept there. The Pretty Things were now coming and going at all hours, using the bedrooms at the very top of the house. They would come charging in at three in the morning and appeared to claim the beds on a first-come, first-served basis. If their roadie did not feel like driving home with the equipment, he would stay the night as well, along with their friend Phil the Greek.

Although I still had the flat in Barnes as a base, it was often too late for me to make my way back there and I sometimes joined in the scramble for a bed. More often than not, I just stayed up all night.

I did not know much about Phil, but he seemed OK and we got on. He was another guy who always looked smart whenever you saw him. He seemed quiet and somewhat out-of-place with the Things. Some of the band thought he was strange as he would never undress in front of anybody when he was going to bed, preferring to leave the room or lock the door. Others whispered he was a crook and carried a cosh but I never saw any evidence of this. As far as I could tell he was a hairdresser who looked as if he was doing OK as he owned a Ford Zephyr car similar to Mick's. He disappeared during the day but always showed up again each night.

The Things' drummer was a guy named Viv Prince who we referred to as a "looner." For Viv there was no such thing as one drink or one party too many. If there was something happening Viv just stayed with it until he fell over, even if it meant staying up for a week. One night he came back around three in the morning having been drinking nonstop for about two days. We sat chatting and drinking a bottle of whisky. As it began to get light he put his drink on the table and passed out on the sofa as if he had died. I had gone through the barrier of wanting to go to bed and felt wide awake, so I decided to simply sit around and smoke. About five hours later the phone rang and Viv sat straight upright like an awakened corpse. Opening his eyes he said, "Hey man, where's my drink gone?" Seeing the half-full tumbler of whisky that he had left on the table earlier, he picked it up and swallowed it straight down in one big gulp before pouring another one. The guy was crazy and we got on great.

Viv had organized himself at Chester Street with a small bedroom at the very top of the house. Despite his penchant for making every occasion a rave-up his room looked remarkably clean and tidy. We continued to make use of the nearby Queens Head pub during what remained of the summer and if Brian was around he would join us.

In September Andrew surprised everybody by disappearing for a few days and announcing on his return that he had been to Scotland to get married. I had met him over a year ago and had seen no indication that he even had a girlfriend. Though he worked as a seeker of publicity, Andrew was also able to keep his private life secret if he wanted. I never did meet his wife.

Although I didn't like it, Marianne's first record had done well and reached the Top 10. She was also now in demand to perform the

---

song on television and progressing well on the road to success that Andrew had intended.

Along with Reg and Andrew I spent an afternoon at the BBC studios in Wood Lane watching rehearsals for a show on which Marianne was appearing. It was probably the biggest building I had ever seen. Hundreds of adjustable spotlights on metal scaffolding lined the ceiling way above us. In the center of the floor several makeshift partitions surrounded a simulated theater stage. The vastness of everything made Marianne seem even more small and frail than she already was. The producer was a fussy man who required Marianne to keep doing the song over and over until he was satisfied. With his repeated request for "one more time," Marianne seemed to become increasingly nervous and lacking in confidence. Finally, after what must have been seven or eight "takes," it was wrapped up. I never wanted to hear "As Tears Go By" again as long as I lived.

While the Stones were touring around the country again, I took a trip back to the Eel Pie with my friend Fengey. The main reason for going as far as Fengey was concerned was to see Jeff Beck. During the evening various other musicians joined Beck on stage, including Rod Stewart. While that was going on below I was in the upstairs bar listening to music from the jukebox. Someone had inserted a coin and selected "It's All Over Now," and about halfway through the song a guy in an army combat jacket wandered over to where I stood.

Recognizing me as being a friend of the Stones he came up and said simply, "Hi, you're Phelge, aren't you?" For a second I thought it was my old friend Willie who played the banjo. I was just about to greet him when he said, "My name's Shanghai."

"Yeah, hi, that's a weird name man, kinda cool though." I liked it and wondered whether Shanghai Phelge would be a good name.

"Yeah, all my friends call me that, so I stick with it," said Shanghai.

"Uh huh, it's OK. So what's happening, Shanghai?" I was asking him politely what he wanted, hoping he was going to say, "Hey, it's really me, Willie!" He sure looked like him.

"The Stones don't play the clubs no more," Shanghai stated.

"They're doing a tour right now," I told him. He was right; they had not done a club for a while now.

"Yeah, man, they don't play blues either, gone all commercial now. Listen to this shit," he said, nodding toward the jukebox.

"Well, it's good record, I think it's great," I said honestly.

"It's commercial, that's all. It's not blues," complained Shanghai. "They're only interested in money now; they've deserted their fans."

"Yeah, well, they've starved enough, man," I said.

I could see Shanghai's point but felt it was more disappointment at not being able to see the band any more—he was probably just harking back to the old days. Things had changed and most people had moved on. I did not tell him how the band had been virtually penniless back at Edith Grove and had performed for next to nothing. Neither did I tell him they wanted to make as much money as they could over the next two years while they were popular. Shanghai would not have understood. To him it was an ideal; you played blues or whatever because that's what you did, even if it meant starving in the process. Any success that came your way would inevitably be achieved through compromise and by pandering to popular taste. Maybe the Stones had compromised a bit, but as I'd said to him, they'd had their share of struggling. I wondered if he would like the next record. It was likely to be another chart hit, so I guessed he probably wouldn't.

WHEN THE LATEST tour came to an end, Brian went back to Reading to see Linda and the baby. He had just about relinquished any claim to his bedroom at Chester Street but he came to visit the following evening. We ended up drinking in the nearby pub with Viv Prince before the three of us moved on to the Ad Lib. Around two o'clock Brian and I left to go somewhere for a meal. Viv was not the sort of person who would leave a club when its bar was still open and selling alcohol, so he remained behind.

Brian and I went to an all-night restaurant in Earls Court and ran into some girls we'd known since the Ealing days. After the meal Brian offered them a lift to their flat in nearby Warwick Road. It was another big house, similar to the building at Edith Grove only in much better condition. It was almost 4:30 A.M. by the time we arrived and joined them inside for coffee. Brian picked up an old classical guitar that was lying about and started fooling around playing calypso songs. He soon became bored—the tunes sounded virtually the same without any words—and switched to reggae before that too became boring. The time was now approaching six o'clock. I looked out of the window down into the street. Cars were starting to hurry past at the beginning of the morning rush hour, and for some reason this triggered an idea.

"Hey man, let's make a dummy!" I called across to Brian.

"What do we want a dummy for?"

"We make a dummy from some old clothes. Lay it in the middle of the road like it's a body of someone who's been run over. Then we come up here and watch all the Ernies on their way to work trying to avoid it. See if any of them stop to help," I explained to him.

Brian liked it and asked the girls to find some clothes. They provided us with some old jeans and a coat. Stuffing the clothes with newspapers and cushions from the lounge floor we built something that vaguely resembled a body. It didn't look very realistic with a square head and no face, but it might have passed for a corpse. We carried it down the stairs in pieces and out to the street. Once there was a lull in the traffic, we moved to the middle of the road, reassembled it, and then ran back into the house. The first car to appear slowed down and steered around the body, the driver opening his window to take a good look before moving on.

"This is great," said Brian. "We'll have a big holdup soon." Another car pulled up and this time the driver got out and walked toward the body. He shone a torch on it.

"Shit! It's a fucking copper!" said Brian.

"Shit! We left the street door open. I'll see if I can get down and close it." I got halfway across the room toward the door.

"It's too late. He's seen the street door open. He's coming over," reported Brian.

One of the girls was quickest to react and suggested we go into the bedroom and jump into bed. She said she would talk to the police.

The rest of us scampered into the bedroom and jumped fully clothed beneath the covers of the three available beds.

Two cops came clumping up the stairway and stood outside the room.

"What's been going on here? Who's put all this stuff outside in the road?" asked one. They had carried the dummy back up to the flat.

"There's nothing going on," the girl answered. "I'm just getting ready to go to work."

"Why is the street door wide open?" the same voice asked.

"I didn't know it was open," the girl said. "There were some boys here earlier. Maybe they left it open when they went."

"Well, who else is in this flat?" The policeman obviously did not believe her and wanted to look around.

"No one," said the girl, moving into the front room. The two cops followed her to see for themselves, then came back out.

"What about this room here?" the other cop asked. He must have indicated the bedroom we were in. Someone turned the handle and opened the door. A torch shone across the room. I lay there making out I was asleep, expecting the search party to come over for a closer look.

"Who's in here?" asked the cop. It sounded as if he meant to find out for himself.

"Some girls I know—please don't wake them up," the girl explained. I lay there holding my breath, trying not to move.

"How many are there?" the cop asked, still flashing the torch.

"Four, some friends stayed late. Please don't wake them; they have to go to work soon," the girl pleaded to the cop. The torch went out and the door closed.

"Make sure nothing like this happens again," said the cop. "And next time someone leaves, make sure the street door is closed. It might not be us who comes in."

"Yes, I will do," the girl said. The cops trundled back down the stairs and closed the street door after them. We all leapt out of bed. Brian was laughing.

"That was brilliant," he exclaimed. "They thought we were girls in there." This time it had paid to have long hair.

Later that day, after a few hours' sleep at the girls' flat, Brian and I went into the West End in his car. We drove down Shaftesbury Avenue toward Piccadilly Circus. The traffic was at a crawl and Brian waved to a few people who had spotted him driving. I was scheming again, fiddling in my pocket with a small firework I had bought. The traffic began to move a little more quickly, and as we got closer to Piccadilly Circus I pulled the firework out of my pocket for Brian to see. The pavement looked crowded with people on their lunch breaks strolling around the shops. As we approached the Eros statue the area was packed.

"You have a light for this thing?" I asked Brian. He looked across at the small firework.

"Oh, no. You're not gonna let that off here, are you?" He knew I was.

"Ideal spot for it. Slow down as much as you can when you reach Eros. I'll throw it out the window into the crowd," I told him.

The firework was a jumping cracker, and I reckoned it could create a bit of havoc bouncing around in the middle of about five hundred people. I wound the window down and waited, then I took Brian's cigarette lighter and held the flame near the blue touch-paper.

"As we reach the newspaper seller," said Brian. He meant the man with no face.

"OK, it's lit," I said. "Slow down." I lifted my arm and was about to toss the firework when it went BANG and jumped out of my hand.

"Shit, it's gone off!" I shouted.

"Where is it?" said Brian

"In the fuckin' car, man!" The cracker popped as I saw it in the seat well, then shot past my ear, hit the ceiling of the car, and landed on Brian's side.

"Jesus Christ! It's down here on the floor somewhere," shouted Brian. "Get it quick!"

I looked over but could not see it. "Keep still. I can't see." It popped again, hitting the windscreen, then bounced out of sight. Brian put his arm up to protect his face and instinctively touched the brakes. The guy behind blew his horn impatiently and we moved forward slowly. I looked around for the cracker but could not see it. There was smoke inside the car now. Then it went pop again.

"It's somewhere in the back of the car; I can't find it," I told Brian as I knelt on my seat looking in the back. Then it cracked again, landing on the seat. The flame from the end was burning the uphol-stery. We were now on the Eros roundabout.

"You'll have to stop the car, it's on fire. Stop!" I shouted to Brian. The firework jumped back into the front.

Brian stopped the car. "Quick, get out, get out," he yelled at me. We opened the doors and jumped out right in the middle of the round-about. Smoke poured out of the car and traffic stopped behind us. The firework was still jumping and popping.

"The seat's on fire!" Brian screamed.

"Quick! Put it out," I told him, but he was already onto it. The traffic was now severely locked up around Piccadilly Circus and a crowd of people had gathered, many of whom no doubt recognized Brian. I never knew how police officers perfected the art of appearing just when you least wanted them to, but within seconds a cop was on hand.

"All right, what are you two doing?" he demanded. I think he recognized Brian too. The cracker had now gone out.

I looked at him and said the first thing I could think of, "Someone threw a firework into the car."

"Back there," said Brian, catching on quickly. "As we reached the corner. It set fire to the seat. We had to get out."

The police officer looked inside the car and Brian shot me a quick grin as the cop examined the black mark on the seat—he knew we must be telling the truth now.

"There's some bloody idiots around with these things," he said. "There's nothing burning inside; you'll have to move on; you're blocking the traffic." We thanked him and moved on, having a good laugh as soon as we got out of sight.

We drove across to Belgravia and Brian stopped by Dawn's house to pick her up before going for a drink at the mews pub. Dawn's pregnancy was in its final weeks, but Brian still had no strategy regarding what he intended to do. I left them talking to each other while I chatted at the bar with some of the regulars I knew. When the pub closed we bought a bottle of Scotch and some Cokes and the three of us went back to the flat at Warwick Road and continued drinking. Being relatively drunk I ended up in the kitchen making a nuisance of myself while Brian spent more time with Dawn in the front room. In the early evening Brian decided to head back to Reading for a few days and left Dawn at the flat.

The situation with Brian and Dawn had now reached the same melodramatic stage as the relationship with Linda had during the latter part of her pregnancy. Both women seemed to have been driven to desperation and sometimes hysteria by Brian's noncommittal attitude toward them. Dawn had also been drinking that night and after Brian left she became very emotional and distraught, seemingly convinced he was going to desert her. Dawn eventually became sick and threw up all over the floor. I thought she was ill and was either going to have the baby or a miscarriage right there and then. I wondered if Brian had purposely encouraged her to get drunk in order to make his departure easier. Knowing there was nothing I could say on behalf of Brian, I told the others in the flat that Dawn was unwell and then left myself. I never saw Dawn again after that day.

At the very beginning of October the Stones were present at the Granville Theatre in Fulham Broadway, a venue that was often used to record television programs. Several other bands were also in attendance, including the Beatles who were recording a show called *Shindig* for American television. The place had a drab feel about it, and the canteen we were sitting in had long ago stopped serving refreshments.

I found myself sitting alongside Paul McCartney and joining in the general banter going on around our table. The various drummers, including Ringo and Charlie, had their usual withdrawal symptoms when removed from their natural habitat behind a drum kit. Fingers, pens, and combs were now substitute sticks with which to keep practicing their craft, and they constantly tapped out annoying tattoos on the wooden tabletop. Paul turned to me and began talking about the new Beatles album and one song in particular he liked called "Eight Days a Week." The title was another play on words similar to "Hard Day's Night," and I told him I liked the idea. He went on explaining about the song and others on the album and talking about writing techniques and ideas. He had seen "Nanker-Phelge" on the Stones' song credits and assumed I was involved in the writing. No one had bothered to tell him otherwise and I went along with the pretense. Later when I told Keith, we had a good laugh. Keith turned to Mick and Brian saying, "Old McCartney still can't figure out how Phelge fits in."

While Brian's life seemed to be full of self-inflicted turmoil, Charlie's world was one of contentment. As if to emphasize that the

Rolling Stones and pop music were not the be all and end all of his life, he and Shirley decided to secretly get married while the band had a few days off. A week after the ceremony had taken place at Bradford Registry Office, with the secret still intact, he and the Stones flew to America to begin their second U.S. tour.

Though the band was away in America, most of the team in Andrew's office carried on as normal, including Reg who was still in charge of the blue Chevrolet. Following what had almost become a routine, we continued to visit the *Ready, Steady, Go!* studios on Friday evenings. A rumor had somehow begun circulating that the Pretty Things' friend, Phil the Greek, was also at the studios. Phil was rumored to be looking for Reg so he could take him down a peg or two with his hidden cosh. Knowing Phil the Greek was a relatively quiet person I thought it was all nonsense, but the word had filtered back to Reg who now wanted a confrontation. Reg had not met Phil and consequently stuck with me the whole time so that I could point Phil out when I saw him. I intended to drink in the Green Room but Reg wanted to tour the crowd looking for Phil, so we toured. Someone eventually told Reg that Phil was up on the stairway looking for him.

"So, which one is this Phil the Greek?" Reg asked me impatiently. I pointed him out across a lobby.

"C'mon, follow me," said Reg. I followed him as he walked straight up to Phil.

"Are you Phil the Greek?" Reg asked him outright.

"Yeah," said Phil the Greek.

"Are you supposed to be hard or something?" Reg asked him.

"Not really," said Phil politely.

"I hear you carry a cosh," said Reg. "Let's see it."

"No, I don't have a cosh," Phil said, adjusting his gold bracelet for something to do.

"I hear you are looking to have a go at me," said Reg, then as an invite said, "Any time you're ready."

"No," said Phil, looking nervously around. "I don't know where you heard that. It's not true."

Reg looked disappointed and told Phil, "Well, if you change your mind, let me know." Phil said he would do that.

We left the studio in Andrew's car and spent the next part of the evening cruising along the Kings Road toward World's End. Whether Reg would have been preferred a more physical conclusion to his confrontation with Phil the Greek he did not say, but I'm sure he had been ready for it if necessary.

"Didn't you live around here somewhere?" Reg asked me.

"Yeah, just up here on the left, Edith Grove, a real dump," I told him as we approached Morgan-Morgan's dairy shop across the street. "That's the landlord's shop over there, the dairy. Maybe I should throw a bottle through the window or something." The last remark about the bottle was a joke, but also a mistake given that I was with Reg.

"Yeah?" said Reg. "That's what we'll do then."

"I was just kidding," I said.

"You said that was what you should do. So we'll do it! I'm going to drive past and turn the car around," said Reg. "When I stop outside the shop, jump out and grab a bottle from one of the crates outside."

I wished I had never mentioned it. Reg turned the car in a side street then headed back to the dairy.

"We'll probably get caught," I said, in the hope that he would forget the idea.

"Don't piss me about, Phelge. Get out and get a bottle," he ordered. I walked over to the stack of crates and returned to the car with a milk bottle.

"Right," said Reg, opening the electric window on my side of the car. "I'm going to drive back round again. When we come back past the shop I'll slow the car down. Then you hurl the bottle through the window. Don't chicken out or we'll come back and do it again!"

He drove back along Kings Road toward the dairy, which was now on the passenger side of the car. As we approached the shop he slowed the car, but not as much as I expected. I had the bottle ready to lob in the direction of the shop window and as we reached it Reg yelled, "Now!" I threw the bottle.

There was a big crash and the sound of broken glass as Reg gunned the car's accelerator. The bottle had missed the window and caught the brickwork next to it.

"You did that on purpose!" accused Reg.

"You were going too fast as I threw it," I told him, trying hard not to sound relieved. Reg was thinking and I knew he was going to say we had to go back and try again.

"OK," he said finally. "We'll leave it for now and come back another time." I lit a cigarette and closed the window as we sped off.

The Stones enjoyed far greater success on their second tour of America and their popularity had soared to a similar level to the one they had reached in England before their first hit record. On this side of the Atlantic the follow-up to "It's All Over Now" was released a few days before they arrived back from the United States. This time it was a blues number called "Little Red Rooster," and the B side was another composition by Keith and Mick attributed to Nanker-Phelge entitled "Off the Hook." The first weekend the band was home, "Little Red Rooster" became their second number one record.

As the band basked in the success of achieving consecutive number ones, news of Charlie's marriage somehow leaked out. When Mick, Keith, and Andrew were confronted with the news they stood stunned in near disbelief. The band was going from strength to strength and news of the marriage could jeopardize this success for everyone involved. There was still a considerable stigma attached to pop stars who were married—many people thought this heralded the beginning of the end. Illegitimate children, though in many ways undesirable, were something that fitted the Stones' image and would cause it less harm. Keith saw Charlie's getting married, to begin with at least, as a treasonable act.

For all the initial shock, the final verdict on the marriage was that the deed was done and that the only sensible course of action was to live with it. Andrew hoped that having two married Stones would not adversely affect the group's fortunes. Mick and Keith may also have seen the situation as one of questionable commitment and loyalty to the band. Everyone had worked hard achieving the success and did not expect it to last forever. This was a one-off chance for the Stones, whereas getting married was something you could do anytime. They showed their displeasure by ostracizing Charlie for a brief period until they calmed down and grew used to the idea.

Mick and Keith had now moved to a new flat—10a Holly Hill, in upmarket Hampstead. Finally they had moved on from the messy living conditions that had prevailed at Edith Grove and Mapesbury Road. The flat was a chalet-style apartment with an extended lounge decorated with pine wood paneling. A few steps took you down to a sublevel bedroom complete with fitted wardrobes and an adjoining shower. A young girl came in a few times a week to keep the place looking immaculate. Even the clothes now lived in the wardrobes instead of their usual places on the nearest floor. Keith had a Gibson 12-string acoustic guitar and matching 6-string on one of the walls. The record player was in its usual home down in the bedroom. Mick was away and I was in the brand-new kitchen boiling a saucepan upon the stove and stirring the contents with a spoon. Knowing full well that there was no food in the house, Keith came in to see what I was cooking.

"I'm just boiling my watch, man," I said, prodding it with the spoon.

"Boiling your watch?" Keith came over and looked in the steaming pan and saw for himself.

"Yeah, it's stopped. I'm teaching it a lesson," I told him.

"Teaching it a lesson. Why don't you just wind it up?" he asked.

"No, I mean it's stopped. Like packed up. It needs boiling."

"Yeah? Well, what good is boiling it up?" Keith wanted to know. That was his problem, he knew plenty about music but nothing about watches.

"Well, apparently if you have a clock or watch that doesn't work you can sometimes fix it by boiling it," I explained. Keith looked doubtful.

"Fuckin' rubbish," he said at last. "Where did you hear that?"

"It's not rubbish; my grandmother told me. It saves having them cleaned and they go again. She had a clock she used to boil. I'll leave it on for a while."

"It sounds like one of those old wives' tales to me," scoffed Keith with a laugh.

We went back down to the bedroom for a smoke. Keith had his Epiphone guitar out and kept playing the chords to "Rag Doll," the Four Seasons song that had recently charted. He was quite taken with the song and knew all the words to it. When the cigarette ran out I went back to the kitchen with Keith wandering behind, still playing "Rag Doll."

The water had boiled away, and the watch lay sizzling in the bottom. I turned on the cold tap and filled the saucepan to cool everything down.

"What shall we do later?" Keith asked before answering his own question. "Ad Lib, I reckon."

"Yeah, what's the time? I'll put this thing right." I held the watch up and gave it a shake to see if it was dry, then moved the hands to the correct time.

"It's not going again," I informed him.

"I told you it wouldn't work. Fucking boiling it. Waste of time," he said flatly.

"Probably the wrong kinda water around here. All fucking snobs' stuff," I told him. I shook it some more but nothing moved.

"The strap's clean," said Keith. "C'mon, let's go out." We walked to the bottom of the hill and caught a cab.

Sitting at our regular place on the side seats at the Ad Lib we were drinking miniature bottles of Scotch. I looked over and saw a group of people being made a fuss over at one of the top tables. Keith looked over and identified them as Judy Garland and her family. He seemed to recognize all of them and reeled their names off just as "Little Red Rooster" came over the speakers.

"Rooster" sounded fantastic; everything was so clear and you could not help but like the sweet sound of Brian's bottleneck sliding over the guitar strings. It was the most professional-sounding record the Stones had done to date, the only aspect of it I did not like were the lyrics. I couldn't understand whether Mick was singing like someone who imagined himself as a chicken, or whether the song was expressing the view of a chicken. It confused me and as it played reminded me of a black chicken we had when I was a kid. I used to chase it around the garden and one day I came home from school and painted it white using a can of paint. The chicken came after me and I knocked it out with the garden broom. My aunt had to wash the chicken under our old brass tap and give it brandy to bring it round. One day at dinner I asked whatever happened to that black chicken we used to have, and she replied, "You've just eaten it." Maybe the blues were supposed to bring memories back.

We got back to Holly Hill well past two in the morning. With no nearby pie stall we were still looking for something else to do.

"We could go for a drive," Keith suggested.

"You got a car?" I asked him.

Keith grinned mischievously and said, "No, but Mick's Zephyr is parked up the road." That seemed a good idea and we wandered out to find it. We walked up the road to where it opened out into a small grassed area. A mist had come down and we walked round for a few minutes looking for Mick's car. There were two others of the same model and the colors looked similar in the dark. Keith did not know the car's registration plate and after trying the key in the doors of the various cars we found one that opened and guessed it was the one we were looking for. I got in and put the key in the ignition.

Neither of us held a driving license, and Keith said he had never driven before. I had been behind the wheel of a friend's car a couple of times and knew basically how things worked, but I was by no means a capable driver, as I had proven with Brian. We had totally forgotten the fact that Mick had been fined for a driving offense a few days previously and had left the car behind in case he'd received a ban.

The car started at the first turn of the key and I moved the column shift into first gear, let the clutch out, and pressed the accelerator. The car moved about three feet, then the engine went silent, and the car rolled back into the curb. I tried again and it made a noise, but the engine would not catch. I pulled something that I thought might have been a choke and the windscreen wipers started moving. After a couple more tries I told Keith it was probably too cold. He got in the front seat to see if he could coax it into starting. In the end nothing was happening when he turned the key. I guessed the battery was flat.

"Does Mick have this problem with it?" I asked Keith, as the mist began settling on our clothes.

"No, it always starts first time when he does it," said Keith.

I looked at the car trying to think what we were doing wrong. Keith lit cigarettes for us both while we figured out what to do next. "Try it again," I suggested. Keith turned the key and the starter croaked meekly before falling silent.

"I think the battery is flat," I said to him.

"We've had it then," said Keith.

I wasn't quite ready to give up, and suggested that if we turned the car around we could let it roll down the hill and start it that way. We both knew the hill was a one-way street, but there was no other choice. We could not push it farther up the hill; that was for sure. We began pushing the car backward and forward in the narrow road, turning the steering wheel until the car was pointing in the opposite direction. Keith got in beside me and I took my foot off the brake. The car picked up speed as it coasted down the hill and I put it in first gear and let out the clutch. The car lurched and kept going, but the engine was still dead. I tried a few more times as we approached the traffic lights at the bottom, but it still would not start. I brought the car to a stop across the main road outside Hampstead tube station, which had long since closed for the night.

"I dunno; it won't go," I told Keith. "Maybe it wants boiling." We both laughed.

"Leave it here," said Keith. "Sort it out later." We locked the doors and left the car almost in the middle of the main road, then walked back up the hill and went to bed.

We woke around midday and decided to see what we could do about Mick's car, assuming it was still there. We went back and saw the Ford Zephyr exactly where we had left it 10 hours previously. Keith got in and tried to start it. The starter whirred but it did not fire the ignition.

"We can't leave it here. It'll get towed," I told him.

"We'll dump it in some side street somewhere and let Mick sort it out," said Keith. We coasted downhill looking for the first available turn off. Over on the right a petrol station came into view.

"Hey, see if you can make it across the road," I said, pointing toward the garage.

Keith touched the brakes and kept the car moving at the right tempo to cross between some oncoming cars and roll onto the forecourt of the garage. I happened to look at the petrol gauge and saw the needle was flat on the bottom.

"Hey, man, maybe it wants some petrol. Let's try that," I said. We weren't sure how to operate the pumps, so we waited for an attendant to come and fill it for us. We were going to look stupid filling a car with petrol when it was broken, but perhaps someone could start it for us afterward. Keith paid the attendant then turned the ignition key and the engine suddenly roared into life. We looked at each other, really pleased with ourselves, we were ready to roll.

Neither of us was confident enough to risk driving through the busy daytime traffic, so we put the car back in the original parking space where Mick had left it and caught a cab to Andrew's office. At the office I decided a license would be useful if we were ever to be stopped. I told Tony Calder we were using Mick's car but that we did not have a driver's license between us, then cheekily asked if I could borrow his. Tony went to his wallet and dug his license out, then handed it to me with instructions not to lose it. Now Keith and I would at least appear legal on the road.

That night Keith drove us to the Ad Lib without any hitches. He quickly got the hang of the column change and hardly missed a gear. His steering was accurate enough, except for a few corners where we were either too wide or too close to the curb. When we left the club we checked the petrol gauge and decided upon a drive round Hampstead. The roads were completely deserted in the early hours, and it was plain sailing until we pulled up at some traffic lights. After waiting at the red light for a few seconds, a police car pulled up behind us.

"There's some cops behind us," said Keith, looking in the mirror. I glanced over my shoulder and saw two of them in the car.

"Don't panic, man. Just pull away nice and smooth like you've been doing all night. They're probably going somewhere anyway," I said, not worried at all.

The lights changed to green, Keith put the car in gear and slipped the clutch to pull away. The car lurched forward and the engine stalled. Instead of pulling around us the police car waited patiently behind and the lights changed to red again.

"Shit," said Keith.

"Stay cool. Just drive like you did earlier," I told him as he started the car again.

The lights turned green and Keith let the car go. The engine faltered but kept going and we pulled away, keeping to the speed limit. The police car followed us for about a mile before the siren and flashing lights started up. Keith pulled the car up and wound the window down as the policeman walked up to us.

"Let me do the talking, man. I've got Tony's license," I said quickly to Keith. The cop shone his torch in and stuck his face through Keith's open window.

"What have we here, then?" he asked. I decided to go in head first.

"Good evening, officer," I said cornily. "We're just on our way home. This is Keith Richards of the Rolling Stones and I'm Tony Calder, his manager."

The cop looked at me and then Keith. "I thought it was. Would you mind giving me an autograph for my daughter?"

"Yeah, sure. It'll be a pleasure," said Keith. The policeman walked back to his car for some paper.

"Jesus, I don't fucking believe it. He wants a fucking autograph," I said. "Sign it and let him drive off."

The cop came back with a pen and paper and Keith signed the autograph.

"Thanks very much," said the cop. "My daughter will love that."

There was one more nervous moment when Keith asked for some wholly unnecessary directions to Hampstead, but eventually the policeman returned to his car and drove off.

We let out sighs of relief. "I don't believe that," I said.

"Yeah, we've no license, no insurance," said Keith. "If only he fuckin' knew."

The next day followed a similar pattern. The cleaning girl came by and vacuumed the flat and made the beds. My watch was still clean but stuck, and Keith was still playing "Rag Doll." That night we had a few drinks then ate steak sandwiches at the Ad Lib before taking Mick's car on another early-morning run. This time we drove to Alexandra Palace and parked on top of the hill and looked across London as the dawn came up. When we decided to head back, I suggested we take a short cut I knew back to the main road. It was a little-known way out I had been through before without any problems.

Keith turned off into the short cut, which was no more than a gravel country lane, not much wider than the car and probably designed for horse traffic. Keeping the car under control on the descent we twisted our way through the tight bends toward the exit onto the road. As we approached the junction, Keith stopped suddenly. Some new black-and-white posts stood cemented across the exit to block access to and from the track. We got out and looked at the poles. They appeared to be too close together for the car to pass between them. I asked Keith to get the car as close as he could so we could judge how much clearance there was. We had to try and get through as the only alternative was to reverse the car back up the narrow twisting hill for about a mile.

"It ain't gonna go through there without damaging the sides," I said.

Keith cast his eyes over the gap. "We could fold the wing mirrors in then get the car a little closer to see," he suggested.

We angled the wing mirrors so they did not over hang the sides of the car. Keith got back in and brought the car forward until I told him to stop and take a look.

"What do you think?"

"It's too tight. We won't do it," he replied. "Let's see if the poles move."

We tugged the poles, but they were tight in the ground. I even wondered about taking the wings and doors off the car, but that was not a realistic option. The only thing I could think of that resembled a tool in any way was a metal comb I carried in my pocket.

"Let me try, see if we can edge through somehow," I said, getting into the driver's seat. Keith waved me forward and I smiled before closing my eyes and waiting for the crashing noise. Opening my eyes again to make sure I was not about to run Keith over, I found the car had miraculously passed through the gap. A slight mark showed on the paintwork, but it was nothing Mick was ever likely to notice.

IN 1965 THE Stones' popularity had become truly global, and they had an itinerary to match. The first part of the year took them across the world to Australia and New Zealand ahead of more visits to Europe and America. I continued to deal with Andrew's output of publicity literature but only saw the band occasionally. On the few times when they were back in London they seemed to have an army of hangers-on. All of a sudden, people who would not have bothered to gob on them a few months before were now announcing themselves as "friends of the Stones." Andrew and others who followed behind him would be referred to as the "Sixth Stone." Some of them even announced themselves that way. People forgot that it was Stu who truly owned the title. The best you could ever hope for was to be dubbed an "Honorary Stone" by Keith or another member of the band. The sixth Stones' place was always taken.

New bands continued to spring up and jump on the R&B band-wagon. The club scene had changed so much and I didn't like a lot of the new music. Whenever I ran into Peter Meadon, he would do his best to drag me off to see a new band he had recently become a fan of called the Who.

"You must come and see these guys," he would say. "They're mad; they smash all their equipment up at the end of the show." I kept putting him off and never did see them, mainly because I didn't like the clubs anymore.

Keith and I sat in a cinema one afternoon watching a film called *Zazie*, which has us in stitches. We had not particularly sought the film out, but just entered the cinema on the spur of the moment to kill some time.

We stopped briefly after leaving the cinema. Keith was bound for France and a concert at the Paris Olympia. I asked when he was due back but he was not sure—there was another tour of America on the horizon. We just said we would see each other later, like friends do, and left it at that. Neither of us knew it was the last time we would ever do anything together again.

I went down to the pub in Shaftesbury Avenue for a drink to see who was around, but even that place was now attracting the hangers-on. I drank a beer and thought about things. The Stones were going to be away for a while, making the most of their popularity span, which, as Keith, Mick, and Brian had estimated, would probably be about three years. I looked around and decided not to become labeled as a hanger-on. I figured I would catch up with the boys when their moment had died down. I thought it was time to go and do something different and decided there and then I would begin the next stage of my life as Mr. Ripoff.

Vowing not to come back to the West End again, I waved farewell to some guy I knew and walked out into the street. At the end of the road I bumped into Pretty Mick, who was now wearing a coat like mine. We had not met for a while, but I knew he had been taking a few pills and smoking pot. I asked him how he was doing.

"Great, man, I'm drinking meths right now," he announced, almost proudly. As we chatted I looked down and scuffed the toes of my boots against the curb. I felt sorry for him, but I also wanted to be gone. Looking in his eyes I thought what a waste it all seemed, but at the same time I felt reassured that it was the right time to leave.

Although I had vowed not to go back into London again, I missed seeing the boys and did visit the office a few times to keep up with how they were doing.

The unstoppable Andrew's latest venture was Immediate Records, and he asked me to produce the record labels and ancillary stationery. Immediate was mainly a vehicle for releasing American records that had not been picked up by the majors but which Andrew fancied could be hits. Several of the records he was considering were lying around the office, and he asked me what I thought of them. One was "Hang On Sloopy" by the McCoys and another "The Slide" by Freddie Scott. I took a shine to "Hang On Sloopy" but was not so keen on the Scott record. Reg was in the process of trying to follow in Andrew's footsteps and had a band called Thee who he was managing. He asked me to produce a logo for them—it was easy stuff so I did it.

When I next returned to the office—it was to prove my last visit—Andrew was leaping about all over the place. "Hey, Phelge, come in here and listen to this." He dragged me into his den. Over in the corner was a turntable on which played the next Stones release. This was the best I had ever heard the band sound on record.

"What do you think? How does this sound?" asked Andrew.

"It's fantastic. How do they get that distortion?"

"I dunno," said Andrew. "Something they do in the studio. Listen to it again."

We played the record over and over again. I guessed this *Satisfaction* was going to be a massive hit.

LATER

Like most people I ended up accidentally stumbling upon a career. After the last visit to Andrew's office, I spent the next two years just looning around and eventually started working in a guitar store. I continued to watch the fortunes of the Stones rising until the band entered a period where it looked as if their popularity had peaked. Their records were charting but were no longer automatic big hits. There was an increasing number of articles concerning drugs, arrests, and the like. Articles would appear in the social columns of newspapers featuring some well-known socialite describing a member of the band as a longtime friend. Often the papers cautiously referred to the latest Stones' friend as a rich ex-drug addict.

The success of the Beatles and the Stones seemed to have opened the door for anyone on the street to become a pop star. Guys who bought guitars and had only a basic knowledge of the instrument would have recording contracts a few months later. Forming a group became a do-it-yourself kit to fame for the masses. Even I ended up playing and singing with a few small country bands in the evenings.

The incident with the Perry Como record when I arrived at Edith Grove was bizarre enough. I often wondered how Keith would have reacted if I'd been wearing the Como overcoat I owned at the time. Back in the early '60s one of the most popular shows on television was *The Perry Como Show* every Friday evening. During the program Como wore an almost white overcoat patterned with a large but faint fawn-colored check. Being a fan of his at the time I obtained a coat that was identical that I used to wear before knowing the Stones. While at the guitar store I still owned the coat but now used it for a different purpose.

I had a flat and a small car, which I parked outside on the street. Some winter mornings the car engine froze making it difficult to start. Someone gave me a tip to keep the engine warm overnight by covering it with a blanket. I chose to use my discarded Como coat instead. Every night I lifted the bonnet of the car and covered the greasy engine with the white overcoat, which by day I kept in the car's boot.

One lunchtime I was standing in a pub with my friend Tommy Rich. We'd been drinking but I was running out of money for any more drinks. Tommy played drums with one of the country bands and also enjoyed a good drink, so much so that he never had any money left over for food. He drank about 20 pints of Guinness each day and still remained thin—he cannot have weighed much more than 100 pounds.

"Geez, it's bloody freezing outside," said Rich, rubbing his hands together for warmth. "I wish I had a bloody coat to wear."

After downing three beers I sensed an opportunity. "Hey man, I got just the thing for you," I said. "I have an overcoat outside in the car you can have for four pounds."

"Geez, that's fantastic," said Rich. "I'll have it."

Thinking I would warn him in advance I said, "It's sorta white. Perry Como had one just like it."

"Did he really?" said Tommy. "I don't care what color it is or who's got one the same, as long as it keeps me warm."

I went out to the car then came back in the pub carrying the over-coat and gave it to Tommy to try for size. It hung down on him in the shape of a tepee. Tommy turned the collar up around the back of his neck.

"How does it look?" he asked.

"It looks great, man. Made for you," I said. "There's a couple of grease marks on it here and there. The car broke down one night when I was wearing the coat. I had to get under the bonnet in the dark."

Tommy looked at the marks. "They should wash off OK; what do you think?"

"Yeah, they'll wash out easy enough. It looks great on you." To close the deal I reminded him how warm he would be.

"Yeah, great," said Tommy. He handed me four one-pound notes and I bought him a beer. Years later I was reminded of the Como record and coat again when a late-night radio phone-in program held a guess-the-record spot. I must have been the only person in the country who knew the correct answer. The record was none other than Perry Como and the Ted Weems Orchestra performing "I Wonder Who's Kissing Her Now."

A few months later the news came on television that Brian had drowned at his home. I read all the papers describing the events that took place leading up to his death. I felt sad at what had happened to my old friend at the height of his success. He had become the head-lines that we did not want to read. The Stones' management team had moved to plush new offices in Maddox Street near Savile Row, and I went in seeking details of Brian's funeral. On the way in, I ran into

Charlie on the stairs. "Hey, wait till I tell the others I've seen you," he said.

The new office was full of American accents coming from mohair suits behind big desks. The word *limousine* seemed to be in constant usage. I waited around for a while but everyone was occupied with the forthcoming Hyde Park concert so I left. I never intended to go to the gig but ended up there anyway. It felt the right thing for me to do at the time—Brian's death had given it added poignancy.

It was hot and sunny and the park was crowded with thousands of "flower power children" lazing around on the grass waiting to see the Stones. The concert stage stood close to the Serpentine, on the grass we had used as a short cut home from our Serpin' evenings. On entering the park I managed to place my car as close as possible to the exit to help me make a quick getaway. I guessed the band would be out of the area quickly after the concert and wanted to meet up with the boys after the show. I figured they would return to their nearby office but was not sure.

At the back of the stage the Stones sat in a mobile home chatting as the other acts played their sets. I could see Charlie clearly through one of the windows and considered attracting his attention but somehow felt silly about doing that. Eventually the Stones took the stage and silence covered the park as Mick read some words from Shelley especially for Brian. Then thousands of butterflies were released and drifted up into the sky as the Stones began to play.

I stood and listened to the whole set, but the band sounded shitty all afternoon. The rhythm section lacked its usual tightness and everything seemed a mess—both the choice of songs and the way the band played them. Brian would not have been pleased.

At the end of the gig an ex-army truck crawled out of the backstage area and I instinctively knew the band was inside it. I made my way back to my car and followed the vehicle as it slowly left the park and turned onto the main road. Some fans in a white car had also worked out that the army truck contained the Stones and had fallen in behind.

The route we were following made it obvious that Maddox Street would be the destination. I began to wonder if going to see them was such a good idea after all. They would be covered in sweat inside the van and probably the last thing they needed after a show was a social visit. I wondered what I would say to them anyhow. Their experiences and success had taken them around the world several times and I considered that we would probably no longer relate very strongly to each other. As the truck approached the office in Savile Row, I turned off and went home.

By the early '70s I ran my own guitar store in a South London suburb and carried on with my life without taking too much notice of the Rolling Stones, unless I caught an occasional TV appearance. A van parked opposite the store one afternoon and the familiar figure of Stu climbed out and wandered over, his pockets full as usual. He came in and said, "Hey! What are you doing here?"

I smiled and told him that this was what I did now. We chatted a while and he took a few things he needed for the Stones, who were playing the Albert Hall that night. He asked if I wanted to go along with him but after thinking for a second or two I declined. I knew things had changed and did not want to be chasing after something that was already gone. As he left Stu said, "Wait 'til I tell them who I got these things from."

Mick and Keith eventually bought houses in Cheyne Walk, a mere hundred yards from the Edith Grove flat. Both houses overlooked the very embankment where we had ventured on our late-night walks to the pie stall and the pier where their first publicity photos were taken. The nearest I ever came to going back to my Rolling Stones roots was when I moved my guitar store to central London and would drive within half a mile of Edith Grove each week. But I never went there again.

My new guitar store was in Denmark Street directly opposite the now defunct Regent Sound Studios used by the Stones for their early recordings. I looked across at it every day for over 20 years but never thought of the Stones being there. It remained just another building.

The biggest flashback to the Edith Grove days occurred not in London, but in Spain. On holiday a few years back I stood in a late-night bar in Lanzarote drinking and listening to Buddy Holly music playing in the background. A woman took a position a little farther down the bar from me and after a while she came up and asked, "Do I know you?"

Taking the wary view that I could be the father of some unknown kid, I replied, "I don't think so."

"Did you ever live in Chelsea?" she asked.

"Yeah, well sort of at one time. If you call it living," I replied. I had no idea who she was. She was not my Immaculate Dolly who I used to see from the bedroom window.

"World's End?" she enquired.

Trying to figure out how much child support I might owe her, I replied, "I lived in Edith Grove down there with some guys at one time."

"Yeah, the Rolling Stones," she said. "I was one of the girls from across the street who used to visit."

Many words have been written putting forward opinions and theories about the Stones, and the result has been to create myths out of simplicity. Although these people thought they knew the guys and understood what they were about, it was obvious they never had an inkling about these things and never would. The band never deliberately cultivated a "bad boy" image to gain publicity or notoriety. The Stones started off as just some guys doing what they wanted to when they felt like it, and this has remained true. If a person found them outrageous it was probably just because the band did things he or she would not have done. Much of the Stones' attitude was just daring to do things no one else would. The money and the fame have made little difference in this respect, and it continues to be a big part of their way of thinking.

Other bands following the Stones have since gone out of their way to try and prove themselves with orchestrated actions just to be controversial. Appearing on television swearing or hitting photographers are not things the Stones have ever done—they are actions that carry little thought that anyone can do. The band is far more likely to ridicule a preconceived notion. Social commentators described the Rolling Stones as being "leaders of the '60s revolution." It was, as I said, just a few guys with guitars having a good time. Society was bound to change through the natural process of social evolution, rather than because some guys in Chelsea were acting like lunatics. The Stones were only an image that people saw on television or read about in newspapers and objected to. People may have copied how they looked and even their attitude, but not their minds. Maybe you have to drink Edith Grove milk or water for that.

All in all I do not think they have really changed that much. They have enough money to go wherever they want and do whatever they like anytime. They now travel in jets and limousines instead of an old van—they probably have a van each now. They do not worry about anything nor care what others think about them. If they want to play music and have a good time that is what they do. In other words, apart from money, their attitude remains much the same as always.

Someone said to me that no one ever writes anything nice about Brian. I tried to think of something I could say to correct that, but could not come up with anything. I have only been able to relate some of the things Brian said or the situations we found ourselves in at the time. You have to judge Brian's character for yourselves from his own actions. I cannot say that he went around giving flowers to old ladies because it would not be true. Brian was like an artist who could never paint the perfect picture. However brilliant he was or however hard he worked, there would always be a flaw. Everything could always be better; there was always one more brush stroke.

I think Brian's much-talked-about isolation from the band started back in the Edith Grove days. His choice to use the lounge as his own bedroom and not share with the others perhaps became the starting point for his estrangement. Nobody thought much of it at the time, but by not sharing the bedroom Brian missed out on the closest parts of the friendships that developed. When you shared one room with someone, you talked to each other at all hours. You could lay awake for a couple of hours talking and joking as Keith, Mick, and I would, and that seemed to make you closer. In missing this, Brian created a gap between himself and the others. It was as if somehow a small piece of his relationship with Mick and Keith always remained missing. Despite all that has been said and written about Brian, no one would have wished him harm. When you are with someone sharing your last food and money to survive, it makes a bond you never forget. You may fall out with someone, but it never lasts forever. I like to think that in due course Brian would have played with the Rolling Stones again had he survived.

I do not know what became of all the people mentioned in this book, other than those who remained famous. I have no idea what happened to the fat lady at the bus stop, but did hear that Peter Meadon went on to be come one of the managers of the Who—another band, along with the Everly Brothers, that I never did get to see. The nearest I ever came was when I once knocked about with six guys in a van who played blues . . .

VOODOO LOUNGE
Wembley. July 11, 1995

KEITH HEARD MY name called out to him and turned round. I just
smiled and climbed the few steps up into his mobile home. He held
his arms open wide and we hugged each other for almost a minute.
Then he held me at arm's length and looked me over. Finally he said,
"Hey man, your hair's gone all gray!"

Index

Adams, Bob, 84
Alexander, Arthur, 24, 58
Andrews, Pat, 65, 96, 120, 139
Applejacks, the, 228
Asher, Jane, 237
Asher, Peter, 237, 258

Baldry, Long John, 27, 259
Ball, Kenny, 67
Bart, Lionel, 213–14
Beach Boys, the, 204, 206, 261
Bean, George, 205, 257, 258
Beatles, the, 28, 29, 68, 84, 104–7,
  110, 112, 120, 143, 152, 158,
  173, 179, 185, 187–88, 192,
  198, 201, 231, 254, 279
Beck, Jeff, 272
Bennett, Tony, 201
Berry, Chuck, 3, 14, 24, 25, 29, 30,
  56, 75, 125, 196, 236
Bilk, Acker, 67
Blake, Lionel, 266
Blues Incorporated, 5
Boone, Pat, iii, 251
Brando, Marlon, 4
Brown, Joe, and the Bruvvers, 215,
  227, 228
Brown, Ricky, 27, 108

Calder, Tony, 203, 204, 241, 287
Cash, Johnny, 33, 179, 215
Charles, Ray, 173
Clapton, Eric (Eric the Mod), 4, 5,
  30, 36, 60, 102, 205

Colyer, Ken, 66, 67, 151, 158, 174,
  186
Como, Perry, 13, 14, 57, 58, 82, 185,
  294
Cymbal, Johnny, 154

Dave Clark Five, the, 228, 229
Davies, Cyril, 4, 27, 40, 47, 108,
  158, 206
Davis, Miles, 44, 244
Deucher, Big Pete, 27
Dickens, Charles, 213
Diddley, Bo, 6, 24, 25, 72, 96, 110,
  186, 236
Douglas, Craig, 181
Downliners Sect, 198
Dutch Swing College Band, 245
Dylan, Bob, 216–17, 227

Easton, Eric, 112–15, 118, 121, 123,
  125, 152, 162, 163, 167, 181,
  184, 187, 192, 265
Epstein, Brian, 113, 143, 256
Everly Brothers, the, 8, 38, 39, 104,
  154, 185, 186, 215, 252, 300

Faith, Adam, 8, 240
Faithfull, Marianne, 226, 250, 269,
  271
Fenge, Mickey (Fengey), 4, 5, 6, 8, 9,
  10, 60, 272
Forsyth, Bruce, 265
Four Seasons, the, 289
Freddie & the Dreamers, 219

Gerry and the Pacemakers, 143
Gibbons, Doug, 4, 257
Gilchrist, Ian, 69
Gomelski, Giorgio, 54, 59, 60, 61, 66, 77, 90–91, 96, 99, 104, 107, 113, 114, 121, 139, 148, 151, 212

Harrison, George, 105, 201
Hawkins, Ronnie, 179
Hayley, Bill, 180, 265
Herman's Hermits, 204
Hollies, the, 159, 167, 198
Holly, Buddy, 173, 298
Hooker, John Lee, 241, 251
Hopkins, Lightnin', 88
Hopkins, Nicky, 27
Hugg, Mike, 62

Irwin, Big Dee, 260

Jacobs, David, 229, 251, 262
Johns, Glyn, 71, 121, 144
Jones, John Paul, 257
Jones, Paul, 198
Jones, Peter, 108, 112

Kane, Eden, 228–29
Kennedy, Jackie, 193
Kennedy, John F., 192–93
Kennedy, Robert, 268
Kid Martyn Band, the, 67, 174
Korner, Alexis, 4, 47, 158
Kramer, Billy J., and the Dakotas, 143

Lang, Don, 180
Lawrence, Linda, 50, 65, 74, 100–1, 129, 225, 261, 265, 267, 270, 274, 278
Lennon, John, 104–5, 176, 192, 201, 255

Lester, Ketty, 58
Lewis, Jerry Lee, 58
Little Richard, 188
Little, Carlo, 27, 108, 206
Loss, Joe, 228

Mann, Manfred, 62, 198, 206, 228
Marsh, Tony, 238–40, 244, 251, 259
Martin, Dean, 247
McCartney, Paul, 105, 176, 201, 237, 255, 279
McGowan, Cathy, 219, 250
Meadon, Peter, 241, 242, 251, 259, 291, 300
Merseybeats, the, 219, 228
Molloy, Dawn, 225, 262, 265, 278
Most, Mickie, 154
Murray, Pete, 155, 181

Noseworthy, Austin, 83

O'Rahilly, Ronan, 221, 266
Oldham, Andrew Loog, 112–14, 118, 121, 125, 128, 139, 152, 161, 184, 199, 203, 205, 226, 231–32, 249

Perkins, Carl, 236
Pitney, Gene, 195, 198, 206
Poole, Brian, and the Tremeloes, 181, 228, 229, 230
Posta, Adrienne, 205, 226
Powell, Jimmy, and the Fifth Dimension, 198
Presley, Elvis, 24, 84, 139, 252
Pretty Things, the, 259, 270, 280
Prince, Viv, 271, 274

Reed, Jimmy, 23, 58, 72, 106, 110
Rich, Tommy, 294

Richard, Cliff, and the Shadows, 8, 13, 32, 82, 162, 228
Rowe, Dick, 120–21, 212

Saville, Jimmy, 229
Searchers, the, 181, 219, 228
Shannon, Del, 47
Shapiro, Helen, 154
Shrimpton, Chrissie, 74, 107, 129, 141, 250
Smith, Terry, 187
Spector, Phil, 198
Starr, Ringo, 105, 201, 279
Steele, Tommy, 180
Stevens, Guy, 103, 148
Stewart, Rod, 272
Sutch, Screaming Lord, 27
Swinging Blue Jeans, 206

Taylor, Dick, 259

Tillotson, Johnny, 223

Valens, Ritchie, 58

Waller, Gordon, 237, 258, 267
Waller, Mickey, 206, 208–9
Waters, Muddy, 72, 247
Watson, Bernie, 27
Weems, Ted, 57, 295
Wheatley, Dennis, 33, 62
Who, the, 196, 291, 300
Wickham, Andy, 203–4, 206, 261
Wilde, Marty, 206
Wolf, Howlin', 24
Wright, Ruby, 82
Wynter, Mark, 113

Yardbirds, the, 212, 259